Race
AND
Writing
Assessment

Studies in Composition and Rhetoric

Leonard Podis
General Editor

Vol. 7

This book is part of the Peter Lang Education list.
Every volume is peer reviewed and meets
the highest quality standards for content and production.

PETER LANG
New York • Washington, D.C./Baltimore • Bern
Frankfurt • Berlin • Brussels • Vienna • Oxford

Race
AND
Writing
Assessment

EDITED BY

Asao B. Inoue AND Mya Poe

PETER LANG
New York • Washington, D.C./Baltimore • Bern
Frankfurt • Berlin • Brussels • Vienna • Oxford

Library of Congress Cataloging-in-Publication Data

Race and writing assessment / edited by Asao B. Inoue, Mya Poe.
p. cm. — (Studies in composition and rhetoric; 7)
Includes bibliographical references and index.
1. English language—Rhetoric—Study and teaching (Higher)—United States—
Evaluation. 2. English language—Rhetoric—Study and teaching (Higher)—
Social aspects—United States. 3. Discrimination in higher
education—United States. I. Inoue, Asao B. II. Poe, Mya.
PE1404.R34   808'.0420711—dc22   2012005699
ISBN 978-1-4331-1815-9 (hardcover)
ISBN 978-1-4331-1816-6 (paperback)
ISBN 978-1-4539-0809-9 (e-book)
ISSN 1080-5397

Bibliographic information published by **Die Deutsche Nationalbibliothek.**
Die Deutsche Nationalbibliothek lists this publication in the "Deutsche
Nationalbibliografie"; detailed bibliographic data is available
on the Internet at http://dnb.d-nb.de/.

Table of Contents

Foreword

William Condon

This volume enriches the conversation about race, class, and assessment in at least two ways. First, the essays here look at all kinds of writing assessment: assessments in classrooms—grading, of course, but other forms of evaluation as well; writing programs, and writing across the curriculum programs; and large-scale assessments of writing as well. Rather than focusing on what every test-taker should know—the focus of standardized assessments in the United States since at least the late 1800s (Elliot, 2005; Gould, 1996)—these essays focus on what test-takers should be able to do, and on how well. This change, which has been in progress within secondary and higher education since at least the 1980s, puts attention where it belongs: on learners and on teachers. Second, this volume deepens the conversation about race, class, and assessment by raising far more relevant questions than the assessment industry has done to date.

Large-scale traditional testing—primarily based in multiple-choice question tests and other short and therefore reductive formats—has ruled assessment for almost three quarters of a century to date, yet we know surprisingly little about the effects of race, class, or other marginalizing statuses on writing assessment, and vice versa. Moreover, what we *do* know is painfully obvious. The testing industry has put all of its eggs in the limited-format basket (Elliot, 2005), despite the questionable validity involved in these methods (O'Neill, Moore, & Huot, 2009; Condon, 2011), leaving the effectiveness of such tests to the people who write the questions. No wonder, then, at the perennial messages about the so-called achievement gap. When questions are written and tested by highly educated middle- and upper middle-class psychometricians, of course test-takers from the working classes will under-perform relative to test-takers from the middle class or above (Sacks, 1999). As a result, we know that large-scale tests are generally inequitable in their treatment of marginalized populations—non-white, non-Asian students; students from lower and working classes; students from homes where the language spoken is not English; and so on (Gould, 1996). These are so clearly the wrong kinds of test that the debate over them obscures the fact that the questions the testing methods raise are really the wrong set of questions. Instead of focusing on the tests and the testing environment, we need to focus on students, on classrooms, on teachers, on writing programs—and then move toward solving the problems of large-scale testing. Who is being assessed (Inoue; Lewis Ketai; Yancey), where are they being assessed (Jordan; Lioi & Merola), who assesses them and by what means (Balester; Fowler & Ochsner; Behm & Miller; Herrington & Stanley), and under what institutional conditions are they being assessed (Anson; Kelly-Riley; Yancey; Bautier & Donahue) are some of the questions that chapters in this collection ask.

Starting in the classroom means starting where—by *far*—most writing assessment happens, where programs set outcomes for students to achieve and where teachers express their values about writing in feedback and in grading practices. Especially as writing across the curriculum takes firm hold, writing assessment happens everywhere in a student's academic experience. As instructors provide formative and summative feedback, they need to ensure that their practices are equitable as well as rigorous. Instructors need to account for patterns of difference and find ways not to penalize some students for where they come from or for aspects of their learning over which students have no control. Learning to express their values in high standards and in sound methods provides a clear path for students of all kinds to meet those standards. On a broader level, assessment also happens in writing centers, in program- and university-wide assessments, and in other sites that assess students' achievements in writing beyond individual classrooms. The assessment practices and standards in those settings need to match what happens in the classroom, to be fair, and to allow students to show as much of their learning as possible. And as this collection suggests, assessment in these contexts should take into account explicitly the classed, gendered, and racialized students it affects. While these goals are possible at a local level, the political economy of the commercial testing industry prevents traditional testing from matching them.

What happens in classrooms, between students and teachers, and between students and their peers, matters profoundly. No nationally normed, multiple-choice test has ever helped a student learn anything. The commercial testing industry simply—and necessarily—overlooks what happens during the learning process. Yet that is the most crucial location for good assessment, for the kinds of assessments that do help students improve as writers. It is fitting, therefore, that a book dedicated to understanding ways of making those local assessments fairer should focus on learning contexts in order to provide as much access to success as is humanly possible.

Finally, this volume continues a shift in the assessment conversation that I noted in a recent issue of *WPA: Writing Program Administration*. For most of the history of writing assessment, local contexts have been challenged to meet the standards and practices of traditional tests. The past twenty-five years, starting with Elbow and Belanoff (1986) have seen that challenge met, and now the local contexts are challenging the commercial testing machine to meet the standards of validity, of fairness, of equity and access, that the local contexts have demonstrated are possible. Portfolio-based writing assessments, along with various other authentic assessments (Cambridge et al., 2001), have demonstrated that even large-scale writing assessments can be fairer and more thorough than their first five or six decades might indicate. This volume extends the challenge to local contexts to keep pushing equity, access, and achievement, even as the conversation turns and the models shift to those articulated by the authors represented here.

In the modern era, it has become apparent that responsible writing assessments must be grounded in the various locations in which students learn, in which they become better writers. Thus, teachers, administrators, and assessors in those contexts must continue the push to ensure that the practices of evaluating writing are not only valid in traditional ways, but also meet the standards of multiple, continuing validity that have emerged since the pioneering work of Messick (1989b) and Moss (1994) and that are confirmed in the standards of the American Psychological Association, the American Educational Research Association, and the National Council on Measurement in Education (O'Neill, Moore, & Huot, 2009, p. 27). In plainer terms, assessments need to provide ways for students of all kinds to demonstrate what they have learned. Traditional assessments have tested only for certain aspects of writing performance that the test-makers have decided students *ought* to have learned. The latter standard is far narrower and more arbitrary than the standards set in colleges and universities around the country over the past three decades. As a result, assessment practices—in classrooms and across the curriculum—have emerged that are far more open to discovering what students can do. These assessments are fairer by orders of magnitude than traditional tests. Yet they can be more equitable still, and that is the challenge the authors in this collection present. We can all benefit by trying to meet it.

Acknowledgments

This project grew out of our desire to engage with contemporary writing assessment scholarship in ways that specifically addressed the issues of racial inequality. In the process of collecting the chapters for this volume, we have come to see how racial identity is deeply interconnected to issues of socioeconomic status, language, and nation. The construction of racial formations relies on these identity markers to embed race in institutional and cultural structures in ways that are often invisible. In making those connections visible in writing assessment technologies, our contributors have raised provocative questions for future researchers. We are humbled that so many individuals generously participated in this project and are indebted to them for their honesty, hard work, and dedication to the field and to racial equality.

We are also deeply grateful to the following individuals who have served as mentors and reviewers in the process of putting together this collection. Without their support, it is impossible for emerging scholars to gain a foothold in the field.

- William Condon
- Frankie Condon
- Norbert Elliot
- Tom Fox
- Keith Gilyard
- Jaime Armin Mejía
- Beverly J. Moss
- Sandra Murphy
- Peggy O'Neill
- Malea Powell
- Eric Darnell Pritchard
- Victor Villanueva
- Edward M. White
- Kathleen Blake Yancey
- Morris Young

Without the patience and support of these individuals as well as our reviewers, Peter Lang series editor Len Podis (Oberlin College), Peter Lang senior acquisitions editor Mary Savigar, and our families, this project would have not been possible.

Introduction

Asao B. Inoue and Mya Poe

This book emerges out of our experiences as teachers, researchers, and writing program administrators. In each of those roles we struggle to find writing assessments that suit our institutional needs and are "fair" as well as meaningful to our students. In selecting and implementing practices in our classrooms and programs, we often have lingering questions about the impact of our assessments, especially on students of color. Are our assessments affecting students differently? What kinds of changes might we make to existing practices to ensure that all students are assessed in a fair and culturally sensitive manner that is also context based? What kinds of data should we be gathering to answer these questions?

Indeed the issue of race in writing assessment is not just a concern at our institutions. Across the U.S., the educational system is undergoing a major demographic shift. For example, this year in Texas, 52% of entering first-year students are students of color (Associated Press, 2011). According to the U.S. Census Bureau, 47% of children under the age of 5 in the U.S. are children of color with 25% of those children being Hispanic (U.S. Census, 2009, para. 1). Overall, 44% of children under the age of 18 in the U.S. are "minorities." Among college-age students, the National Center for Education Statistics (2009) estimates that by 2018, the enrollment of traditionally underrepresented minorities in higher education will include a 26% increase in black students, a 38% increase in Hispanic students, a 29% increase in Asian Pacific Islander students, a 32% increase in American Indian students, while only a 4% increase in white students.

The U.S. is not the only country to witness such remarkable changes in demographic composition. Australia, France, England, the Netherlands, and many other European countries are also experiencing similar racial and ethnic changes due to immigration patterns. According to Organization for Economic Co-Operation and Development (OECD) reports, migration from non-OECD countries such as the former USSR, India, and China is significant, and "migration to a number of European countries (e.g., Sweden, Germany, Austria, Greece or France) is significantly higher than is generally reported and approaches levels that are as high in relative terms as observed, for example, in the United States" (OECD, 2005, p. 133). Today's global demographic changes, which include socioeconomic shifts as well as racial and ethnic changes, are made further complex by the transnational movement of people, ideas, and businesses in which children may find that they are citizens of multiple countries, speak multiple languages, and have shifting racial and class identifications as they move across national borders.

Such changes in student populations are having notable effects on teaching and learning in schools. Ranging from second-language issues, such as the "myth of linguistic homogeneity" (Matsuda, 2006) in composition teaching practices, to an increasing awareness of complex oral- and text-based histories in literacy research (Duffy, 2007), the changes in our practices necessitated by the new student populations are numerous and challenging. These pedagogical shifts bring additional changes in the ways we develop, engage in, and validate writing assessment.

This collection looks specifically at issues of racial identity in classroom and large-scale writing assessments. Certainly, issues such as gender and socioeconomic status work in tandem with race, and this collection notes some of those intersections. Indeed, the sociocultural backgrounds that students bring to our classrooms are complex, but to collapse all of those issues into the variable of "culture" means that we do not scrutinize any one factor, as has been done in various assessment studies on gender (e.g., Black et al., 1994). We need studies that look at the mix of sociocultural variables that students bring to our classrooms as well as studies that focus on individual variables such as gender or race. This second perspective means that we ignore gender, for example, when we study race but that race is "starred" in our analysis; however, it doesn't mean that we forget about other influential factors in students' lives, such as gender and socioeconomic class. This dual approach to research will open possibilities for validating assessments, especially in terms of response processes and consequences, as it will allow us to look within and across group formations. To ignore race because attention to it will reinforce stereotypes misses the value in exposing how racial identity organizes institutions in our society, ranging from housing to health care to education. Consider the statement from the American Sociological Association on the importance of collecting data and doing social scientific research on race:

Sociologists have long examined how race—a social concept that changes over time— has been used to place people in categories. Some scientists and policymakers now contend that research using the concept of race perpetuates the negative consequences of thinking in racial terms. Others argue that measuring differential experiences, treatment, and outcomes across racial categories is necessary to track disparities and to inform policymaking to achieve greater social justice. The American Sociological Association (ASA), an association of some 13,000 U.S. and international sociologists, finds greater merit in the latter point of view. Sociological scholarship on "race" provides scientific evidence in the current scientific and civic debate over the social consequences of the existing categorizations and perceptions of race; allows scholars to document how race shapes social ranking, access to resources, and life experiences; and advances understanding of this important dimension of social life, which in turn advances social justice. Refusing to acknowledge the fact of racial classification, feelings, and actions, and refusing to measure their consequences will not eliminate racial inequalities. At best, it will preserve the status quo. (2002, para. 4)

The ASA statement goes on to acknowledge that even in countries such as France, where race data are seldom collected, racial discrimination remains: "The 1988 Eurobarometer revealed that, of the 12 European countries included in the study, France was second (after Belgium) in both anti-immigrant prejudice and racial prejudice (29)" (American Sociological Association, "Social Reality and Racial Classification," 2002, para. 2). The ASA's statement on the importance of race in research provides a finely articulated rationale for why the study of race is important in writing assessment research.

For the purposes of this collection, the unifying concern is the interrogation of race or local racial formations. We invite readers to make race a central element in their writing assessment inquiries, or at least, central as they consider the chapters in this volume, and consider what their next steps are in their own writing assessment endeavors. We further invite our readers to consider how a focus on racial identity allows them to see their assessment practices in new ways that may also illuminate new questions about gender, socioeconomic status, geographic location, and other contextual factors. We see our contributors working to ensure that all students can reach high levels of writing ability and that we have the appropriate technologies to do that, but that it is not a simple matter of "holding standards" or applying them unilaterally.

Assessment, Race, Culture, Ethnicity, And Racial Formations

Assessment, as used in this volume, is not simply a test. Ruth and Murphy (1988) offer one way to understand "assessment." They explain that assessment is "formal" or "informal" and it occurs "whenever one person seeks and interprets information about another person." Writing assessment, they explain, "occurs when a teacher, evaluator, or researcher obtains information about a student's abilities in writing" (p. 6). Because assessment refers not only to our practices, but other things that are a part of the assessment environment, we use the term "assessment technology" in this introduction to refer to the entire system, environment, and even agents that make up what most call a writing assessment. We take our cues for thinking about assessment as a technology from several sources (Madaus, 1990; O'Neill, 1998; Madaus & Horn, 2000; Huot, 2002a; Inoue, 2009b). Conceiving of assessment as a technology allows us to always acknowledge explicitly the shaping effects that various racial, socioeconomic, gender, and other sociocultural and sociopolitical formations have on any writing assessment, even when we make decisions from our assessment outcomes without any consideration of the racial identity.

Race, as used in this collection, is not simply a box that we mark on a form to identify ourselves. Race is a social and political construction that has created and sustained human hierarchies and domination, ones we have not fully escaped, and that often inherently provide (or withhold) value (Goldberg, 1994; 2002; Hannaford, 1996; Omi & Winant, 1994). Race is a sociological concept that helps us see and understand trends in assessment technologies. In this manifestation, it does not help us interact with or understand individuals very well. At the individual level, race is often ambiguous and elusive. But at the social level, which is often the level where WPAs and writing assessment researchers work, race can be explanatory and helps us tap into the worlds our students come from, and see groups of students, competencies, and social patterns.

Often the term *culture* is used as a synonym for race. A typical example of this can be seen in Murphy's laudable account of cultural validity (2007). Murphy explains through a review of the literature that at the heart of validity is the way "students make sense of test items and test situations" (p. 236), which come from students' cultural dispositions. Certainly any cultural bias in a writing assessment technology could easily cause racist effects. But "culture" and "race" as concepts that refer to social dimensions are different in explanatory nature, and should be clearly distinguished. One way to think about these terms is to consider culture as constructed through practices and the way practicing groups talk about their practices. In other words, culture is constructed from within the group. Race, on the other hand, is usually (or has been) socially constructed by external institutions, agents, and groups. Since the term's history has served to group people and create hierarchies from those groups, "race" is artificial. Neither term, though, denotes inherent properties, abilities, or capacities of people.

Using the terms "race" and "culture" interchangeably raises two potential problems: First, it can reduce race to relativism (it's just about acknowledging "difference" and accommodating subaltern or "other" voices and subjects), which still leaves intact racialized hierarchical values, methodologies, and other institutional structures that leave race unattended; and, second, it allows us to continue to ignore the racialized, social, historical, and institutional structures that construct the lived experiences of all students, teachers, and stakeholders who come to the university in uneven ways. *Ethnicity*, in a similar fashion, is often used to mean a common culture (i.e., religion, language, customs, nationality, and political identification) or a common descent (i.e., heredity and group origins). While many sociologists might argue that ethnic identity is a fairly stable feature of one's identity based on the belief of heredity, Waters (1990) has shown that for many Americans, ethnicity is "a social process that is in flux" (p. 16). Over time, Waters shows, Americans may change their ethnic affiliation through marriage or a desire to seek affiliation with a more socially favorable group. Yet, despite the slipperiness of the term *ethnicity*, it remains a preferred term in sociology and much of educational research on testing. For writing assessment scholarship, we believe there are two problems with using the term "ethnicity" alone to identify student populations. First, using the term "ethnicity" tends to place everyone, African Americans, Italians, Mexicans, etc., on the same footing. Everyone's differences often appear to amount to the same thing, but each group is located differently in relation to power, and each group stands at a different distance to the prestige dialect of English promoted by any writing assessment technology. Second, ethnic terms change over time, so even if an ethnic identity term does refer to a stable group identity at one point in time, it's likely to change in a few decades or even years (and be tied to equally shifting definitions of race). For example, the term "Mexican" was used until the 1930s in the U.S., with "Hispanic" becoming the preferred term for census data on ethnicity in the 1970s.

Ethnic (and racial) identity terms become complicated in cross-national research as well. The term "Chinese," for example, is often used as an ethnic term in the U.S., but "Chinese" is not an ethnic designation used in China. The Chinese government recognizes 56 ethnic groups, including Uyghur, Tibetan, Zhuang, Manchu, and Mongolian. One solution is to use country-specific terms. The OECD, for instance, uses nation-specific terminology in reporting educational outcomes for various racial and ethnic groups but also uses cross-national terms such as "Roma" in other reports.

Given the problems with the terms *culture* and *ethnicity*, we believe that the term *race*, if theorized in particular ways, can be useful, especially in U.S. contexts. However, the term *race* is not without its problems. Specifically, race can be used as a static term imposed on a group of people or be used to collapse groups into artificial categories based on a perceived set of common traits, such as skin tone and physiognomy. Such usages of race and racial terms, like "black" or "white," tend to be ahistorical and essentialist. They, too, elide many of the complexities of race in the U.S. today, ignoring, for example, those who may be identified for various reasons as multiracial. While race has its problems as an organizing term for data collection and has been proven not to have any scientifically biological grounds, it is somewhat useful as a term that refers generally to a theoretical, sociohistorical, and structural concept of hierarchical groups. The fact is everyone has been touched by the concept of race, regardless of how we feel or think about the term.

Racial formation may ultimately better serve our future goals for writing assessment scholarship. Among theorists, a racial formation is "the sociohistorical process by which racial categories are created, inhibited, transformed, and destroyed" (Omi & Winant, 1994, pp. 55–56). Racial formation acknowledges the "racial projects" that are constantly going on around us, often for different goals and purposes. Racial formation, for example, allows us to speak of black racial formations in a particular historical moment and location in a writing assessment technology without reducing that racial distinction to a static category because it acknowledges the social construction, the formation, of race by forces in history, local society, schools, and projects–such as writing programs. Part of what makes racial formations "local" is how those formations are historically situated in particular communities with particular social, political, economic, and cultural histories. What makes racial formation useful for assessment purposes is that it allows researchers to account for race without essentializing racial identity in the conclusions they make about writing assessment outcomes.

If racial formations are about the historical and structural forces that organize and represent bodies and their lived experiences, then racism is not about prejudice, personal biases, or intent. Racism is not about blaming or shaming white people. It is about understanding how unequal or unfair outcomes may be structured into our assessment technologies and the interpretations that we make from their outcomes. This could mean, for example, that a placement exam is racist because it creates a racial hierarchy in a school, placing most African American and Latino/a students into "remedial" courses. In doing so, the exam reproduces social outcomes that arrange groups of people along ostensibly racial lines (e.g., African Americans end up failing more consistently in courses than their peers). One cannot assume that just because a test identifies a student as "remedial," for instance, it is a function of the student's abilities as a writer, especially when larger racial patterns can be seen, and the construct of "writing ability" is likely associated with dispositions that are historically linked to whiteness. Classical measurement theory cannot account for such a view of race because it is limited to the boundaries of the assessment, not the psychological or social consequences of assessment. Current conceptions of validity also would not consider outcomes problematic if the assessment had been validated using the five-part model of validation offered in the Standards for Educational and Psychological Testing (AERA, APA, &

NCME, 1999). Our job is to understand how unequal outcomes may reflect larger socially organized forces and suggest ways that we could account for the effects of these racial formations in our processes of validating assessments. It's our ethical responsibility.

The Consequences Of Writing Assessment For Students Of Color

The last 20 years have witnessed rich changes in writing assessment scholarship in what Yancey calls overlapping waves, "with one wave feeding into another but without completely displacing waves that came before" (1999, p. 483). Throughout this history, scholars have worked to validate new approaches to assessing student writing, such as establishing portfolios for assessing competency, making decisions about students, and training teachers (Belanoff & Dickson, 1991; Black et al., 1994; Yancey & Weiser, 1997). Other advances have been in understanding validation theories and practices for holistic scoring of essays and portfolios (Williamson & Huot, 1993). Yet other scholars have focused on displaying, explaining, and theorizing large, locally grown assessment technologies that move students from placement, Junior-rising portfolio, to writing in the major courses (Haswell, 2001; Carter, 2003). And finally, writing assessment researchers have developed alternative ways to assess writing, such as Broad's Dynamic Criteria Mapping (Broad, 2003; Broad et al., 2009), while others have explored using the WPA Outcomes Statement for teaching and assessing writing (Harrington et al., 2005) and designing and implementing directed self-placement (Royer & Gilles, 1998; Royer & Gilles, 2003) (For an early review, see Huot, 1990. For more recent essays, see Huot & Neal, 2006; Huot & O'Neill, 2009)[1].

Much of the current writing assessment scholarship draws on newer conceptions of validity that come from the field of psychometrics, which look to the uses, social effects, and consequences of writing assessment technologies (Cronbach, 1988; Messick, 1989a; Messick, 1989b; Moss, 1992). As Huot et al. (2010) explain, "[t]his contemporary view of validity not only includes all notions of validity and reliability, it also demands that test consequences and implications for the local, educational environment be considered as well" (p. 507). For Samuel Messick, who spent his career at the Educational Testing Service, test scores should be used with caution because of their potential deleterious effects on poor students and students of color. Messick was deeply concerned with the role that bias as a social and ideological phenomenon plays in validity, and he called for the testing community to validate tests by considering an assessment's decisions and consequences (1989b, p. 13). Messick also argued forcefully that testing and its validation are inevitably politicized. Citing Lee Cronbach, Messick explains: "testing serves multiple ends inherently embroiled with contending or conflicting social values. As a consequence, the interpretations and uses of tests need to be justified not only in scientific and professional forums, but in the public arena as well" (1989b, p. 91). Today, there are a number of well-articulated standards for assessing individual tests and test items based on consequential validity (see AERA, APA, & NCME, 1999, pp. 80–83).

Along the way, some scholars have looked specifically at the effects of newer forms of assessment on students of color and their relationship to educational contexts (Kamusikiri, 1996; Supovitz & Brennan, 1997; Davidson Howell, & Hoekema, 2000).[2] An early notable example published in *College English* was "Racial Minorities and Writing Skills Assessment in the California State University and Colleges" by White and Thomas (1981), which showed that direct writing assessment on the English Placement Test (EPT) yielded smaller variations in test performance between racial groups than the multiple-choice Test of Standard Written English (TSWE). Equally notable, Smitherman (1993) analyzed NAEP scores from 1969 to 1979. She found that African American English "correlated significantly and negatively with rater score for both primary trait and holistic scores" on essays written by African American junior high students (p. 16). In another study, Smitherman (1992) analyzed NAEP scores for the 1984 and 1988 writing assessments. She again found that African American English continued to affect holistic scores for the essay, i.e., "the more [African American English], the lower the holistic score" (1992, p. 56). In other research on holistic scoring, Ball (1997) compared holistic scores for six students of different races; she found that the European American teachers scored essays hierarchically along racial lines, with white students receiving the highest scores, "even though teachers had been given no prior details concerning the demographics of the sample population, other than the fact that the student writers were 5/6th graders from diverse backgrounds" (p. 178). African American teachers scored all essays lower and with less variability than their European American counterparts.

In addition to the work of individual scholars, there are discipline-based organizations that have contributed to making newer forms of assessment fair. The American Psychological Association's Committee on Psychological Tests and Assessment (APAb, 2012) maintains bibliographies on the assessment of students of color, culturally diverse populations, and non-English-speaking individuals. *Educational Measurement* (NCME and ACE, 2006) includes a chapter on "Test Fairness" and the entire second section of the *Standards for Educational and Psychological Testing* (AERA, APA, & NCME, 1999) focuses on fairness in testing. The CCCC position statement on writing assessment (Committee on Assessment, 2009) acknowledges publicly that the "best as-

sessment practice respects language variety and diversity," and a similar statement is made in the NCTE-WPA White Paper on Writing Assessment in Colleges and Universities (NCTE-WPA Task Force).

Despite this good work, there remain many unanswered questions about
the impact of writing assessment on students of color. Do more recent conceptions of validity as inquiry into the consequences of assessment results on
various stakeholders provide a robust enough theoretical framework to understand the complex and varied ways our students interact with writing assessment technologies? Does an emphasis on creating site-based, locally
controlled, context-sensitive, rhetorically based, and accessible writing assessment technologies (Huot, 2002a) allow us to address informed and self-
conscious ways of assessing the diverse students we teach?

Overview Of The Collection

In part, the chapters in this collection attempt some responses to the
above questions. In the first section, "Identifying the Absent Presence of Race
in Writing Assessment," our contributors identify how race is often elided in
the practices of composition studies but is still very much silently present.
Chris M. Anson discusses how race has been invisible in writing-across-the-
curriculum practice, considering possible reasons for this invisibility, and suggests the role race could play in future work as assessment in WAC programs
and in classrooms across the curriculum. **Diane Kelly-Riley** calls for validity
inquiries of "shared evaluation writing assessment practices" that identify students of color and offers a framework for such inquiry.

In our second section, "Technologies of Assessing Racial and Linguistic
Variation," our contributors provide insightful research on technologies of
assessment at work in writing classrooms as well as teacher and student responses to those technologies. **Anne Herrington and Sarah Stanley** offer a
critique of the machine scoring program $Criterion^{SM}$ and consider the ways that
such programs cannot respond to linguistic variation. **Valerie Balester** analyzes 14 different writing assessment rubrics to show how "standard" English
conventions are embodied in various ways. Finally, **Asao B. Inoue** examines
the usefulness grading contracts for three racial formations in first-year writing
classrooms at California State University, Fresno's First Year Writing program.

In the third section, "Responding to Racial and Linguistic Variation,"
Zandra L. Jordan explores HBCU students' attitudes toward African Ameri-
can English and their implications for writing assessment. **Judy Fowler and
Robert Ochsner** conduct a study of the way teachers rate Latino/a and Afri-
can American student writing at two different universities (the University of
California, Merced, and Fayetteville State University), the first marked as a

Hispanic-serving institution and the second as historically serving African American students. **Nicholas Behm and Keith D. Miller** use Edwardo Bonilla-Silva's rhetorical framework of color-blind racism to explicate the assessment discourses of the classroom for new teachers.

In the fourth section, "Composition Placement Assessment," our contributors consider approaches to assessing writing for the purpose of determining placement in an appropriate first-year writing course. **Rachel Lewis Ketai** analyzes Directed Self-Placement (DSP) guides of two universities, Grand Valley State University and California State University, Fresno, in order to understand how they ask students to conceive of themselves and their writing competencies, paying special attention to the way the language of the guides may reproduce racialized placement outcomes. **Anthony Lioi and Nicole M. Merola** discuss different writing placement technologies at two schools to show the consequences that ill-conceived placement mechanisms have on students and how, as WPAs, they attempted to implement more-context-sensitive assessments.

In our final section, "Beyond Composition Placement Assessment," our contributors look beyond writing programs to ask about writing assessment in college admissions and international testing. **Kathleen Blake Yancey** examines trends in college admissions that point to non-cognitive areas worth considering, since they offer more equitable treatment for students of color, who traditionally have been excluded because of such assessment technologies. **Élisabeth Bautier and Christiane Donahue** discuss the effects of the international PISA exam in France for students *"en difficulté."*

We believe this collection does something important for the field of writing assessment. It gathers together in one place writing assessment research and scholarship that explicitly considers race and local racial formations. We are aware that this collection misses many important topics, including Writing Center perspectives, service learning courses, and community literacy programs, and we realize that several notable writing assessment scholars are absent. We also are aware that several of the chapters, while being deeply engaged with race and racial formations, do not always engage equally as well with the assessment scholarship related to their inquiries. And we also are aware that a few chapters do engage more deeply with the assessment scholarship but less so with the scholarship on race. We see these issues as representative of the way our field and its training practices prepare future writing assessment researchers and race scholars. We either read deeply in the literature of writing assessment, which does little with the literature on race, or we read deeply in the literature on race, which does little with the writing assessment literature. Just as Brian Huot (2002a, p. 21) called for writing assessment scholars in composition studies to learn more about the good work in educational measurement, we urge members of our field to incorporate more of the literature on race in order to help us do writing assessment in ways that have so far eluded us. Our contributors have taken up this challenge admirably. The chapters in this collection both illustrate this need and valiantly attempt to answer the call for examining race and racial formations in writing assessment.

Notes

[1] It is important to note that contemporary writing assessment is not without its counter-voices and critics. Peggy O'Neill argues that the field of educational measurement, which includes its practices, has been controlled too much by psychometric theories, such as validity and reliability, which have assumed positivistic notions of literacy and writing (1998, p. 15). Patricia Lynne makes a similar critique about the field of writing assessment, and argues for new principles for governing writing assessment theory and practice, ones that come from composition studies (2004, p. 6), suggesting "meaningful" and "ethical" assessment (pp. 117-18). As Chris Gallagher (2010) points out, "local assessments might not serve local needs and interests well. They may be poorly constructed, unaligned (or misaligned) with curriculum and instruction, and even blatantly unfair and discriminatory" (p. 11).

[2] The effects of standardized testing on students of color have been well documented (Madaus & Clarke, 2001; Hong & Youngs, 2008; Plata, 1995). Educational measurement scholars, for example, have documented many of the effects of traditional testing on students of color. For example, in addition to scholarly articles, *Measuring Up: Challenges Minorities Face in Educational Assessment* (Nettles & Nettles, 1999), *The Black-White Test Score Gap* (Jencks & Phillips, 1998), and *Raising Standards or Raising Barriers? Inequality and High-stakes Testing in Public Education* (Orfield & Kornhaber, 2001) offer three book-length treatments related to race and educational testing. Recently, Roy Freedle's (2003) research on the SAT raises new questions about differential item functioning (see also Santelices & Wilson, 2010).

Identifying the Absent Presence of Race in Writing Assessment

In "Race: The Absent Presence in Composition Studies," Prendergast (1998) draws on critical race theory to read Shirley Brice Heath's seminal ethnography, *Ways with Words: Language, Life, and Work in Communities and Classrooms,* "for the way race appears and disappears in other tropes, while racism doesn't enter into the symbolic level of the text at all" (p. 47). Through her analysis, Prendergast shows that by making race invisible, we neither see the way that students in Heath's study are "*already* socialized into discourses of race and power relations" (p. 49, emphasis in original) when they come to school, nor do we see the ways that race is subsumed into color-blind explanations for educational and social outcomes. Pointing to composition studies, Prendergast writes that we need to be more attuned to the ways that tropes such as "basic writer" get attached to certain racial formations. She explains:

> If we are to understand the mechanisms (like racism) that prevent some students from being heard, we need to recognize that our rhetoric is one which continually inscribes our students as foreigners. We might observe, for example that Asian-American students don't exist in composition studies—they are either ESL students or unnamed (white). (p. 51)

The authors in this first section, like Prendergast, explore the various ways that we may account for the absent presence of race in writing assessment by re-reading the literature of writing-across-the-curriculum and shared evaluation.

In "Black Holes: Writing Across the Curriculum, Assessment, and the Gravitational Invisibility of Race," Chris M. Anson offers an extensive literature review of writing-across-the-curriculum, noting that "empirical research on WAC is far outpaced by the voluminous instructional, programmatic, and administrative literature, which [...] has not adequately spoken to issues of student and teacher diversity." Anson rightly explains that the lack of articles on the topic does not mean that WAC researchers do not care about such issues; in fact, many WAC scholars have spent their careers arguing for equity and issues around diversity, but various historical, political, and disciplinary forces have kept race from the center of the movement. Like Prendergast, Anson calls for making race visible in the field. He notes that "[w]e know little about students' experiences as writers across the range of their college courses, and even less about the experiences of students of color. And we know almost nothing about the experience of teachers of color as they support students' writing development in their disciplines." Anson concludes by providing specific suggestions on how to make race visible in WAC practices: in faculty development (to focus on students as individual learners with attention to the different literacy practices that students bring to disciplinary classes and to open up "discussions of the evaluative complexities of difference in small-group revision"), in research (to study teacher evaluation of linguistic variation in student writing-across-the-curriculum and generate site-specific data on different racial formations).

In "Getting Off the Boat and onto the Bank: Exploring the Validity of Shared Evaluation Methods for Students of Color in College Writing Assessment," Diane Kelly-Riley discusses theoretical considerations in examining the results of shared evaluation approaches on diverse populations. A student inquiry about failure rates for African American students on the Washington State Portfolio exam was the impetus for her research in which she developed and validated a quantitatively based methodology that examined students' experiences on the portfolio assessment. Kelly-Riley was not content to consider only students' results on the portfolio assessment—what she calls, invoking historian James Ronda's metaphor, a view "from the boat." Instead, she wanted to "get off the boat; get on the bank," which led to inquiring about how certain outcomes came about: were the lower scores on the portfolio assessment for black students the result of rater bias, construct irrelevance, or other sources? Kelly-Riley explains: "The findings suggest that race—as an overt variable—did not seem to contribute to faculty's assessment of students' writing [...] More surprising, the findings from the study also suggested that the raters employed non-programmatic criteria"—including variables related to students' comfort and confidence with writing—"more than the assessment criteria articulated by the Writing Assessment Program."

Much like Broad's (2003) conclusions about the faculty's judging practices at City University, Kelly-Riley concludes that the differences in student performance on the Writing Portfolio might not have been overt rater bias but "idiosyncratic faculty criteria applied in the shared evaluation construction of the definition of 'good writing'" in the portfolio assessment. In the end, Kelly-Riley's research is instructive as she employs a range of methodologies informed by contemporary conceptions of validity to study differences in assessment outcomes as well as the intended and unintended consequences of those assessment practices.

CHAPTER ONE

Black Holes:
Writing Across the Curriculum, Assessment, and the Gravitational Invisibility of Race

Chris M. Anson

A quick visit to most writing-across-the-curriculum (WAC)[1] websites typically yields plentiful resources, including information for instructors, writing guides, and links to other programs, networks, conferences, and published scholarship. Assuming that these sites are the most visible representations of a program's philosophy and working assumptions, the absence of information on the relationships between writing and racial or ethnic diversity is strange—once we see it. Although also limited (Center, 2007; Prendergast, 1998), scholarship on diversity has played a more important role in the broader field of composition studies, from theories of racial identity in the classroom to the conundrums of dialect and style differences in students' work. WAC has especially lagged behind in helping scholars, administrators, and teachers across a broad range of disciplines to implement best practices in assessing the writing of diverse learners, both at the classroom and programmatic levels. As a closely allied branch of composition studies that shares its journals, its research base, its administrative practices, and its scholars, how can WAC have neglected issues of race and racial identity in its literature and its practices, especially in the crucial area of assessment?

This essay, like Diane Kelly-Riley's essay in this collection, explores the possible reasons for this neglect from the perspective of complex academic, pedagogical, political, and institutional forces. This chapter then considers what role racial diversity might play more specifically in the future of writing assessment in WAC at both the programmatic and classroom levels, with some thoughts about its role in faculty development, assessment of student achievement, and programmatic assessment initiatives. By considering what has been left out of the conversations about race in cross-curricular writing assessment, we may be able to adopt what Villanueva (2001) describes as a "culturally sensitive and politically conscious edge in how we approach literacy" across the academy (p. 166).

Invisibility Unseen

The history of the writing-across-the-curriculum (WAC) movement is characterized by attempts to reach out to academic communities beyond the usual source of its impetus—composition programs and departments of English. Early work in program development described the joys of creating "communities of scholars" (Fulwiler, 1984) and embracing faculty in other fields. It also acknowledged emerging research on discourse communities (Bizzell, 1982; Kent, 1991; Porter, 1986) and a respect for their varying genres, textual conventions, and ways of creating and mediating knowledge. Scholars attracted to WAC were "people who marvel at the diversity and unpredictability of culture" (Thaiss, 1988, p. 92) and preferred to view the disciplinary work of teachers, students, and administrators as taking place in an "interrelated system" (Herrington & Moran, 1992, p. ix).

As WAC continued to strengthen alongside composition studies in the 1980s and 1990s, shifts from a cognitivist to a sociocultural orientation led to an interest in the interrelationships between textual production and other dimensions of human interaction within situated practice (Prior, 2006). While some WAC leaders were actively collaborating with faculty in other disciplines, even coauthoring essays that appeared in their discipline-based teaching journals (e.g., Strauss & Fulwiler, 1987), research on the genres, processes, contextual influences, and "relationships between rhetoric and ways of knowing and thinking in disciplinary communities" (McLeod, 1989, p. 340) continued apace. Much of the move from writing *across* the disciplines (WAC) to writing *in* the disciplines (WID) owes to broader trends in the study of literacy throughout the 1990s. As WAC experts examined various approaches to cross-disciplinary writing, its research took on a kind of anthropological ethos, withholding judgment in favor of understanding how, what, and why people write in different disciplines and respecting the "dynamics that [make] these discourses distinctive" (Bazerman & Russell, 1994, p. xvi).

The pedagogical side of the WAC movement (in symmetry with the emergence of basic writing programs) had its genesis in equally embracing principles that were a consequence of increased access to education starting in the late 1960s. For Russell (1991), WAC filled a need for greater access and equity, setting out to "assimilate, integrate, or (in the current phrasing) initiate previously excluded students by means of language instruction" (p. 271). In the push to close achievement gaps, colleges and universities were confronted with the new task of "teaching dominant language to excluded populations" (Russell, 1991, p. 274; see also Shaughnessy, 1976). In its idealistic emergence, WAC was oriented toward the values of student-centeredness and a focus on discipline-based courses as communities of learning where writing could play a central role (Russell, 1991, p. 273; see also McLeod & Soven, 2006).

In the historical context of WAC's focus on student development, its openness to diverse forms and communities of discourse, and its scholarly interdisciplinarity—where one might expect the influence of language experts such as Smitherman (e.g., 1979), Anzaldúa (e.g., 1987), Lu (e.g., 2006), Canagarajah (e.g., 2006a), and Ball (e.g., 2005)—the general absence of the subject of racial and ethnic diversity is puzzling. At the same time, that lack of attention, so conspicuous once we recognize it, has been itself nearly invisible, like a black-hole sun whose powerful gravitational force draws back in its own light.

We can detect this invisibility in some of the most heavily used resources for WAC scholars and teachers. Expertly managed, the WAC Clearinghouse—the world's largest online portal focusing on WAC, WID, and related areas—provides links to journals, books, program descriptions, networks, research exchanges, and other resources for teachers and scholars. Yet the hundreds of webpages linked from its site, including the archives of five WAC-oriented journals and a bibliography divided into a dozen subject headings, contain little about racial or ethnic diversity. Twenty categories of dissertations include one on "race and ethnicity issues," but it contains only two entries—one on a cognitive apprenticeship approach to algebra (Retzer, 1998) and one that reports on differences in fifth-grade writing skills instruction in Pennsylvania schools (Bishop, 1986).

A search of CompPile, the largest bibliographic database of published work in composition, tells a similar story. The search terms "race" and "WAC" yield a single entry to an article on the role of race and gender in an Internet-based history course (Butler, 1998). "Diversity" and "WAC" produce 10 entries focusing on varieties of academic discourse and contrastive rhetoric; six are documents archived in ERIC rather than publications in major, peer-reviewed journals. Three essays that appeared in edited collections do explore important issues of diversity in WAC: in peer response groups (Nelson, 1997), in teaching assistant preparation across the curriculum (Gottschalk, 1991), and in adapting language across the curriculum to diverse populations (Hirsch, Nadal, & Shohet, 1991). But these contributions still represent a tiny percentage of the 3,196 entries indexed under WAC in CompPile.

Similarly, almost none of the over 1,000 works in the most comprehensive annotated bibliography on WAC (Anson, Schweibert, & Williamson, 1993) focus on race or ethnicity. Based on the corpus of work that had accumulated to the point of publication, my colleagues and I were unable to include the terms "race," "diversity," "multiculturalism," or "ethnicity" in its extensive subject index ("ESL" yielded one entry). Recent compendiums of research on writing fare no better; the *Handbook of Writing Research* (MacArthur, Graham, & Fitzgerald, 2006) includes 29 chapters that expertly review accumulated scholarship in areas ranging from writing process theory to writing and brain research to the influence of gender on writing development (with one chapter focusing on multilingual writing in preschool through 12th grade and another on teaching writing in culturally diverse classrooms); but as a reflection of 40 years of writing research across multiple curricular settings, it includes very little on race, ethnicity, and diversity (terms that are also absent from its extensive subject index). Of special interest here is the total absence of race in the two chapters focusing specifically on assessment.

Many of the most important books on WAC also skirt issues of race or ignore them entirely. In none of the collections that now chronicle the development of WAC—*Language Connections: Writing and Reading Across the Curriculum* (Fulwiler & Young, 1982), *Roots in the Sawdust: Writing to Learn Across the Disciplines* (Gere, 1985), *Writing Across the Disciplines: Research Into Practice* (Young & Fulwiler, 1986), *Writing in Academic Disciplines* (Jolliffe, 1988), *Programs That Work: Models and Methods for Writing Across the Curriculum* (Fulwiler & Young, 1990), *Writing to Learn: Strategies for Assigning and Responding to Writing Across the Disciplines* (Sorcinelli & Elbow, 1997), and *Direct from the Disciplines* (Segall & Smart, 2005)—to name just a few—can be found serious, systematic attention to racial and ethnic diversity of any kind, much less in the area of assessment. Bazerman and Russell's *Landmark Essays on Writing Across the Curriculum* (1994), a collection of previously published articles that represent the history of scholarship on WAC, includes no articles focusing overtly on race or diversity. In my edited collection of cases for faculty development in WAC (Anson, 2002), the hundred or so fictitious teachers, administrators, and students include a few who, directly or by suggestion, are people of color, but among the 45 instructional worlds depicted in these scenarios, only three focus thematically on issues of racial diversity in the context of supporting writing in all courses. This absence is noted by Tolar-Burton (2010) in a review-essay of *The WAC Casebook* and five others on WAC (Bazerman et al., 2005; Herrington & Moran, 2005; McLeod et al., 2001; Thaiss & Zawacki, 2006), finding a significant gap in research on the experiences of ethnically diverse students in writing-intensive courses.

With some notable exceptions, (LeCourt, 1996; Villanueva, 2001), the invisibility of race and diversity is itself undiscerned even in most of the historical publications that forecast certain futures or propose new directions for WAC. In "The Future of Writing Across the Curriculum," for example, Thaiss (1988) pointed to several important areas for continued concern, including the nature of WAC textbooks, problems with top-down WAC administration, tensions between "method" and "content," general-education reform, and articulation between colleges and high schools, but said nothing about diverse student populations. Based on national surveys, McLeod's (1989) article on WAC's "second stage and beyond" described the expansion of approaches, resources, and structures of WAC and warned of rigidity that could lead to faculty resistance or unhealthy pedagogy, but she was silent on issues of race and ethnicity. Likewise, Bazerman's (1991) review of four late-1980s books (Brodkey, 1987; Jolliffe, 1988; McLeod, 1988; Simons, 1989) proposed another "second stage" for WAC: a movement away from "missionary zeal" and toward a "realistic assessment of the roles written language actually takes in disciplines and disciplinary classrooms" (p. 209). But although it was "too early to prejudge which concepts [would] produce the most useful analyses" (Bazerman, 1991, p. 212), race was not among them. Jones and Comprone's (1993) "Where Do We Go Next in Writing Across the Curriculum" focused on systemic issues and the tensions between general-education reform and discipline-specific needs but not the needs of diverse populations. My essay "The Future of Writing Across the Curriculum: Consensus and Research" (Anson, 1993) proposed a stronger emphasis on assessment, especially as "competing beliefs surface about the nature and function of writing in different disciplines and about the most appropriate implementation of WAC programs" (p. xv); however, the impact of race on assessment was missing. Walvoord's (1996) "The Future of Writing Across the Curriculum" offered a compelling analysis of the competing forces at work in higher education reform, including the need to accommodate diversity. But Walvoord's solutions (work with other movement organizations, define WAC's relationship to institutional administration and to technology) remained generalized. Thaiss's more recent "Theory in WAC: Where Have We Been, Where Are We Going?" (2001) defined a "core" of WAC principles that have endured over the previous three decades of WAC's development (p. 299). In an interesting analysis of the unresolved tensions in WAC, Thaiss predicted that theory would be needed to respond to the "blurring of the differences between school and community" (p. 319); "difference" is unexplored.

These and other retrospective and projective essays spanning three decades of WAC history—Miraglia and McLeod's "Whither WAC?" (1997), Maimon's "Writing Across the Curriculum: Past, Present, and Future" (1982), Yood's "The Next Stage Is a System: Writing Across the Curriculum and the New Knowledge Society" (2004)—give little or no voice to the complexities inherent in addressing the diversity of students in the classrooms and programs where WAC is implemented and how their diverse backgrounds and experiences affect teaching, learning, and assessment. This problem is not unique to WAC; Prendergast (1998), for example, argues that "while it is often called upon as a category to delineate cultural groups that will be the focal subjects of research studies, the relationship of race to the composing process is seldom fully explored. Instead race becomes subsumed into the powerful tropes of 'basic writer,' 'stranger' to the academy, or the trope of the generalized, marginalized 'other'" (p. 36).

Shedding Light

Not one of the scholars who have produced all the previously mentioned books, articles, chapters, websites, and search engines is unconcerned about educational equality, access, and the relationship between writing and students' identities; many have spent their lives in the service of a fairer and more inclusive system of higher education, and increasingly, they are analyzing students' experiences in cross-curricular writing in ways that account for their unique backgrounds and developing identities, particularly in upper-level classes (e.g., Herrington & Curtis, 2000; Sternglass, 1997; Walvoord & McCarthy, 1990). Racial invisibility in WAC comes not from conscious exclusion. Instead, various historical, political, and disciplinary forces appear to have filtered race and diversity from central consideration in the WAC movement.

These forces affect WAC leaders as much as they affect teachers within the disciplines. For example, the subject of race is perceived to generate layers of additional complexity over principles, theories, and pedagogies already challenging to faculty in various disciplines to interpret and apply to their teaching. Although approaches to deeper, longer-term faculty development in WAC are gaining in popularity, such as learning communities (Zawacki & Williams, 2001) and semester-long seminars (Anson, 2006b), the brief, onetime workshop still enjoys a dominant position as the most common form of WAC delivery (Thaiss, 2009). In such contexts, workshop leaders may be reluctant to complicate their agendas by opening up discussions of race and diversity before faculty have fully internalized and applied new ideas about how to rethink their roles as literacy coaches, how to design effective, goal-driven writing assignments, how to evaluate student work fairly and efficiently, or how to support students' developments as writers through methods such as peer response and revision that require expert attention to students' behaviors, attitudes, and learning processes. That issues of diversity are often at the center of these instructional challenges is beside the point when students become the subject of abstract principles operationalized in generic classroom strategies or when "best practices" focus on heavily genre-based assignments and rubrics without attention to how students with diverse backgrounds will understand and respond to them and how teachers will read and evaluate those responses. Administrators on campuses and guest presenters alike are complicit. Of the many dozens of occasions I have been invited to campuses to lead WAC workshops or consult on curriculum or administration, the subject of race or diversity has rarely come up. In deference to my hosts' desired focus and coverage, I have not given it sustained attention.[2]

The codependency of this avoidance has deeper roots in the compartmentalized and bureaucratized structures of different disciplines. As Russell (1990) puts it, "cross-curricular writing programs, past and present, are negotiated by many competing interests, which have a cultural, economic, or political stake in the expansion (or restriction) of advanced forms of literacy" (p. 66). Because most WAC leaders occupy disciplinary homes in the humanities, they are acutely aware of how faculty in other areas construct their identities, and they often try to distance themselves, or their programs, from their own affiliations. Beneath WAC leaders' delicate negotiations of their disciplinary identity lies a fear that colleagues in fields such as economics, nuclear physics, soil science, or music history will resist the imposition of the leaders' values, processes, and language. Or they fear that if they too strongly identify as English specialists, their colleagues—often teachers of narrowly defined content areas—will think they are expected to feign expertise in stereotyped writing subjects they are unprepared to teach, such as grammar, style, and the principles of classical rhetoric—or, worse, will loudly proclaim ignorance of such matters.

WAC scholarship heightens such concerns about disciplinary identity by challenging the motivations for outreach. Walvoord (1992) admonishes WAC leaders not to adopt a "training" approach that arms faculty with procedures that they mindlessly apply to their instruction or a "conversion" model in which "faculty in other disciplines are heathen who must be converted to the Right Way" (p. 11). Although they are often made to seem logistical, these dangers are as much about the social and interpersonal dimensions of WAC and the way they are imbricated with the political and the territorial. Understanding the complex and often idiosyncratic (inter)personal and structural conditions in specific institutions, departments, and courses helps us to make sense of both resistance and potential for change and, therefore, how to adopt the most appropriate roles for collaboration (Halasz et al., 2006; see also Donahue, 2002). But politically charged subjects such as race may be too great a risk for those who perceive themselves to be walking delicate lines as they enter into other disciplinary spaces for the purpose of motivating educational change and innovation.

Acting on these complexities of role and identity, WAC leaders may also fear invoking subjects that are more often associated with their own and affiliated disciplines. They may acknowledge the strong interest in cultural and racial diversity in the arts, humanities, and social sciences but mistakenly believe that research in the hard and even applied sciences focuses exclusively on human-free objects and phenomena. Fear or misunderstanding of scholarly difference can cause WAC leaders tacitly to adjust their approaches to match certain disciplinary audiences—to make WAC "relevant." When such an audience represents a blend of many disciplines (as is often the case in a campus-wide workshop), its very "multipleness" forces WAC leaders to make more singular their strategies of implementation or generalize them beyond consideration of diverse groups of students. Pedagogically, it may feel safer to focus on assumed institutional goals, such as helping faculty to achieve certain definable outcomes of communication competence for their students that often relate to career preparation.

However we might explain the lack of attention to race and diversity in WAC, it clearly has its source in the methods that WAC advocates have used to engage colleagues who work in diverse disciplinary and curricular contexts that are shaped by institutional practices and traditions, disciplinary identity formations, and the push and pull of territoriality arising from competition for resources and recognition. As Mahala (1991) has observed about the need for broader educational reform, "[i]nstead of addressing the most contentious issues, WAC programs have often maintained a political invisibility, tailoring theory to institutional divisions and the demands from teachers for 'methods that work,' rather than really interrogating prevailing attitudes about knowledge, language, and learning" (p. 773). Tightly interwoven in those attitudes are largely unexplored dimensions of diversity and its relation to the assessment of writing.

Toward Visibility

In one of the few exceptions to the invisibility of race in the literature on WAC and its future, Villanueva (2001) argues that we need to consider the relations among discourse, culture, economics, and politics (both as ideology and as power). This "third stage" of WAC will involve a far greater obligation to bring into our cross-disciplinary conversations those issues, theories, research, and reflections about racial diversity that have been absent, "enter[ing] into a dialogue across the disciplines so as better to understand the social processes that could relegate such a large number to the trouble-heap" (p. 170). Although assessment would seem to be the last place to start such conversations—reinforcing the use of writing as a test of ability or knowledge rather than as a tool for learning and development—it is also, for almost all disciplines, an unavoidable pedagogical and curricular reality whose neglect comes at a price. Assessment, as Kathleen Blake Yancey points out in her chapter on the Insight Resume, nevertheless challenges faculty and administrators to broaden their understandings of writing.

With WAC's roots in individual pedagogy, the classroom presents itself as the first context where race and assessment deserve heightened attention. Work on student evaluation and assessment in WAC has been dominated by teacher-focused strategies such as designing grading rubrics, easing the paper load, and responding effectively to students' papers based on specific learning goals. When it is acknowledged that problems such as garbled sentences or deviations from the conventions of a disciplinary genre may have their roots in confusing assignments or lack of support for the development of students' papers, improvement may involve working on assignment design, creating grading guides that students can use formatively, practicing more focused response strategies, learning about campus resources such as the writing center, and becoming familiar with online and text resources such as handbooks. All of these are helpful teaching strategies, but they are often generalized and decoupled from issues of diversity, such as the language varieties students bring from their homes and communities into academic/disciplinary contexts whose linguistic codes may be unfamiliar. In many courses across the curriculum, the process of evaluation is especially challenging in the context of English Language Learners, who often become a "problem" that discourages faculty from paying more attention to writing. Even as teachers wish that all students could come into their classes able to write "clean" prose devoid of surface errors, writing is especially sullied to them by the complexities of "language interference" among international and ELL students. The economies of scale in most models of WAC create outliers of such students, who require additional support from specialists and thereby alleviate the need for all faculty to engage in sustained, collective discussion of the social and cultural issues associated with difference (see Zamel, 1995).

What would it take to bring race into the assessment of writing in discipline-based courses? First, a far more conscious effort in faculty development in WAC is needed to focus on students as individual learners. Practices of discursive socialization are always about identity, yet much of the composition scholarship in this area—crucial to advances in WAC—focuses on students as a generalized construct, not as individuals who bring specific histories, experiences, and "vernacular literacies" to their learning. How students view their relationship to a discipline or major is a formulation of its institutional ideology, which includes its history of diversity or lack thereof, the presence or absence of role models, and how its various constituent communities look on the value of its work. In a series of longitudinal case studies, for example,

Roozen (2008, 2009a, 2009b) documents the way that students of color must negotiate the "resonance and dissonance of multiple and diverse textual ways of being in the world" (Roozen & Herrera, 2010). Drawing on identity theory and activity theory, Roozen uncovers multiple kinds and sources of literate practice that students bring into the classroom. In focusing only on conventional academic tasks, teachers can entirely overlook these practices and experiences. The effects can be unfortunate, as students' diverse literacies become squelched through routinized evaluations imposed quickly on the results of stereotypical academic tasks. The solution comes from an awareness of "how our sense of ourselves as literate persons is forged in the interplay of multiple encounters with literacy, private as well as public, and how authoring a literate life means engaging in the ongoing work of reconciling the conflicts and synergies among them" (Roozen, 2009b, p. 541).

Of course, models of writing development, attention to students' composing processes, and methods of evaluation often do form the basis of discussion and advice in faculty workshops, but they are treated as general principles applied uniformly across different populations of students. To mitigate the most commonly mentioned source of resistance to WAC—the time it takes to read, respond to, and evaluate student writing—WAC leaders are reluctant to advocate even more attention to the needs of individual students, including the advantages of learning about those students' literate histories and making principled, humane decisions about the best responses, resources, and advice to give them. The problem intensifies in the context of larger classes, where students are anonymous, where the conventional delivery mode is lecture, and where WAC leaders must sell the prospect of frequent writing along with promises (and methods) to keep additional burdens as light as possible. Beyond the course—in the department, college, or entire institution—the very idea of sensitivity to language variation can set off protests or fears about the loss of standards (see Baron, 1992).

The often tacit effects of racial identity on teachers' evaluation of writing also cry out for more focus in faculty development. For example, in a case study, Matarese and I examined teacher response to the writing of students who demonstrated definable features of African American English (Matarese & Anson, 2010). In spite of their training as writing instructors, the teachers in this study demonstrated so little knowledge of dialect differences that in some cases they were hindering their students' learning with bad advice or overcompensating their assumptions about their African American students' writing by erroneously correcting perfectly good sentences. In a study of evaluation practices among instructors in Fresno State's composition program, Bulinski et al. (2009) found uneven relationships between certain kinds or frequencies of comments (praise, criticism, marking of error, etc.) and both students' and teachers' race or ethnicity, suggesting that many unconscious elements of instructional and racial ideology affect teachers' complex processes of reading and reaching judgments on students' work. If such findings emerge from the pedagogy of professional writing teachers, we can imagine the faculty-development needs of instructors across the curriculum who readily admit that they were not trained to teach writing.

Other, more formative methods of evaluation offer further starting points for discussions of race in WAC. Peer response groups, for example, are among the most often abandoned formative classroom strategies to support writing development across the disciplines. Without expert coordination, modeling or direct training, clear expectations, follow-up, and accountability, peer response groups fail to yield meaningful information to writers, fortuitous revisions to their texts, or improvements in long-term discursive and rhetorical knowledge. But far deeper concerns than the mechanics of turn-taking or how to evaluate students' participation arise when we consider such groups as contact zones (Pratt, 1991; see also Bizzell, 1994), where students of different backgrounds work with each other on writing that often represents their beliefs, experiences, constructions of identity, habits of mind, and discursive practices shaped by their home communities. Simply showing faculty the logistics of peer revision conferences neglects to make them aware of how student collaboration can erase difference through the creation of artificial consensus, usually through the imposition of dominant social and cultural values and "authoritarian leveling toward the norm through peer pressure" (Johnson, 1986; see also Myers, 1986, and Smit, 1989). Even more complicated is orchestrating such groups when the subject matter of the students' writing deals with issues of race and diversity, as it will in many courses in the arts, humanities, and social sciences. Faculty new to such student-centered approaches to supporting writing development—and even experienced faculty yet to break through the surface of logistical matters such as timing and accountability—may be unaware of the need for students to establish common ground prior to collaboration or of the likelihood that students of color will feel silenced in the process of peer evaluation (see Henry, 1994). Opening up discussions of the evaluative complexities of difference in small-group revision conferences also provides faculty with opportunities to consider broader questions about the role of diversity in teaching. Such questions also apply to contexts, especially in the applied sciences and engineering, that involve collaborative writing and oral presentations (often by way of preparing students to do similar work in business and industry).

The challenges of preparing faculty to address students' needs in the assessment of their writing are not limited to what goes on in their classrooms. Highly tacit racist assumptions perpetuated by social mythologies and educational lore can affect instructors' beliefs about support programs such as writing centers, sites where they might send students for additional help with their writing. Arguing that critical race theory needs to inform the work of writing centers, Condon (2007) proposes a "sustained consideration of whether, how, and to what degree writing centers have historically been used as or complicit with racial projects within our institutions and higher education writ large" (p. 21). Just as WAC has been unable to attend to issues of race and racism in its work, writing center administrators, busy with multiple responsibilities and constituencies and sometimes tacitly endorsing assimilationist approaches to literacy instruction, unwittingly allow issues of race to "go underground" as they carry on their work (p. 20). Issues of race, language difference, and the contradictory dispositions teachers and programs bring to the table should be central in faculty development, curricular design, and departmental consultation; they inevitably emerge when the focus is on the assessment of students' work.

WAC's slow development in the area of program-wide assessment offers another likely explanation for racial invisibility—and a space for new activity. Assessment on a scale beyond individual classrooms may provide the impetus to learn about new perspectives, research, and pedagogical approaches that can realize greater equity in student achievement. Historically, WAC programs have taken the form of designated writing-intensive courses cut off from the rest of the curriculum, or grassroots efforts that focus on changing individual faculty through collective activities such as workshops. When WAC programs broaden their focus to program- or department-level implementation and assessment (Anson, 2006a; Anson, Carter, Dannels, & Rust, 2003; Anson & Dannels, 2009; Carter, 2003), common interest in student achievement often pushes faculty and administrators to begin acknowledging the important relationships between performance and demographic factors (see Yancey & Huot, 1997). Especially when program-level assessment is conducted formatively, faculty may begin to recognize the reasons for disparities in students' work along the lines of race, ethnicity, or immigrant status, or how to approach such disparities in the full spirit of reflective practice. WAC programs can gather site-specific student data so that a picture of racialized institutional effects can be understood more clearly. Such awareness driven by large-scale assessment has been demonstrated in other contexts, such as engineering programs' concerns about the low rates of minority student success, retention, and recruitment (e.g., Moller-Wong & Eide, 1997; Seymour & Hewitt, 1994).

Scholarship on assessment from the field of composition studies (e.g., Ball, 1997, 1999; Hoover & Politzer, 1981) can provide helpful perspectives to administrators interested in assessing writing across a major or department. For example, knowing that the use of the past tense in historical writing alienates Native American history majors who do not share the same epistemology of time as their teachers (LeCourt, 1996) can inform the construction of high-stakes exams, papers, and department-level assessments. Knowing that students' construction of graders' racial identities on writing tests changes the way that the students position their arguments and self-representations (Poe, 2006b) can inform the methods used for programmatic and institutional assessment.

It is also important for those in charge of WAC programs to critique the driving force of larger-scale (departmental or institutional) assessment. When imposed from above, writing assessment can undermine the efforts of WAC programs or can lead to the problematic reshaping of WAC efforts. For example, institutions often experience a kind of nervous energy from the specter of accreditation agencies, which demand accountability through quality enhancement plans and various assessments focusing on general literacy and critical thinking skills. Administrators' obsession with reaccreditation can blind them to the linguistic and pedagogical complexities of supporting writing, narrowing their agenda to the eradication of surface features of "bad English" and then calling upon the WAC program to fix the problem. In such a context, the role of a WAC program is to help administrators and faculty oversight groups to understand that textual or linguistic preoccupations represent only one lens for the support of students' writing and to introduce other perspectives (e.g., sociocultural, cognitive, developmental; see Kucer, 2009) that can reveal inequities in student support and gaps in knowledge about the relationship of race to performance. The need is greatest on campuses where a lack of support for WAC opens the door to regressive assessment programs that are unresponsive to student and faculty development.

Developing Foresight

All of these and other pedagogical and programmatic concerns point to the need for increased research and pedagogical activity in WAC, assessment, and diversity. Although it is strengthening, empirical research on WAC is far outpaced by the voluminous instructional, programmatic, and administrative literature, which itself, as I have shown, has not adequately spoken to issues of student and teacher diversity. We know little about students' experiences as writers across the range of their college courses, and even less about the experiences of students of color. And we know almost nothing about the experience of teachers of color as they support students' writing development in their disciplines. As Freedman (1996) has suggested of composition studies more generally:

> Our research will benefit by continuing to be inclusive—of a diverse population of learners, taught by a diverse population of teachers, using approaches that allow for a diversity of ways of learning—with new knowledge gathered from diverse sources and with diverse methods [...] Specific research on the learning of diverse populations pushes us to elaborate existing theories to account more specifically for how writing is learned across varied populations. (p. 184)

Clearly, WAC must make institutional, programmatic, and field-related commitments to longer-term developmental initiatives, where faculty can dig deeper into issues that until now have remained hidden or are dealt with too perfunctorily to have much meaning. Such commitments will mean stronger alliances with other areas of educational support, such as diversity offices, minority student councils, and offices of institutional assessment. WAC faculty development and training needs to refocus some of its efforts, seeing issues of writing assessment across the disciplines as understanding and honoring language differences that may change disciplinary discourses and practices from the bottom up. Such efforts will mean making visible the students who write in our courses and curricula and the teachers who assign, support, read, respond to, and evaluate that writing in the multiple contexts where it is given life.

This work will not be easy. It will often mean finding ways for departments and disciplines to engage in the kind of self-scrutiny that makes their members uneasy or seems like a distraction from their work. And it will mean continuing to reject accommodationist approaches to writing assessment across the curriculum while simultaneously recognizing the dangers of alienating colleagues or creating perceptions that we are engaged in ideological conversion.

Notes

---

[1] For simplicity, in this essay the acronym WAC is used to refer to all initiatives focusing on the integration of communication pedagogies into instruction in all disciplines, including CAC and CxC (Communication Across the Curriculum), WID (Writing in the Disciplines), WTL (Writing to Learn), and ECAC (Electronic Communication Across the Curriculum).

[2] A few WAC programs do focus on issues of race and diversity in their programming, such as the University of Vermont's Writing in the Disciplines Program, which has co-sponsored sessions on diversity with the Center for Teaching and Learning.

CHAPTER TWO

Getting Off the Boat and onto the Bank: Exploring the Validity of Shared Evaluation Methods for Students of Color in College Writing Assessment

Diane Kelly-Riley

Scholars in writing assessment have advocated adopting evaluation methods that arise out of local context, opening the possibility of integrating classroom learning, faculty expertise, and student agency into the undergraduate curriculum (White, 1985; Smith, 1993; Huot, 2002a; Haswell, 2001; Inoue, 2009b). As a result, shared evaluation methodologies—*practices in which local context drives the articulation of assessment standards*—have become more widely used. In contrast to traditional educational testing methods that sit apart from teacher input, shared evaluation procedures attempt to integrate college classroom standards as well as experiences of teachers into evaluation criteria and the assessment process; these practices have been the trademark of emerging writing assessment practices that are attentive to local context (Yancey & Weiser, 1997; Broad, 1997, 2000; Haswell, 1998a; Hamp-Lyons & Condon, 2000). Shared evaluation practices include the expert-rater methodology in which teachers make placement decisions based on student writing (Smith, 1993; Haswell & Wyche, 1996); directed self-placement in which faculty articulate the outcomes of a particular composition curriculum and then have students choose the most appropriate placement (Royer & Gilles, 2003); hermeneutic standardization in which faculty articulate standards for the end of a program and measure how well students have met those standards (Broad, 1997, 2000); and student reflection in which students document their own academic progress (Yancey, 1997). Shared evaluation methods are not specific to any one mode of assessing writing—portfolio, eportfolio, impromptu essay exam, self-analysis—as all of these can be and are evaluated with different methodologies (non-shared evaluation methods would include holistic, primary trait, and analytic scoring). The hallmark of shared evaluation is the articulation and application of standards by a community that attempts to connect context-rich assessment to the complexity of the classroom experience,

faculty practice, and the learning environment. In other words, shared evaluation methods rely on the assessors to articulate and apply criteria that are derived from a specific local context; these methods differ from other forms of
assessment that impose standards and criteria and ask the raters to apply them
to students' work.

Unfortunately, research into shared evaluation writing assessment practices has not fully attended to the shifting conceptions of validity, much less
the impact of these evaluations on various demographic groups, particularly
students of color. Murphy (2007) argues that "the issue of validity is critical
[...] because test scores provide the basis for long-term decisions about students
concerning placement, selection, certification, and promotion. These long-
term decisions can have significant consequences for students and, as we all
know, not all of those consequences are good" (p. 228). Because most shared
evaluation methods used for large-scale writing assessment programs have not
undergone validity scrutiny, as several in this collection have noted, there is
not a clear sense of the consequences of these context-rich assessment methods
for student populations. Specifically, the consequences of this type of writing
assessment remain largely unknown for students of color. This essay advocates
for more rigorous validity inquiry of shared evaluation writing assessment
practices in line with the revision to the concept of validity in the *Standards for
Educational and Psychological Testing* (AERA, APA, & NCME, 1999). In addition, this essay discusses a useful framework from historical interpretation that
considers both wider contextual and stakeholder issues to help expand the
exploration of validity in college writing assessment programs that use shared
evaluation practices. As an example, I draw on my previous work (Kelly-Riley,
2006, 2011) in which I developed and validated a quantitatively based methodology that enabled me to examine students' experiences on a large-scale
writing portfolio assessment. In particular, using statistical and methodological
processes, this earlier work focused on how students of color fared in the assessment system and how race factored into the raters' evaluation behavior
(Kelly-Riley, 2006, 2011). The present essay focuses on the theoretical arguments for actively examining issues of validity through the lens of race.

As the director of the Washington State University (WSU) Writing Assessment Program, I have had the opportunity for many years to observe the
dynamics of the expert-rater evaluation sessions used for the first-year-level
Writing Placement Exam and junior-level Writing Portfolio (see Haswell &
Wyche, 1996). The expert-rater system relies on the classroom expertise of faculty to predict a student's readiness for specific writing challenges within different points of an undergraduate curriculum. In the WSU system, faculty are
recruited from the instructional ranks, based on their experience and expertise

in assigning and evaluating writing, to become paid evaluators. These faculty are hired and trained by the Writing Assessment Program to evaluate students' readiness for the various writing-rich courses within the undergraduate curriculum at WSU. These assessments occur before students enroll in the first-year writing curriculum (Writing Placement Exam) and again at the junior level before students enroll in the upper-division Writing in the Major courses within their disciplines (Writing Portfolio).

At the first-year level, faculty evaluate two impromptu exams written in one session; at the junior level, faculty evaluate five pieces of writing—two impromptu pieces and three pieces of writing from college-level coursework. Faculty articulate and apply standards for "good writing" within the specific contexts of the curriculum. Thus, the focus of the assessment is shifted from a barrier exam to a diagnostic exam—one that matches student writing abilities to appropriate writing support necessary to manage the writing requirements of the first-year composition course or the upper-division Writing in the Major courses. In doing so, the evaluation methodology attempts to integrate classroom expectations, student work produced in the classroom, and faculty expertise into the evaluation process (Haswell, 2001).

The inclusion of faculty expertise as part of the assessment process has provided important teacher buy-in, but little to no research has been done related to the effects of faculty articulation and application of standards on students' writing for either the general student population or for more specific demographic groups. As I detailed elsewhere (2006, 2011), an African American student was the impetus for my research project related to race and shared evaluation methods employed in the large-scale writing portfolio assessment at WSU. This student told me that she had heard that black students failed the Writing Portfolio more than other students. I had no answer; since the inception of the program in the early 1990s, we had not collected data about race or ethnicity.

But issues of race and ethnicity are mentioned and surface routinely in the writing assessment program. I have heard faculty raters say that a student's writing sounded "like Ebonics," and some have wondered aloud—rather unself-consciously—about how to evaluate such writing. I have also observed faculty discussions about the level of competency to which a multilingual writer can reach—insinuating that at some point a multilingual writer crosses a threshold in which they must be cheating to be writing so well. Other faculty and tutors have commented anecdotally about the seemingly high enrollments of students of color in their basic writing courses or in the courses that provide the instructional support required by the Writing Portfolio. In a recent internal report, Meloni (2009) documented that nearly 70% of students placed into the basic writing course at WSU were white, 22% were students of color, and 8% had no data regarding their race. Proportionately, though, the placement of students of color into the first-year basic writing course is higher than the university enrollment; approximately 15% of WSU undergraduates are students of color. The data for the other courses have yet to be investigated. Within this collection, Lioi and Merola express similar anecdotal evidence to suggest that the writing assessment systems at their respective institutions have similarly disproportionate results for students of color.

Such anecdotes are compelling and raise questions about shared evaluation practices. Advocates of such methods seem to operate with an assumption that the classroom and undergraduate curriculum are sites of egalitarian, democratic values in which all students, faculty, and disciplines are thought of and treated equally. That is, those of us in composition studies operate with the sense that if teachers are driving the assessment process, the process is somehow better or safeguarded from the type of threats that exist with tests designed by people with educational measurement backgrounds. But if classrooms are microcosms of our larger society—complete with problems of injustice and inequity—then it is not reasonable to think that all students or teachers or disciplines can be safeguarded against intentional or unintentional bias.

Shared evaluation practices evolved in response to objections to and limitations in assessment practices in the field of educational measurement. Since the 1980s, when shared evaluation practices were first used, the field of educational measurement has evolved and developed. In particular, the concept of validity has been revised significantly. Validity was once understood as a concept that was comprised of individual components—construct, content, face, or predictive—and was employed to consider the merits of a test. Recently, the construct of validity used by the educational testing community has been revised in light of innovations in alternative and performance-based evaluations (another revision of these standards is forthcoming). In these revisions, conceptions of validity have shifted to examine the use and interpretation of test scores in particular contexts. The Standards state that "validity refers to the degree to which evidence and theory support the interpretations of test scores entailed by the proposed uses of tests" (AERA, APA, & NCME, 1999, p. 9). The new definition of validity asserts that the test itself is not enough to satisfy the focus of a validity inquiry. Rather, validity inquiries should examine the use and interpretation of test scores and the consequences of those scores to the individuals taking the tests. In theory, integrating teachers' values and standards into the assessment of students' writing should be a good thing. But the open-ended complexity in rating processes presents serious problems for validity. Faculty raters or the other members of the rating community may unwittingly introduce silently held, negative beliefs in these evaluation sessions. Without validity inquiry into shared evaluation rating processes, we will not understand how these assessments operate, nor will we understand if there are unintended consequences to the students who take them.

Ronda's Historical Lens

Moss (1998) advocates studying "the actual discourse that occurs around the products and practices of testing—to see how those whose lives a testing program impacts are using the representations (interpretations) it produces" (p. 119). To help extend the frame for validity investigations for college writing shared evaluation practices, I have found James Ronda's approaches to historical interpretation useful and applicable. Ronda is a historian who has written extensively about the early nineteenth-century Lewis and Clark expedition's search for the Northwest Passage. Ronda's contribution to this research area (1984) opened up traditional academic scholarship about Lewis and Clark to include perspectives and experiences of the native peoples encountered along the expedition. In 2006, I attended his final lecture about the bicentennial of the Lewis and Clark journey. Ronda's observation that "the folks who tell the stories own them" struck a chord for me because it emphasized that the perspective of the story favors the storyteller. Ronda argued that the historical perspective of the story "carries its own implications, its own moral burden," and that "all stories from the past—no matter what they are—impose obligations on us [...] The obligation here is all about choices" (2006). He detailed several narrative approaches in historical research of the Lewis and Clark expedition and the opening up of the American West. These narrative themes include Lewis and Clark as white, male heroes; the expedition as a band of brothers; Lewis and Clark as imperialists bent on subjugating native people; and Lewis and Clark as objective scientists.

According to Ronda, these narrative approaches fall short because they operate with a linear story line with a singular, predictable outcome that suits the narrator's perspective. Instead, Ronda (2006) argues that we must "get off the boat; get on the bank [...] Change the angle of vision; try to see the story through different eyes; try to listen to other voices." Examining the narratives of writing assessment through Ronda's framework can help expand our understanding of validity, shared evaluation, and the experience of students of color in the writing assessment enterprise.

The View From The Boat

Ronda's observation about the narrow perspective of the storyteller echoes the narratives about the emergence of shared evaluation practices and mirrors the narrow themes identified by Ronda in the Lewis and Clark scholarship. These perspectives tend to focus predominantly on the heroics of the field of college writing assessment—venturing away from the perils of standardized testing into the unknown wilds of assessment. The story of Edward White and his colleagues at California State University is well documented. In the early 1970s, they won the responsibility to design the freshman placement exam. White (2001) described the realizations that sank in once they had been awarded this responsibility: these were English people "before the days of composition studies [...] with only the vaguest notions about assessment theory [...]; they wondered, 'Now what?'" (p. 307). Similarly, the Washington State University portfolio designers likened their feat in designing a large-scale writing portfolio assessment system to riding over Niagara Falls in a barrel (Haswell, Johnson-Shull, & Wyche-Smith, 1994); Hamp-Lyons and Condon (2000) refer to their implementation of portfolio assessment for the freshman writing program placement at the University of Michigan as being "poised on the edge of an abyss."

Such narratives of writing assessment, while noting important advances in the field, do not move beyond identification of hazards that lie ahead. There has been a great deal of criticism and many calls for research regarding potential bias in assessment based on race or ethnicity (Mountford, 1999; Farr & Nardini, 1996; Lippi-Green, 1997; Hamp-Lyons & Condon, 2000), but our scholarship and research in this area have not advanced beyond these repeated calls for action. Ironically, our perspective "from the boat" tends to favor regaling others about our heroic administrative accomplishments or issuing new research agendas. For the most part, college writing assessment practices have not paid attention to what these advances in writing assessment mean for the programs in which they are situated, how they operate, or the effects on students who take them.

Stepping Onto The Bank

Ronda's admonition to "get off the boat; get on the bank" opens the possibility for a more complex understanding of the validity of shared evaluation practices for students of color in large-scale writing assessment programs. Once we venture off "the boat," it becomes clear that the view from the bank is quite complicated, especially for diverse student populations. For example, Delpit (1988) observes that such students experience difficulties because of their unfamiliarity with the aspects of the "culture of power" that operates within educational systems. Steele (1997) asserts that negative stereotypes contribute to lower academic performance. Allen and Niss (1990) document the unbalanced treatment of students of color in college classrooms where white and foreign students are rewarded and engaged with more by teachers. Harber (1998) asserts that students of color receive more lenient feedback on their academic performance, giving them a false sense of achievement.

Likewise, research in composition studies documents complexities in assessing the writing of students of color. Piche, Rubin, Turner, and Michlin (1978) discuss the linguistic stereotype hypothesis, which asserts "speech elicits social identifications which in turn trigger those trait ascriptions to the speaker which are stereotypically associated with his social group" (p. 107). They investigated whether teachers could reliably infer the racial identity of writers based on the presence or absence of black nonstandard written English markers, and whether or not those markers affected the qualitative judgments of children's written compositions. The researchers concluded that their study provided "no clear support for the salience of a linguistically-mediated process of social stereotyping" (p. 116). However, the researchers found that there was an "existence of a general stereotype conditioning in teachers' expectations for black students" (p. 117).

Ball and Lardner (1997) document how preconceived notions of students' abilities affected student performance. In the 1979 Ann Arbor case, "the Court ruled that the teachers' unconscious but evident attitudes toward the African American English used by the plaintiff children constituted a language barrier that impeded the students' educational progress" (p. 471). Bowie and Bond (1994) found that teachers "continued to exhibit negative attitudes toward African American English, often stating that African American English [had] a faulty grammar system and that children who [spoke] African American English [were] less capable than children who [spoke] standard English" (p. 112). Finally, Ball (1997) concluded that holistic writing assessment procedures disadvantaged students of color because they do not share the same linguistic features as middle-class European students and the middle-class European teachers who evaluated their writing. These examples document the troublesome relationship between teachers and students, particularly students of color, and the contexts in which student work is assessed. If teachers bring "stereotype conditioning" or "negative attitudes" to the classroom, it is entirely likely that they may be doing so in other arenas in which they are asked to use their expertise to apply writing criteria.

Thus, from the "boat," it seems that we have been short-sighted, seeing mostly our administrative accomplishments. For shared evaluation to work equitably, we need to make clear what the contexts in which assessments occur really mean. For shared evaluation methods, such articulations do not happen inevitably or automatically. In fact, Smith (1993) and Nelson and Kelly-Riley (2001) document that expert-rater processes retain a large amount of disagreement in the evaluation of weak or strong writers. In other words, students who have not met articulated standards and face consequences (of additional course work, time, monetary costs, and stigma associated with not passing an exam) remain those not necessarily served by shared evaluation. Elbow's question—which he originally leveled at holistic writing assessment—remains relevant for assessment methods that use shared evaluation processes: "what kind of proof do we have that students are wrong when they say, 'I do not belong in this dummy class?'" (1996, p. 93). This question should motivate us to step off the boat onto the bank.

Bridging The Boat And Bank

As I have argued elsewhere (2006, 2011), while there have been notable empirically based validity studies in college writing assessment (Smith, 1993; Williamson & Huot, 1993; Haswell, 1998b, 2000; O'Neill, 2003; Elliot, Briller, & Joshi, 2007), few inquiries have examined the experience of students of color for shared evaluation. Instead, validity investigations into race and writing assessment have occurred mostly within the K-12 realm (Callahan, 1995, 1999; Supovitz & Brennan, 1997; Ball, 1997). Bond (1995) asserts, "the available information on performance-based assessments [does not] provide sufficient evidence for a determination of *bias*, narrowly defined as differentially valid test interpretations for different social groups" (p. 22). Bond suggests that the preliminary evidence for equity and adverse impact, defined simply as substantially different mean scores by subgroups, did not look good. Bond also cautions that examination of consequential aspects of validity should "not only [include] the elimination of elements in assessment that unduly *disadvantage minority persons* but also the elimination of construct-irrelevant elements that may subtly *advantage majority persons over others*" (1995, p. 23). More recently, Murphy (2007) advocates for cultural validity in writing assessment—an overt consideration of culture and consequences for students of color; and Inoue (2009b) advocates for racial validity, a call to use such inquiries as a way to change the power and dynamics of institutionalized inequity.

To bridge the newer visions of validity for college writing assessment, we have to know how or if shared evaluation methods might result in unintentional consequences for students of color. Cronbach (1988) anticipated this need for accountability to the stakeholders most negatively affected by the results of a test, stating that "tests that impinge on the rights and life chances of individuals are inherently disputable" (p. 6), and adverse social conditions, in and of themselves, call the validity of test use into question. But do the unresolved issues about shared evaluation writing assessment methodologies represent "adverse social conditions"?

Because shared evaluation practices lack the control inherent in the experimental process as well as a static, "true" psychometric construct to be measured, they present new challenges to writing assessment administrators and practitioners in their efforts to validate these socially constructed methods of assessment. In my own experience, I had to establish separate quasi-experimental research projects conducted outside of the actual evaluation process. Such challenges present opportunities for large-scale writing assessment programs to evolve into more mature programs of validity inquiry that extend beyond the training received in many composition doctoral programs. These validational processes require knowledge of appropriate research design, acceptable numbers of study subjects, and a knowledge of statistics.

Shared Evaluation Practices At WSU

Initially at WSU, validity inquiries of WSU's Writing Portfolio examined more traditional constructs of validity in the expert-rater system. At the time of the Writing Assessment Program's implementation, one of the most controversial and innovative portions of the Writing Portfolio evaluation methodology was the development of the Simple Pass rating. Research (Smith 1993; Haswell & Wyche, 1996; Haswell, 1998b) validated the process of evaluating obviously passable writing based on four separate evaluations of student writing (one impromptu exam and three course papers) instead of relying on two raters to evaluate the same piece, or multiple pieces, of work for confirmation of the score. The Simple Pass rating allowed more time and consideration to be spent by the raters on the more "questionable" writing—writing that was either really strong or really weak. Subsequently, the rates for pass, pass with distinction, and needs work were tracked, and this line of traditional validity inquiry has become the standard for the WSU program in the form of biennial reports (beginning with Haswell, 1995, to Evans & He, 2007). The Simple Pass rating proved reliable and stable over time and did not present the problems that the portfolio designers originally anticipated.

In spite of the warm reception of the Writing Portfolio by faculty and administrators at WSU, student complaints about the Writing Portfolio have provided the impetus for most of our other validity inquiries. For example, students complained about having to complete the requirement and were most vocal about fulfilling additional course requirements if their writing was deemed Needs Work. Initially, these complaints were written off as something to be expected—lazy students, trying to get out of requirements. But Nelson and Kelly-Riley (2001) found that some of the students' complaints, particularly those who were required to take additional course work, were warranted. This study showed that many students were dissatisfied with the supplemental writing support required by the Writing Portfolio—not because of the quality of the course—but because the students had delayed (and the program had allowed) their completion of the portfolio assessment and the subsequent course until their final semester of their senior year. This delay undermined the intent of the midcareer diagnostic assessment; these students actually preferred to take a three-credit writing course instead of a one-credit writing tutorial that could not be connected to any kind of writing course because the students were in their final semesters without courses that assigned writing. This inquiry did not specifically address validity issues for students of color, but it provided the first instance of stepping off the boat and onto the bank to understand students' perspectives of the Writing Portfolio.

A couple of years later, the African American student mentioned earlier raised the possibility that students of color earned higher percentages of Needs Work ratings and triggered a quantitative, descriptive validity inquiry into the performance data by race and another inquiry into the ways in which faculty raters articulated and applied standards in the WSU Writing Portfolio (Kelly-Riley, 2006, 2011). These studies found that racial groups performed differently on the two types of writing in the WSU Writing Portfolio, the impromptu exam and the course papers submitted from college-level classes:

> An analysis of variance showed that the difference in performance by race on the timed writing portion of the Writing Portfolio was significant, $F_{(4, 503)}=6.032$, $p=.000$. Post hoc analyses using Tukey's LSD for significance indicated that Black (M=1.58, SD=.496), API (M=1.59, SD=.509), and Hispanic (M=1.7, SD=.462) students' timed writing performances were significantly lower than White students (M=1.84, SD=.550) [...]. The results indicated a significant difference in the performance on the final Writing Portfolio by race, $F_{(4, 744)}=3.120$, $p=.015$. Post hoc analyses using Tukey's LSD for significance indicated that Black students (M=-1.81, SD=.429) performed significantly lower on the final Writing Portfolio review than all other students: American Indian (M=2.00, SD=.434), API (M=1.97, SD=.412), Hispanic (M=1.93, SD=.411), and White (M=1.94, SD=.493). (Kelly-Riley, 2011, "Validity Inquiry and Writing Portfolio Innovations," para. 3)

In other words, black, Asian Pacific Islander, and Hispanic students performed lower than white students on the impromptu exam, but only black students performed lower on the final review of the Writing Portfolio compared to all other racial categories.

Based on the performance differences by race, a second phase of this study examined how faculty raters evaluate the two different types of writing in the Writing Portfolio, particularly to see if they unwittingly include race as part of their evaluation. The study conducted sequential regression analyses on the different types of writing to identify how faculty raters operationalized their definition of good writing. The findings suggest that race—as an overt variable—did not seem to contribute to faculty's assessment of students' writing in this setting. However, surprisingly, the findings do suggest that faculty employ a limited set of the programmatic criteria published by the Writing Assessment Program and that the variables are slightly different for the impromptu writing versus the course papers. For the impromptu exams, focus, mechanics, and support account for writing quality; for the course papers, focus, mechanics, and organization account for writing quality. For the timed exams, the criteria variables of conception of topic and organization are not utilized by faculty raters; for the course papers, faculty raters do not seem to utilize conception of topic and support. The methods and findings from this study are extensively detailed in Kelly-Riley (2011).

More surprising, the findings from the study also suggested that the raters employed non-programmatic criteria more than the assessment criteria articulated by the Writing Assessment Program. In other words, faculty did not use the full complement of the criteria articulated and published by the program. Instead, more of the writing quality score could be accounted for by distinct criteria not articulated by the program. The non-programmatic criteria accounted for most writing quality and included variables related to writing (coherence, creativity, logic, and grammar). Demographic variables—confidence, comfort with writing, and perceived intelligence—also accounted for writing quality, but to a lesser degree than the Writing Assessment Program criteria. Perhaps the differences in student performance by race on the Writing Portfolio can be attributed to the presence of unstated and idiosyncratic faculty criteria applied in the shared evaluation construction of the definition of "good writing" in the Writing Portfolio assessment.

I share this study as an example of what "stepping off the boat and onto the bank" can illuminate. These findings echo the concerns of other authors, Delpit and then those in this collection—Lioi and Merola, in particular—who express concern about the difficulties for students of color as they navigate codified structures of the university system. Their navigation is made more difficult by these seemingly unstated expectations held and enacted by faculty through assessment systems. Such issues will remain invisible unless we actively try to seek them out and uncover them.

Taking Stock From The Bank

Writing assessment programs that use shared evaluation methodologies need to begin programs of validity inquiry that intentionally examine the experience of students of color. Given that these methods are used in distinct, local contexts, there will be many different ways these inquiries can occur. The *Standards* (AERA, APA, & NCME, 1999) assert that "when test scores are used or interpreted in more than one way, each intended interpretation must be validated" (p. 9). The move to develop writing assessment programs driven by local context will result in new validity issues for program administrators, and issues of race need to be overtly included in ongoing programmatic and validity review. As a result, program administrators and researchers in writing assessment need to take up an active course of inquiry that looks at the interpretation and use of test scores in the contexts in which these assessments are situated.

The negative associations many composition scholars have with educational testing and psychometric traditions should not result in the complete abandonment of obligations we have for investigating the effects of shared evaluation methods in the assessment of writing. As O'Neill (2003) observes, "validation arguments are rhetorical constructs that draw from all the available means of support" (p. 50). In doing so, we should adopt a wider framework, such as the one advocated by James Ronda, that allows us to better understand the complexity of shared evaluation assessments as they intersect with the equally complex lives of the students who take those assessments and as those assessments are situated within the complex organizations of our undergraduate curriculums. We need to keep track of our narratives and open them to accommodate the experiences of students. To that end, the following are some programmatic considerations for large-scale writing assessment programs.

First, we need to develop practices informed by our research on race and writing assessment that are situated in Ronda's call to "enlarge and enrich" the interpretation of our narratives for writing assessment and race. This orientation to exploring race and how it plays out in writing assessment will enable us to develop essential lines of validational inquiry. A useful approach to begin such an inquiry is to examine the intended and unintended consequences of our assessments. Identifying unintended consequences, in particular, is the most difficult because they are not readily apparent. In the end, such considerations are the moral burden of assessment practitioners—to know to the best of our ability what we think our tests do and how well they seem to do it. Just as the historical narratives of the Lewis and Clark journey have evolved, so too should the narratives of writing assessment, especially those related to the consequences of these types of writing assessments for students of color.

Second, race and ethnicity need to be overtly incorporated into ongoing programs of review for locally developed writing assessment practices. The omission of such considerations in the WSU Writing Assessment Program is not unique to WSU. Locally developed programs need to actively collect data related to student performance by race and/or ethnicity as well as other traditional demographic areas. The educational testing community has reviewed tests based on race as standard practice for many years. At a minimum, we need to collect descriptive data about how students from various racial groups perform on our locally developed writing assessments and examine that data regularly. The consideration of these data must be used as the basis to reflect upon and shape our practices.

To begin, administrators should examine the stated purposes of their assessments, how the assessment results are interpreted, and the patterns of particular demographic categories related to those assessment results. Administrators should be able to articulate the purposes of their assessment programs. At WSU, the purposes of the Writing Placement Exam and Writing Portfolio are to ascertain students' readiness to enter the first-year writing curriculum or the upper-division Writing in the Major courses, respectively. All locally developed assessments should have similar statements of purpose. Such statements might be phrased like this: our directed self-placement requires students to make decisions about their readiness to enter various courses within a first-year writing curriculum based on articulations of those courses; or that our program-wide portfolio assessment within a first-year composition program intends to quantify how many students are able to meet the stated outcomes of the curriculum.

Then, the rating processes should be clarified. In the case of the WSU Writing Assessment Program, we recruit, hire, and train the teachers of the courses into which students are placed to become the raters. We ask them to reference their experience in the classroom to determine whether the writer appears to need help with the type of challenges in the course or not. Raters use their classroom experience to inform and articulate the standards for writing. Likewise, similar locally developed assessment programs should be able to articulate how the evaluation process works as well as identify the people who serve as raters and their qualifications for doing so.

Many program administrators are accustomed to calculating the simple percentages of the breakdown of their assessment results to report to their department chair or their dean. Using these data as a starting point, program administrators can work with their Offices of Institutional Research to get demographic data regarding race (or other demographic information) so that they can compare the performances of the general group to others that examine the patterns by particular groupings (race, sex, language background, etc.). This simple comparison allows administrators to get a better understanding of how students perform on the assessment and if there seem to be discrepancies between various groups.

This realm of stated purposes and interpretation of scores mostly considers the intended consequences of our assessments, but it is much more difficult to identify when our programs work in ways that are not anticipated. For me, a good starting place for such inquiry has been the site of student or faculty complaint. Rather than adopting a defensive stance (writing off the complaint to an ill-informed faculty member or a belligerent student), these complaints are worthy of investigation. They point out the places where people are directly affected by the assessment, and their perspectives may lead to sites of contention that, when more closely examined, may reveal vulnerabilities in the assessment process.

Revising and reconsidering our assessment practices can lead to profound changes. Alterations in seemingly innocuous administrative practice can make meaningful differences. The mundane act of allowing a student to register for college classes, for example, seems like a routine activity, but consider James Meredith, the first African American to register for courses at the University of Mississippi in 1962 (Cohodas, 1997). This simple act of course registration led to the integration of the campus of Ole Miss and dramatically changed the opportunities for students of color at that and other institutions. We need to identify the large and small administrative acts that can be the points of change that result in better informed and more equitable writing assessment practices.

Finally, we need to expand our tools to collect information related to race and ethnicity. In the WSU Writing Portfolio study, the definition of race was based upon the limited categories employed by my institution for collecting data related to race. At the time, these were outdated categories from the U.S. Office of Management and Budget. While our inquiries need to start with data that are accessible, developing more complex ways of studying and accounting for the complexities of race, racial formation, and ethnicity are important. James S. Jackson (2007) advocates a more nuanced view of race and ethnicity, and details the pitfalls of combining all similarly defined populations into one racial category. Jackson points to the economic disparity between African Americans who are descendants of slaves compared to recent African immigrants to the United States. Combining these two groups into one category minimizes the dramatic differences in their economic realities. We also need to develop more nuanced ways to gain understanding of our student and faculty populations. As Lioi and Merola outline, students do not fit neatly into single categories; their backgrounds—racially, linguistically, demographically—result in various interactions, and it's important for us to understand the ways in which these variables intersect with the tasks we ask students to complete.

Composition scholars have criticized limitations in methods and tools used in social sciences to examine issues of race and ethnicity, but we have failed to develop suitable alternatives. We can borrow or adapt many approaches from the evolving practices in the social sciences or the educational testing community to develop our own tools for examining race in writing assessment, but we need to begin to articulate a methodology that is applicable and meaningful to locally developed writing assessment programs.

Technologies of Assessing Racial and Linguistic Variation

H anson (1993) has argued in *Testing Testing: Social Consequences of the Examined Life*, assessment technologies are never neutral systems. Like any other "test," grading, responding, and other assessments generally produce the very traits, characteristics, and categories they claim to measure (pp. 284, 287-288). Madaus (1994), likewise, argues that "[t]echnology is not by nature socially unjust. It is, however, inextricably intertwined with the distribution of wealth, race, and gender relations" (p. 79). O'Neill (1998), suggests that "what we name the technology is less important than our purposes and use of the information we gather" (p. 6).

The authors in this section consider various writing assessment technologies and what racialized practices we promote when we use any writing assessment technology. These chapters point to the ways that assessment technologies allow us to see racial formations in certain ways when we attach value to specific dialects or ways of writing and that the *effects* of technologies are very much worth studying.

Anne Herrington and Sarah Stanley in "*Criterion*^SM: Promoting the Standard" investigate *Criterion*, a computerized assessment of student writing designed for classroom-based instruction. They note that the promise of such technologies is to help all writers but that by privileging one dialect, such technologies may have a disparate impact on certain groups of students, namely writers of nonstandard dialects of American English. They go on to explore *Criterion*'s response to an essay written by "Lisa," an "AAVE-speaking student," whose essay appeared in an article written by Ball and Lardner (2005). They find that *Criterion* is incapable of identifying essayistic structures that deviate from the standardized American school essay. As a result, the program informs Lisa that she has no introduction and misidentifies supporting evidence in the essay. The program also flags 33 grammar, usage, and mechanics "errors," of which 23 are not errors. Ultimately, because *Criterion* cannot recognize that writers make rhetorical choices in their writing, such programs ultimately reduce writing to a narrow vision of academic prose, one out of synch with contemporary writing pedagogy. They write:

> To suggest that Lisa made choices in composing her essay points to a different direction for pedagogy: one that respects the multiplicity of languages and dialects of English; one that aims to teach students to write in a variety of rhetorical genres and

contexts, including ones valued in college; one that aims to help them develop the language and rhetorical skills to make choices as they compose based on their intentions in a given rhetorical situation.

Valerie Balester also takes up the issue of linguistic standardization in "How Writing Rubrics Fail: Toward a Multicultural Model." It is not the issue of standardization itself that is problematic, Balester argues, but the valuation of one linguistic variety over others. Balester offers a close reading of writing assessment rubrics to examine how language proficiency—and ultimately race—is constructed through the technology of the rubric. In her analysis of 13 rubrics, Balester traces three logics toward language: an acculturationist view that seeks to eradicate linguistic variation, an accommodationist view that allows linguistic variation but only in certain contexts or genres, and a multicultural view that seeks to value linguistic variation as a resource for learning and expression. In the end, Balester argues that rubrics need to receive more attention in their constructions of multilingualism because they have an enormous influence in articulating values toward language. Like Herrington and Stanley, she enjoins us to design technologies that value the linguistic resources that our students bring to classrooms and programs.

Finally, in "Grading Contracts: Assessing Their Effectiveness on Different Racial Formations," Asao B. Inoue investigates the outcomes of a different technology, contract grading, on different racial groups or formations. Analyzing two years of data from the California State University, Fresno's First-Year Writing Program, Inoue traces the effects of program-wide grading contracts on Asian, black, and white students. Drawing on qualitative as well as quantitative data, Inoue provides a rich portrait of the results of one technology at his institution, considering the ways that grading contracts in a writing program help construct racial formations with particular characteristics. He concludes that grading contracts are most effective at Fresno State for Asian Pacific Islanders (APIs), while only marginally effective for white students. His findings showed that while APIs, who are mostly Hmong, had the highest level of remedial status, lowest parental education levels, and more often spoke other languages at home, they performed significantly higher in a key program outcome ("summary and conversation") in final portfolios, met workload expectations in their chosen courses at some of the highest rates among all groups, and were most satisfied with the grading contract. Inoue concludes:

> The effectiveness of any grading technology often hinges on the assumptions that the technology makes about the nature of quality writing, the relationship of quality to the workload of the course, the assumptions students must accept in order for the grading technology to function properly, and with whom that technology is interacting (about whom it makes decisions and who makes decisions).

CHAPTER THREE

Criterion^{SM}: Promoting the Standard

Anne Herrington and Sarah Stanley

Automated assessment of writing has moved into the classroom. Instead of just being used for some standardized testing programs, including two popular college placement programs (the College Board's ACCUPLACER test using WritePlacer *Plus* and ACT's COMPASS test using e-Write), automated assessment programs are now being sold for instructional purposes. One of the more popular of these is *Criterion*, a product of the Educational Testing Service (ETS), our focus for this essay. A web-based program, *Criterion* is marketed as an aid to both teachers and students for the fast computer evaluation it can provide. As the lead sentence on the ETS *Criterion* On-line Writing Evaluation homepage proclaims, "The *Criterion* service provides instructors and students with reliable evaluations of English-language essays" (2011a, para. 1). With many teachers facing the pressures of large teaching loads and larger classes, students with a range of home language and dialects, and accountability demands, it is not surprising that *Criterion*'s "reliable evaluation" could seem attractive.

To date, while more has been written in composition studies about automated programs in general (Ericsson & Haswell, 2006; Herrington & Moran, 2001, 2006; Hesse, 2005; Williamson, 2003), there have been few independent reviews published on instructional programs designed to teach writing, specifically *Criterion* (Broad, 2006; Chen & Cheng, 2008, Herrington & Moran, 2009; Hutchinson, 2007). All point to the limited capability of the program to do more than identify linguistic and structural features. Much ETS research finds similar conclusions, while still arguing for the validity of *e-rater* judgments.[1] For example, on the basis of their study of *Criterion* in three EFL courses for English majors in a Taiwan university, Chen and Cheng (2008) conclude, "if the goal is to communicate the writer's thoughts effectively to real audiences and demonstrate the writer's creativity and originality, using AWE [automated writing evaluation] is probably not a good choice" (p. 109). Enright and Quinlan (2010) reach a similar conclusion: that human raters respond to a "wider variety of essay features than *e-rater*, such as response effectiveness and quality of ideas and content" (p. 330).

While pointing to the theory of writing programmed into *Criterion*, not even the Chen and Cheng study considers the ideology of language that drives the program. Our purpose, then, is to review *Criterion* in this light, asking the key questions we, as teachers, need to ask of any textbook or instructional technology, recognizing it as promoting particularly ideological orientations (Huot, 2002as; Kemp, 1992): What beliefs about writing, language, and learning is it programmed to follow as it evaluates student writing? What message does *Criterion* send to teachers and students alike about the relationships among language, race, and teaching? As Kemp (1992) reminds us, "instructional software is not merely a set of instructions that drive computers (and sometimes users) but a subtle platform of belief which can [...] carry implicit messages regarding [...] viewpoints which remain invisible even to writing professionals trained to recognize ideology in written texts" (p. 12).

What we will show in our review is that *Criterion* enacts an arhetorical view of writing, a homogeneous view of English as a single standard dialect, and an error-focused approach to teaching and learning. In saying this, we acknowledge that *Criterion* operates on values and practices of some English teachers. It mirrors some portion of our profession, but not in a way that prompts self-examination.

Who are we in writing this essay? Two white teachers of two generations, both of whom grew up in homes where Edited American English was spoken, the dialect of middle- and upper-class white Americans, the dialect of *Criterion*. Because of our privileged dialect we have not had discriminating or erasing experiences because of language, just as we also have benefited and benefit from institutions that privilege the dialect we speak and write. We have some knowledge of linguistics; we strive to enact the CCCC's policy statements on language diversity in our teaching; and, to that end, we profit from theoretical and pedagogical scholarship on ways to do so.

Recognizing And Honoring Multiple Varieties Of English

The chapters in the collection *Language Diversity in the Classroom: From Intention to Practice* (Smitherman & Villanueva, 2003) challenge us "to think about how we enact our belief in the multiplicity of language, of English, in our classrooms" (p. 1). Regardless of where we teach, some multiplicity of languages and varieties of English are used. In the 1970s, the Conference on College Composition and Communication's policy statement, "Students' Right to Their Own Language" (1974), called us to recognize and honor the multiple dialects of American English; the same organization's 1988 National Language Policy Statement called us to recognize and honor the variety of languages present in our classrooms. Ongoing scholarship on dialects of English (e.g., Richardson, 2003a; Smitherman, 1993) and more recent scholarship on World Englishes (e.g., Canagarajah, 2006b) and the myth of linguistic homogeneity in U.S. schools (Horner & Trimbur, 2002; Lu, Matsuda, & Horner, 2006; Matsuda, 2006) make the same call, arguing as well that students' language capabilities in whatever variety of English they speak are resources for learning to write and that an unchecked and/or unmarked policy of monolingualism ill-prepares students for a world of increasing inter- and intra-mixing of languages. This scholarly work rests on what linguistics and rhetorical analysis demonstrate: all varieties have conventions—and standards—for discourse patterns, style, and grammar. While language scholars continue to assert that, linguistically speaking, no dialect is any more "standard" than another, it remains the case that one dialect of English is socially dominant, the dialect of American English taught in our schools and used in institutions—the dialect most associated with middle- and upper-class white Americans: what we will refer to as Edited American English (EAE) to mark it as a particular dialect that has become standardized, and thus, dominant. Recognizing the dominance of EAE does not require, however, teaching students to follow it as the *only* language standard. As Ball (1999) has pointed out, though, in reference to African American Vernacular English (AAVE), many educators still fail to recognize AAVE as a viable language:

> Although linguists and anthropologists have assured teachers that AAVE is a logical language with systematic patterns of expressions, many educators have trouble seeing and appreciating these patterns. Instead of patterns, they see only "mistakes"; instead of "efficacies"—powerful resources that are part of an oral tradition that students can use to produce an effect—they see only "errors." (p. 226)

Unfortunately, *Criterion* enforces the same misconceptions about varieties of English other than EAE.

Marketing Standardization: Overview Of *Criterion*

ETS *Criterion* Online Writing Evaluation website markets *Criterion* as designed for instruction in K-12 and Higher Education and for English Language Learners, an ethnically diverse group of learners. The page foregrounds a smiling brown-eyed, dark-haired woman of color and backgrounds a classroom with computer stations—the other students are out of focus in this picture, but one is clearly a white woman. The implication of the images is that *Criterion* is designed to help all learners. What isn't stated is that *Criterion* recognizes only one dialect of English. In this way, the images further the complicated relationships among language, race, and education on the one hand and the standardizing practices of *Criterion* on the other. In other words, helping all learners becomes, in practice, erasing other languages or dialects.

The website for *Criterion* also prominently displays the seals of three technology awards that *Criterion* has received, including the 2007 Platinum Level Award from the IMS Global Learning Consortium for "high-impact use of technology in learning" (ETS, 2007a, para. 2). Other pages for each of the three main categories contain testimonials from teachers and administrators who use *Criterion* and praise it for saving time for instructors so they can devote more time to individual students, providing pre- and post-testing and placement capabilities, and supporting students in revising their writing.[2] What these awards and testimonials do not speak to are the ideologies of writing and language programmed into *Criterion*.

According to the "*Criterion* Service Overview" for Higher Education, *Criterion* is "a reliable writing assessment tool," "allowing instructors to benchmark writing, make placement decisions, adjust instruction and track progress" (ETS, 2011b, "Using the Criterion Service," para. 1). Not only is it useful for assessment and benchmarking, "the *Criterion* service is a learning tool that does not increase workload and adds value to writing instruction by providing a teachable moment" (ETS, 2011b, "Using the Criterion Service," para. 2). As these two quotes illustrate, ETS draws on the discourses of both accountability (benchmarking, value added) and progressive pedagogy (teachable moment) to market the product. But what sort of teachable moment is it and for whom?

The page *About the Criterion Service for Higher Education* includes a Frequently Asked Questions section. In 2008, the FAQs on the *Criterion* website included a question that linked the standard to racial and national identity. The question was posed thusly, "Does the *Criterion* service discriminate against students who may be bright but who may not have mastered standard English—for example minorities and ESL students?" Not surprisingly, the answer to this question was "No." The program simply measures features in a piece of writing and compares them to features in previously scored essays used to define the rubric. If—and a lot hinges on "if"—the collection of sample essays includes essays that use non-standard English and also earn high scores, then the *Criterion* service will assign a high score to essays with the same features. *Criterion* is "simply" doing what it is programmed to do, and it is programmed against the norms of human readers. Those readers, of course, are ones trained by ETS to evaluate standardized tests. For those raters, there is only one standard, EAE. *Criterion* only perpetuates that view.

At the time of writing this chapter, we noticed that a preceding question that evoked the relationship between standard and non-standard language use had been dropped from the FAQs and replaced with a question about style:

How does the *Criterion* service handle an unusual writing style? The *Criterion* service looks for specific features of syntax, organization and vocabulary. If the essay under consideration is not sufficiently similar to those in its database of already-scored essays, the *Criterion* service posts a warning, called an Advisory, saying that it is unable to give an accurate score. Advisories usually result from essays that are too brief or those in which the vocabulary is unusual or the content is off-topic. (ETS, "Using the Criterion Service in Teaching," 2012)

While the final sentence highlights length, vocabulary, and content as markers of an "unusual writing style," the lead sentence focuses attention on syntax and organization as well. What constitutes a "usual" or "unusual" style, then, is determined on the basis of a corpus of previously scored test essays, the implicit standard. In framing the question as style, rather than language, as unusual rather than non-standard, *Criterion* opts for a scientific explanation about language use. As the scientific explanation forwards corpus-based determinants rather than prescriptive rules, it becomes difficult, ideologically, to argue that the new framing contradicts a belief that language is social and rule-based: after all, the machine is just analyzing what is present in the corpus. Such reasoning continues to be the rationale for these assessments; however, the nature of the corpus, no matter how large, reflects arhetorical testing conditions despite *Criterion* being marketed for classroom use. As Nick Behm and Keith D. Miller point out in this collection, assessment conditions inherit a racial history. Further, as we will show in our analysis of a student essay, *Criterion* is ill-suited for identifying rhetorical patterns other than that of a traditional thesis and main-point-driven school essay, and it is not programmed to identify the "usual features" of a variety of English other than Edited American English (Chodorow, Gamon, & Tetrault, 2010).

A standard is also evident in the response to the following question:

Will the use of the *Criterion* service stifle creative writing among students? Not necessarily. The *Criterion* service is designed to be used for evaluating writing done under testing conditions—situations in which even the most creative writers concentrate on "playing it safe" with straightforward and competent writing. (ETS, "Using the Criterion Service in Teaching," 2012)

And, herein lies another central flaw of *Criterion* for classroom purposes: it is designed for "writing done under testing conditions," where a "straightforward" view of what is "competent" is assumed, and where students are rewarded for "playing it safe" as writers. Unmarked is the assumption that standardized American English for school writing is the standard. This conception of the kind of writing we should be asking our students to do further underscores the impoverished construction of academic writing that *Criterion* teaches. The consequence of such an impoverished view is that *Criterion* reproduces existing linguistic and social hierarchies by erasing the relationships among language, race, and education rather than acknowledging and working from that reality.

As is evident by the section on ELL, *Criterion* does recognize multiplicity of languages and language users and, in general, is better designed for L2 speakers than for speakers of nonmainstream dialects of American English. For example, the online *Writer's Handbook* comes in an ELL version and three bilingual versions: Spanish/English, Simplified Chinese/English, and Japanese/English. Clearly, more is done to recognize the validity of multiple languages than multiple dialects. This difference in valuation is consistent with the finding of the 1996–98 CCCC-sponsored study of high school and college language arts professionals that there is more acceptance for using languages other than English than for using nonmainstream dialects (Richardson, 2003b, p. 52), implying less acceptance of U.S. dialects of English as viable language varieties and pointing to the complex intermingling of dialect, race, and prejudice in the U.S. (See Zandra Jordan's chapter in this collection on how that intermingling affects student writing development.)

Using *Criterion*

Presently, *Criterion* is capable of providing holistic evaluation of expository or persuasive essays. To be specific, *e-rater*, the program used for the holistic evaluation, is normed against impromptu essays written for timed ETS tests that use expository and persuasive prompts. As explained in one of the Frequently Asked Questions, the essay prompts come from "ETS testing programs like NAEP®, the English Placement Test designed for California State University, *Praxis*®, GRE®, and TOEFL®." In other words, *Criterion* is designed to evaluate test-situation writing, not, for example, a researched argument, an interpretation of a short story or essay, an analysis and response to a published text, an oral history interview, a science laboratory report, a website, a digital story—the list goes on. In short: *Criterion* does not present anything like the range of rhetorical genres that students would be asked to write in their college courses, nor engage them in the kind of critical thinking valued in college and professional work.

As teachers, we would have the option of selecting one of the topics *Criterion* provides or creating one of our own, selecting, for instance, from topics for College Level Preparatory, First Year College, or English Language Training. In order to use the holistic rating feature, though, our "teacher-designed" prompt would have to be of the same type as the *Criterion* ones. Further, if one wishes to use the holistic feedback rating, *The Criterion Teaching Guide* advises setting a time limit for writing: "Note that it's very important to assign *the same amount of time* for writing the essay from instructor-generated and modified prompts as is required by the standard higher education prompts" (ETS, 2007b, p. 28). "The standard" is evoked again, here equating timed, impromptu writing with the standard for writing assignments in college classrooms.

Once receiving the prompt, students could first use the "Make a Plan" option, using one of eight planning templates (e.g., outlining, free-writing). They would then draft their essays and submit them for evaluation. Here's where the real focus of *Criterion* lies. *Criterion* is designed to provide two kinds of evaluation: Holistic, using the scoring program *e-rater*, and Trait Feedback, using the scoring program Critique (Burstein, Chodorow, & Leacock, 2004, p. 27). The holistic scoring rubric and standards for comparison are matched to the level selected by the teacher (e.g., College Level Preparatory, First Year College, English Language Training). On the basis of the holistic score evaluation, the draft would receive a holistic score on a scale of 1 to 6, determined by comparing this draft to the bank of essays scored for ETS tests for that level. Following are the holistic explanations for a rating of 6 for three levels of *Criterion* prompts.

First Year College (persuasive)

You have put together a convincing argument. Here are some of the strengths evident in your writing:

Your essay:

- Looks at the topic from a number of angles and responds to all aspects of what you were asked to do
- Responds thoughtfully and insightfully to the issues in the topic
- Develops with a superior structure and apt reasons or examples (each one adding significantly to the reader's understanding of your view)
- Uses sentence styles and language that have impact and energy and keep the reader with you
- Demonstrates that you know the mechanics of correct sentence structure, and American English usage—virtually free of errors

College Level Preparatory (expository)

Excellent

- Develops ideas well and uses many specific, relevant details throughout the essay.
- Is well organized with clear transitions; maintains focus.
- Sustains varied sentence structure.
- Exhibits many specific word choices.

- Contains little or no errors in grammar and conventions; errors do not interfere with understanding.

English Language Training (expository and persuasive)

A typical essay at this level:

- effectively addresses the writing task
- is well organized and well developed
- uses clearly appropriate details to support a thesis or illustrate ideas
- displays consistent facility in the use of language
- demonstrates syntactic variety and appropriate word choice, though it may have occasional errors

Noteworthy is that only for First Year College is the language standard being used explicitly acknowledged: "American English usage." Still, "American English usage" is presented as a singular, homogenous *American* usage—the "national" standard, not even as the usage of a *particular* American dialect of English. Another unmarked standard programmed into the holistic evaluation is the standardized American school essay structure: the five paragraph essay (Burstein, Chodorow, & Leacock, 2004; Attali, 2004). Notice, too, that it is only in the criteria for First Year College that the writer of a top-rated essay is praised for responding "thoughtfully and insightfully to the issues in the topic." Finally, while we understand the merits of evaluating the writing of non-native writers of English in relation to TOEFL tests, it is not apparent what scoring rubric should be used for bilingual students or speaker/writers of AAVE in order to have their rhetorical and linguistic capabilities recognized and not marked as erroneous or "unusual."

The trait feedback, with its focus on deficit, is identified on the online demo as "the key reason why *Criterion* is such a valuable remediation tool" (ETS, 2007b, p. 5). The trait feedback includes five general traits: organization and development, grammar, usage, mechanics, and style. As with the holistic feedback, the trait feedback is of questionable accuracy, implicitly organized around a single standard, and excessively form and error focused. We base this conclusion on our testing of *Criterion*'s evaluation of three student-written essays and also the four versions of the "African American History" essay in Ball (1992b). The essays in Ball's article model four distinct discourse patterns: standard school essay and three patterns that she identifies with African American Vernacular English. Two of the student essays were written by our students. The other one is an essay that Ball and Lardner print in full in *African American Literacies* (2005, pp. 37–49), identifying it as written by Lisa, an

"AAVE-speaking student." We report on *Criterion*'s evaluation of Lisa's essay in the next section.

Criterion Fails The Test: Misreading Lisa's Essay

Lisa's essay was written in response to a Joyce Carol Oates story, "Theft." (See below for the first three paragraphs of Lisa's essay.) It's a 13-paragraph essay written in a pattern that Ball and Lardner (2005) identify as "narrative interspersion," where narrative is inserted within the structure of an expository text in the manner of African American oral tradition (p. 47). Now, if Lisa's essay were to be evaluated by *Criterion*, what feedback would she receive to assist her in revising? First of all, her essay couldn't receive a holistic evaluation because the assignment and essay do not conform to the more simplistic prompts required for *Criterion*'s holistic analysis. It did receive Trait Feedback, however, and we use the feedback the essay received to illustrate each of the trait feedback categories and their operating criteria. We will also refer to the other essays as relevant. Lisa's first three paragraphs read as follows:

> "Theft," by Joyce Carol Oates tells the story of a girl name Marya who has something taken from her. In the beginning Marya had her favorite pen and wallet stolen from her drawer. She did eventually get her wallet but her pen she didn't see anymore. Imogene who's another girl in this story has nothing taken from her. Yet, she becomes Marya's friend and eventually tries to steal her image.

> The meaning of "Theft" in this story can be explained in two different ways. One was when Marya had her wallet and pen taken from her. The other was when Imogene her supposed to be friend, tries to take away Marya's image. It's one thing to steal someone's belongings. It's another when you steal someone's image, identity or reputation. And this story "Theft" is a good example of both.

> Imogene was the most popular around the campus. Marya was not. Imogene had nice clothes and was very pretty. Marya on the other hand was not. Marya did not have fancy clothes and she wasn't as pretty as Imogene was. What Marya did want was the kind of things Imogene possessed. And there's nothing wrong with that. I would want to have those nice things myself. But what seemed to be the problem was that Imogene pretended to be Marya's friend.

Criterion recognizes only structural features, such as organization and development. Further, it is programmed to read for only one culturally specific structure—the standardized American school essay. As the analysis of Lisa's essay illustrates, *Criterion* is incapable of accurately identifying the structure of essays that deviate from this pattern, thus leading to misidentification of aspects of the essay. *Criterion* erroneously tells Lisa that she has no introduction, failing to recognize the first paragraph as likely functioning as such. It also erroneously identifies the first sentence as the thesis, when the thesis seems to appear in the second paragraph. Typical of its other stock comments, *Criterion* hedges a bit in the comment: "Is this sentence really part of your thesis? Remember that a thesis controls the whole content of your essay. You need to strengthen this thesis so that you clearly state the main point you will be making. Look in the Writer's Handbook for tips on doing this."

For identification of main ideas, the program underlines the first sentence of each paragraph—except for the first, final, and one following a quote—with everything following first sentences marked as supporting ideas: for example, the first sentences of the second and third paragraphs of Lisa's essay are underlined as main ideas, although that is misleading also. (With all the other essays, this pattern was also followed—first sentences as main ideas; the following as supporting ideas—whether accurate or not. One student's essay that followed a more inductive pattern was also erroneously flagged as having no thesis. Reflecting *Criterion*'s five-paragraph bias, another essay identified as having only two main ideas was flagged "because a good essay will contain at least three main ideas.") While misleading Lisa with inaccurate information, *Criterion* also fails to provide useful feedback on the actual structure of her essay, feedback that could serve to either reconfirm what she aimed to do or help her discern that structure.

Criterion's grammar, usage, and mechanics analyses are all error focused, programmed to read for errors in Edited American English, represented as "general English grammar." The corpus used for identifying these "violations of general English grammar" is 30 million words of newspaper text (Burstein, Chodorow, & Leacock, 2004, p. 28). Following are the types of errors identified.

Grammar Errors

- fragment or missing comma
- run-on sentences
- garbled sentences
- subject-verb agreement
- ill-formed verbs
- pronoun errors
- possessive errors
- wrong or missing word
- "Proofread this!"

Usage Errors

- wrong article
- missing or extra article

- confused words
- wrong form of word
- faulty comparisons
- preposition error
- nonstandard verb or word form

Mechanics Errors

- misspellings
- missing commas
- compound-word errors. (ETS, 2007b)

For the grammar trait "Proofread this!" we see a human personality being invoked, although what types of "errors" evoke this response is not evident, nor is how the program knows whether it is appropriate for a given paper, say, one written by an English language learner or one written by someone using African American English or Spanglish.

As with the feedback on organization and development, *Criterion*'s identification of these three categories of errors is often misleading and sometimes inaccurate. For example, for Lisa's essay, *Criterion* identified 33 grammar, usage, and mechanics "errors," 23 of which were not errors, reflecting an accuracy rate of only 30%. In other words, at best, this feedback would be distracting, requiring the writer to identify which feedback is correct and which is not and in terms of which standard, tasks which presume the writer has the knowledge to recognize that.

The flagging of grammar errors shows the *Criterion*'s SAE bias and its limited capability to identify features accurately or helpfully. *Criterion* identified 17 grammar errors in Lisa's essay: 12 fragments or missing commas; two run-on sentences, two subject-verb agreements, and two "Proofread this!" The 12 fragment or missing comma "errors" include six instances of page references—e.g., "pg. 452"—that *Criterion* did not know how to read, two missing commas after an introductory subordinate clause, and four fragments, two of them within a quotation. The subject-verb "error"—"if you're the kind of person that basically stay to yourself"—Ball and Lardner (2005) identify as AAVE, which *Criterion* fails to recognize as a viable dialect. The two "Proofread This!" errors were simply additional places where a comma was omitted (e.g., "When you think about it Marya and Imogene [...]"). The three usage errors detected in Lisa's essay were again errors on *Criterion*'s part, reflecting its inability to detect nuances of language: for example, mistakenly flagging a "wrong article" in the phrase "a girl name Marya" and mistakenly flagging "friend" in the phrase "supposed to be friend" as missing an article. For Lisa's essay, *Criterion* flagged 13 mechanics errors, but only two were correctly identified, the failure to use a hyphen in the phrase "so-called," which also evidently misled *Criterion* into thinking an article was needed for "so called friend." Had Lisa followed *Criterion*'s advice, she would have revised to write "so-called a friend."

For style, the trait report summarizes not "errors" but the number of "comments" relating to the following subcategories: repetition of words, inappropriate words or phrases, sentences beginning with coordinating conjunctions, too many short sentences, too many long sentences, passive voice. Obviously, again, *Criterion* presents a reductive and still "error" based view of style, in contrast to viewing style as rhetorically and creatively motivated uses of language and syntax. Before submitting Lisa's essay to *Criterion*, we conjectured that it would flag the "oral-based idioms" (e.g., "See a person like Imogene is phony to me.") as inappropriate words or phrases and the repetitions that structure the entire essay as repetition. Well, it did pick up on repetition but not of whole phrases. Instead, *Criterion* identified 178 "repetition of words," specifically Lisa's repeated and understandable uses of the names of the story's main characters (Marya and Imogene) and of the personal pronouns "her," "she," and "you." The use of "you" reflects Lisa's oral style as does her use of coordinating conjunctions to begin sentences (*Criterion* identifies 13 such occurrences). What *Criterion* is unable to do is identify this as an aspect of a style. *Criterion* also identifies "too many short sentences," flagging 16 of them, with the injunction that reflects the value-judgment of the comment: "Your essay contains too many short sentences. It will be stronger if you combine some of these sentences with others and vary the length of your sentences more."

To appreciate the limitations of *Criterion* and the error focus, instead of rhetorical resource focus of the feedback, consider the third paragraph in Lisa's essay (quoted above). To our minds, Lisa effectively uses short sentences in setting up the contrast between Imogene and Marya although *Criterion* flags both the second and fourth sentences as "too short," along with the third to the last. The third to the last and the last sentence are also flagged for "beginning with a coordinating conjunction." Finally, every use of "Marya," "Imogene," "did," "she," and "I" are flagged for "repetition of words," with the injunction, "You have repeated these words several times in your essay. Your essay will be stronger if you vary your word choice and substitute some other words instead. Ask your instructor for advice." By focusing on these isolated categories—flagged as problems—*Criterion* misses what is happening rhetorically and, in turn, directs the writer's attention to these isolated traits. What doesn't get highlighted is Lisa's rhetorically effective parallel structure—only to be noted if a problem—coupled with her alternation of relatively longer and shorter sentences. Neither are the cues to an oral register noted in the essay overall as that register alternates with a more academic register. In short, the 207 style comments—178 being repetition of words—are distracting and unhelpful.

   Criterion could highlight Lisa's "errors" for her a number of ways. She could call up each category, one by one, and review her draft with each type highlighted: e.g., first view all grammar errors, then view all mechanics errors. Roll-overs would explain the errors in a very limited way, and she could also call up an online *Writer's Handbook* explaining the error. For each category, a bar graph could also be displayed showing how many of each type of error occurred, giving a further sense of objectivity and mathematical power to the analysis. The task for revision would be to reduce these errors. The underlying conception of revision as error elimination is also evident in the ETS paper "Exploring the Feedback and Revision Features of the *Criterion* Service" (Attali, 2004).

   We recognize that in being programmed to recognize error and enforce a single language standard, *Criterion* is programmed to respond as some teachers do. For instance, Ball and Lardner (2005) cite some of the following comments from teachers who have been shown Lisa's essay in workshops: "The writer cannot write properly." "You shouldn't use informal language." "Proofread." (p. 41). Their point is that if teachers were more knowledgeable about AAVE and read not to find mistakes but to discern patterns, they would see in Lisa's paper a rhetorically effective use of repetition as a patterning device for the essay and an effective "intermingling of discourses" (p. 49). In short, they would see that "the choices are purposeful." This is something that *Criterion* cannot recognize either. What's different about our human response is that we can choose to respond differently, especially when we learn more about our students and language difference.

Beyond The Bar Graph: Choosing A Different Direction For Teaching And Learning

   To suggest that Lisa made choices in composing her essay points to a different direction for pedagogy: one that respects the multiplicity of languages and dialects of English; one that aims to teach students to write in a variety of rhetorical genres and contexts, including ones valued in college; one that aims to help them develop the language and rhetorical skills to make choices as they compose based on their intentions in a given rhetorical situation. (See, for example, Lovejoy, 2003; Lu, 1994; Stanley 2009.) The *Criterion* materials imply that *Criterion* can be used for such pedagogy. For example, *The Criterion Teaching Guide* invokes Chickering and Gamson's "Seven Principles for Good Practice in Undergraduate Education," including active learning, prompt feedback, and respect for diversity of talents and ways of learning" (ETS, 2007b, p. 3). However, the automated assessment features of *Criterion* are not central to any of these lessons; instead, what are used are features for posting and sharing drafts with one's teacher and/or peers—features that many other web-based platforms offer, without the additional cost of *Criterion*. Reinforcing this point, a recent study of ELL students finds they learned more from giving feedback than receiving it (Lundstrom & Baker, 2009). Tellingly, there are not examples in the *Teaching Guide* of lessons that would make visible to students the language values programmed into *Criterion* or involve students in critically examining those values and standards. Such lessons would be at odds with the ideology of language promoted by *Criterion*. Yes, *Criterion* does enable "active learning" but using a narrow and limited range of prompts and no more so than any writing course that asks students to write; it provides prompt feedback, but feedback based on a single standard and often either inaccurate or misleading; fundamentally, while it aims to "respect diversity of talents," it does not respect "the multiplicity of language, of English, in our classrooms."

If the findings of the 1996-98 CCCC survey of English teachers are still valid—and we suspect they are—*Criterion* mirrors beliefs that some of us hold about a single appropriate standard of English, beliefs that are at odds with our own organization's position statements and scholarship on language, rhetoric, and composition. We should look at the mirror self-critically, then, for what it reflects about ourselves and our values. That is the anti-racist work that Keith Gilyard (1999b) calls us to in "Higher Learning: Composition's Racialized Reflection." What unacknowledged ideologies are implicit in our beliefs about language and our students, and what ideologies do we promote using the technology of *Criterion*—not only ideologies about language, but also about the function of response to student writing?

We can also learn by reading scholarship on language, race, rhetoric, and ethnicity and by studying our students' writing. An automated assessment program with bar graphs of errors will not help us discern language and rhetorical patterns in our students' writing—especially patterns that may reflect standards other than the program's implicit "standard"—patterns that should be seen as resources for their writing and learning, not hindrances.

Notes

---

[1] Quinlan et al. (2009) conclude that "whether defined in terms of process or product, the e-rater scoring engine provides partial coverage of the construct, with the majority of measurement capturing the low-level aspects of essay quality that reflect basic writing skills" (p. 24). Enright and Quinlan (2010) find that while e-rater scoring often agrees with human scoring,

human raters' evaluations include such higher-level aspects of quality as "response effectiveness and quality of ideas" (p. 330). The latter study and Chodorow et al. (2010) also reflect a focus of ETS applied research on the capability of *e-rater* for reliably identifying "errors" of Edited American English made by English Language Learners. Weigle, a Georgia State professor and member of the TOEFL Committee of Examiners, has also evaluated the validity of TOEFL, which also uses *e-rater*, concluding in one study that "Correlations between both human and *e-rater* scores and non-test indicators were moderate but consistent, providing Criterion-related validity evidence for the use of *e-rater* along with human scores" (2010, p. 335). Her focus is on the use of automated assessment for large-scale testing, not instructional purposes.

[2] The five "case studies" are rather sketchy, showing a range of uses and degrees of use: for instance, Dallas County Community College where one teacher is reported to use it for his writing classes; East Texas Baptist University where it is used primarily as a proficiency exam; Wayne State University where it is reported to be used by the School of Social Work and is endorsed by the Associate Director of the English Language Institute, although it is not clear how it is used by the Institute; and Lawson State Community College, Alabama, where it is reported that at least 500 students use *Criterion* each semester and that faculty find it is efficient for tracking student progress.

CHAPTER FOUR

How Writing Rubrics Fail: Toward a Multicultural Model

Valerie Balester

Rubrics are commonplace in today's writing assessment processes and play a central role in writing instruction—a role less innocent in both cases than merely an aid to efficiently and reliably measure performance (Mabry, 1999; Huot, 2002a; Wilson, 2006). In teaching, writing rubrics share the spotlight with textbooks as a means to train novice teachers and to express and enforce common standards. Because of their powerful influence in instruction, rubrics announce forcefully how we define "good" writing. Unfortunately, rather than opening a dialog about culturally specific notions of "good writing," rubrics have become a means for defining a standard in the service of inter-rater reliability. In this case, efficiency trumps dialog. I argue for another vision of rubrics—one that enables us to judge writing quality as reliably as possible within the context of "power, politics, and economics, to say nothing of the subjective dictates of style" (Martin & Penrod, 2006, p. 67). This vision acknowledges that writing skill and writing evaluation are "dynamic, variable, and contextually-dependent" and require "negotiating sets of expectations and purposes that may vary across readerships" (Martin & Penrod, 2006, p. 71). Those expectations of readership, of course, are always influenced by identity and how we construct language use in relation to it. The problem with uncritical uses of rubrics, as I suggest in this chapter, is that they oversimplify and standardize writing, thus failing a significant segment of our student population, namely, students of color or students whose first language is not always Edited American English.

The knotty problem with rubrics is that in the attempt to standardize scoring and instruction, they also standardize prose (Mabry, 1999, p. 674). On one hand, standardization is exactly what *is* desired in much academic writing. Inculcating members into a discipline requires imparting standards of practice (Lave & Wenger, 1991), including stylistic regularities that identify one as an insider to that community. Like the mechanized grading software reviewed in this volume by Herrington and Stanley, rubrics are also convenient and efficient for training novice graders; they are, for example, widely used in cross-curricular literacy programs as well as in many programs that use holistic, analytic, and primary trait scoring. Standardization, on the other hand, can be a means of marking otherness. When a non-expert cannot use the jargon, we know we are confronting an outsider. At its worst, standardization can be inflicted as a punishment, a way to castigate the non-believer or keep out the undesirables (Miller, 1991). Too often in teaching writing we assume standardization is what we owe students.

Castigation may be most severe for "error" (as defined by deviance from a standard) (Widdowson, 1994; Rubin & Wilson-James, 1997). And it may be particularly severe for those who embody difference, who write with the "accent" of non-native speakers or the stylistic variation of writers from multilingual backgrounds, for example, students who identify with varieties of English spoken in many African American, Latino/a, or Native American communities (Garcia & Menken, 2006, p. 175). Focus on error can unnecessarily interfere with students' forms of expression (and ultimately identity, as observed by Huot, 2002b). Focus on error in evaluation can also potentially lead to focus on error in instruction, to the neglect of developing students' sense of rhetorical awareness (Rubin & Wilson-James, 1997, p. 150). This focus on error ultimately reinforces the stance that academic English is best served by enforcing rigid, monolingual, and unified standards (Horner & Lu, 2007, p. 141).

It can be argued that contextualization will lead to better assessment. Huot makes a strong case for the potential of rhetorically based, context sensitive assessment at a local level (2002a). Huot, O'Neill, and Moore celebrate the field's "establishing the efficacy of designing local assessment methods" (2010, p. 512) because local assessment means honoring and using teacher knowledge. Broad (2003) suggests "Dynamic Criteria Mapping," which restores local control by helping programs discover what is "really" valued in the writing local professionals teach, how these values will be reflected in an assessment tool, and how they will be made transparent to students being assessed (pp. 4–5). Broad assumes that improvement will come from a better fit between what writing teachers in the classroom value and what is valued in assessing student writing. But even local, context-based assessment can present problems for writers from different language backgrounds. Often teachers, with the best intentions, may want to exclude some kinds of language from academic writing. Both teachers and students may believe that employing stylistic and rhetorical variation and experimenting with discourse norms must be reserved for advanced writers. And often they may see no possibility for alternative expression and interpret "appropriateness" to mean nothing more than Edited American English. As Wilson points out, "sometimes we have no idea of what we value until we run into it" (2006, p. 41).

With this context in mind, I advocate revising rather than rejecting rubrics, at least for the short term. Rubrics need to embrace language variety because multilingualism reflects the variety of human experience and reminds us that conventions change, that English is a "living language" in a world of other Englishes (Cooper, 2004, p. 100; Lu, 2006, p. 608). But even if we revise rubrics to encourage judging writing rhetorically, they must be interpreted by trained readers who can make a case for multilingualism. If teachers and students alike can be educated to value linguistic diversity as a rhetorical choice, then assessment may push us to confront the ways that racism and language intersect.

A Closer Look At Rubrics

I examined 13 rubrics from grade 11 through higher education, all publicly available, focusing my attention mainly on the criteria of grammar and mechanics, style, and voice. (The appendix to this chapter lists all 13 and their URLs.) I make no claims about discovering all possible types of rubrics. The taxonomy I present emerges from the interpretive approach that I used, which I draw on to discuss the philosophies of composition embodied in this sample of rubrics. Moreover, my assignment of a rubric to any one category might be challenged, since the rubrics do not always neatly follow one philosophical position. For example, sometimes they fit one philosophy on the criterion of grammar and another on that of style. I focus on grammar, mechanics, style, and voice because these are the areas where the drive toward standardization is most persistent, visible, and resistant to change.

To find a framework for my examination of rubrics, I turned to Horner and Lu (2007), who, based on the work of other scholars in composition and sociolinguistics and their own observations, theorize four predominant "approaches to differences in student writing," namely, (1) eradicationist, (2) second-language acquisition, (3) accommodationist, and (4) multilingual, the last being their own contribution (p. 144). The first three approaches:

> [R]einforce a tacit English-only policy insofar as they not only assume that all students will be writing in and only in English but also support beliefs underlying the politics of English Only: specifically, the beliefs treating language and identity as fixed, linked, and uniform, and that treat fluency in standardized English, thus understood, as either a valid mark of national identity or a key that unlocks the doors to global opportunity. (Horner & Lu, 2007, p. 145)

In my own analysis of rubrics, I use roughly analogous categories: (1) acculturationism, (2) accommodationism, and (3) multiculturalism.

Acculturationist Rubrics

Acculturationist rubrics aim for "standard" English, posited as a stable and single entity, appropriately the sole language variety to be used in schools or academic circles. The goal is to eradicate "substandard," "slang," or "bad" English. Acculturationist advocates see conformity as a means of providing opportunity by "providing students access to English as an International Language" (Horner & Lu, 2007, p. 141). While most compositionist scholars and teachers do not adhere to this view, it continues to be reflected in many large-scale writing assessments, such as those used on state-mandated scoring rubrics.

A hallmark of acculturationist rubrics is error counting—e.g., more than three errors is evidence of some problem in the writing; in addition, these rubrics employ terminology such as "rules," "standard," "correct," or "proper" and espouse the ultimate goal of an "error-free" paper, the core assumption being that what counts as error is stable and easily identifiable. The pedagogical principle corresponding with the acculturationist approach is that a single standard, appropriate for all audiences, can be summarized in a textbook and taught through drill and practice. Herrington and Stanley (this volume) demonstrate how completely the ETS product *Criterion* also falls into this category and does further damage by limiting the range of acceptable rhetorical genres available to a teacher. Their analysis also highlights a problem with error counting: depending on who counts and what criteria are used, it is often done incorrectly or inconsistently (Williams, 1981).

A rubric used at Fordham University (2009) derived from Advanced Placement exams (Appendix, rubric #1) displays this philosophy, describing the mechanics of superior, good, borderline, "needs help," and failing papers as follows:

The Superior Paper (A/A-)

Mechanics: Sentence structure, grammar, and diction excellent; correct use of punctuation and citation style; minimal to no spelling errors; absolutely no run-on sentences or comma splices.

The Good Paper (B+/B)

Mechanics: Sentence structure, grammar, and diction strong despite occasional lapses; punctuation and citation style often used correctly. Some (minor) spelling errors; may have one run-on sentence or comma splice.

The Borderline Paper (B-/C+)

Mechanics: Problems in sentence structure, grammar, and diction (usually not major). Errors in punctuation, citation style, and spelling. May have several run-on sentences or comma splices.

The "Needs Help" Paper (C/C-)

Mechanics: Big problems in sentence structure, grammar, and diction. Frequent major errors in citation style, punctuation, and spelling. May have many run-on sentences and comma splices.

The Failing Paper

Shows obviously minimal lack of effort or comprehension of the assignment. Very difficult to understand owing to major problems with mechanics, structure, and analysis. Has no identifiable thesis, or utterly incompetent thesis.

This particular rubric reflects the assumption that comma splices and run-on sentences are egregious errors and that comprehension from the reader's point of view is tied to grammatical correctness. Other examples of acculturationist rubrics include the Northeast Community College Writing Rubric (2008), which states that an essay must have "Correct punctuation, spelling, mechanics, usage, inflection, and agreement" (Appendix, rubric #2); a general holistic rubric accompanying *Writer's Choice* for grade 12 (2008), which scores an essay high if it demonstrates "sophisticated and consistent command of Standard English," is "free of spelling, capitalization, and usage errors" as well as errors in punctuation and displays "precise syntax" (Appendix, rubric #3); and the College Essay Writing Assignment Scoring Rubric (2009), which quantifies error and sets four as the number allowed at the mid-level (Appendix, rubric #4). (More than four results in zero points for the category represented.)

Accommodationist Rubrics

The acculturationist category and the accommodationist category share some similarities, in particular a tendency to refer to a standard; however, the accommodationist seeks to embrace multilingual students with the goal of bridging home and academic literacies. ("Home" language means anything other than Edited American English.) The goal is to give students a stake in mainstream culture, often by using home language as a bridge to teaching Edited American English. In the accommodationist view, students must accommodate to school language, usually through code switching. Code switching is thought to mean using Edited American English in school and work settings and reserving language variation for other settings, drafting, or prewriting (Horner & Lu, 2007). Thus, although accommodationists profess a respect for language variety, they usually cast linguistic variation as appropriate only for personal or private use (as if there were no public settings that use different language varieties; see Nunley, 2004 and Canagarajah, 2006a). Language variety is painted in opposition to the standard, which is perceived as "the language of power" (Horner & Lu, 2007, p. 146). As Keith Gilyard explains, other language varieties are "equal to Standard English but not quite equal enough" (1991, p. 74).

Besides "appropriateness," accommodationist rubrics frequently mention comprehensibility, which suggests a rhetorical effect. Too many or too egregious errors and inappropriate language or voice will hamper comprehensibility. For example, the College-Level Writing Rubric from Saint Mary's College (2009) relies on the concept of appropriateness while also conflating severity of error with interference, as shown in the following portion of the rubric dedicated to mechanics and presentation (Appendix, rubric #5).

Mechanics and Presentation

Masterful. Virtually free of punctuation, spelling, capitalization errors; appropriate format and presentation for assignment

Skilled. Contains only occasional punctuation, spelling, and/or capitalization errors. Few formatting errors. Most errors likely careless

Able. Contains several (mostly common) punctuation, spelling, and/or capitalization errors. Several errors in formatting or formatting is inconsistent

Developing. Contains many errors of punctuation, spelling, and/or capitalization. Errors interfere with meaning in places. Formatting incorrect in most places

Novice. Contains many and serious errors of punctuation, spelling, and/or capitalization; errors severely interfere with meaning. Formatting weak

(Way Off). Frequent errors in spelling and capitalization; intrusive and/or inaccurate punctuation, communication is hindered. No formatting as appropriate to assignment

At the Novice level, severity and quantity of error come together to create incomprehensibility: "Contains many and serious errors of punctuation, spelling, and/or capitalization; errors severely interfere with meaning." The novice writer's paper is also inappropriate in that it "lacks an awareness of a particular appropriate audience for [the] assignment; tone and point-of-view somewhat inappropriate or very inconsistent" (Saint Mary's College, 2009). In other words, we have a rhetorical effect caused by an accumulation of errors.

Behind this rubric is the assumption that writing "with an accent," writing that stretches us to listen a bit more closely, is incomprehensible and impolite, or worse yet, "Way Off." Poe observes that violating reader expectations and norms is often considered, according to the autonomous model of literacy and psychometric theories of literacy, as a signal of cognitive deficiency (2006a, p. 16).

The accommodationist philosophy does not share the impulse for eradication of error. Since writing is a process, a measure of willingness to allow error in the spirit of experimentation is often evident. In a holistic rubric used by the University Writing Center at the University of Central Florida (2011), the writer at the highest level "demonstrates facility with the conventions of standard written English but may have minor flaws" (Appendix, rubric #6). "Flaws," deviations from the standard, are minor when they do not affront the reader or interfere with comprehension. Likewise, in the highest score for the influential rubric used statewide by the Texas Education Agency (TEA), which administers the Texas Assessment of Knowledge and Skills for grade 11 (Appendix, rubric #7):

> When the writer attempts to communicate complex ideas through sophisticated forms of expression, he/she may make minor errors as a result of these compositional risks. These types of errors do not detract from the overall fluency of the composition. (2008)

What, we might ask, are "sophisticated forms of expression"? That's the crux—the accommodationist seldom defines sophistication as embracing difference, or does so only in limited and usually private discourse.

In the accommodationist rubrics, the notion of sophistication is tied to voice. Voice is an especially important element in the TEA rubric discussed above. The required voice must not only be "appropriate," but it also must be playful, inventive, creative, and original. And how might a writer achieve a high score? In part by creating an "authentic" voice and in part by "correctly apply[ing] the conventions of the English language." In the language of the rubric there is no recognition that voice may be tied to multilingualism. Since the essay must be "readable," it must conform to the "conventions of the English language." The very fact that these conventions need no definition makes it clear: they are the norms of Edited American English, of course. To make this even clearer to graders and teachers, voice is defined in terms of connecting with the reader—the representative of the educational system, naturally: for example, in the "somewhat effective" essay, "the writer engages the reader but fails to sustain the connection"; at the same time, the writer must "sound authentic or original" and express "his/her individuality or unique perspective," all without errors that "weaken the overall fluency of the composition."

Likewise, the rubric endorsed by the State University of New York's Writing-Discipline Committee (2008), intended for assessing academic argument, is based on narrow notions of academic audience (Appendix, rubric #8). At the highest level:

> [The] essay exhibits a solid command of word variety and a tone and diction appropriate for the subject and its implied audience. Mechanics (grammar, punctuation, spelling and documentation, if needed) are nearly flawless. (State University of New York's Writing-Discipline Committee, 2008)

On the other end of the scale, in a paper that does not meet standards:

> [Diction], tone, and word choice are not appropriate for the subject or for the implied audience. Mechanics (grammar, punctuation, spelling and documentation, if needed) disrupt reading and often obscure meaning. (State University of New York's Writing-Discipline Committee, 2008)

In some ways, "implied audience" is a refreshingly enlightened term, offering possibility for readers who are open to language variety. But how should we judge obscurity in meaning? How seriously can we take this invitation to envisage an audience open to a more multinational, multiracialized approach to language?

The University of Central Florida's (2011) rubric highlights writerly control, which, as I will argue shortly, exemplifies some aspects of a multicultural rubric (Appendix, rubric #6). The highest scoring writer "demonstrates facility with the conventions of language, including syntactic variety." Still, it clings to the requirement for Edited American English, which seems designed to protect academic English from *too much* variety. Goucher College's English Writing Assessment Program (2007) rubric goes a bit further in rhetorical sophistication by relating language to genre and purpose in addition to audience (Appendix, rubric #9). In the highly rated essay, it is the artful control of language that distinguishes the strong writer: "A *strong* paper presents and executes a careful plan for its material" (Goucher College, 2007). But for the enjoinder that in the strong essay "[s]tandard usage is employed, and errors either are not present or do not interfere with meaning," we might envision this as an invitation to experiment with language variation and classify it as multicultural (Goucher College, 2007). Like the Texas assessment, it leaves us wondering how we might engage a reader with anything but a white academic voice.

Multicultural Rubrics

Multicultural pedagogies recognize the value of language diversity and the equal stature of all language varieties. Multiculturalists adopt the CCCC position that students have a right to their own language (Conference on College Composition and Communication, 1974; see also Jordan in this volume) and that all students benefit from exposure to language variety. Educationally, while multiculturalists advocate providing instruction in the dominant forms of academic discourse, they also advocate education in the politics of language and making room for alternative discourses. Multilingual students bring many creative resources to language production; these should be tapped, not discouraged or relegated to spoken discourse (Canagarajah, 2006b; Horner & Lu, 2007). External social pressures already motivate conformity to mainstream language patterns. Because these pressures may be destructive to student identity and ultimately work against educational goals, multiculturalists affirm language variety and support linguistic choice. Because World Englishes are fluid and multifaceted with many equally influential and important varieties, rhetorical power is gained by learning to negotiate between and integrate different texts, genres, languages, audiences, or dialects (Campbell, 2005; Canagarajah, 2006b; Horner & Lu, 2007). The writer is empowered to use all available resources to create a text rather than to master and then re-enact a narrowly defined linguistic code; in the process, the writer asserts or invents an identity and may also challenge the norms of a community of practice. As Canagarajah (2006b) observes in his case study of a multilingual writer: "the author is not only being creative in shuttling between communities, he is also choosing the terms in which he wants to represent himself" (p. 600). Appropriate language is judged based on the whole rhetorical situation, the identity of the writer included.

Campbell (2005) expresses the ideal of the multicultural pedagogy for native English speakers: "The inclusion of vernacular discourse in our writing pedagogies would affirm the cultural identity and community of many African American students whose identity and community are often questioned, if not categorically denied" (p. 472). Campbell's vision, extended to all students, returns us to the question raised by critics of rubrics: namely, whether they can fairly and reliably assess writing without standardizing it and without creating an unequal playing field for writers using anything different from the norm defined by the rubric and the raters. Student involvement in assessment and

the creation of rubrics is one measure of a multicultural assessment philosophy (Inoue, 2004).

Another distinguishing characteristic of multicultural rubrics is encouragement of a writerly agency that privileges meaning-making through rhetorically based choices. Other multicultural rubrics invoke writerly agency, also
expressed as judgment and control, placing it more squarely with the writer
than with the reader. Reader control usually means the writer has to conform
to unspoken standards of appropriateness, whereas writerly control means the
writer sets and executes a plan for reading. For example, the James Madison
University Writing Rubric (2008) states that the advanced writer "demonstrates mastery of spelling, punctuation, usage and mechanics" and "may use
language and punctuation to enhance meaning" (Appendix, rubric #12).

> **Traits**: Usage & Mechanics: Generally includes issues dealing with writing conven-
> tions. Features considered may include: clarity, sentence structure, grammar, spelling,
> punctuation, and capitalization.
>
> Beginning. Contains pervasive errors in mechanics, usage, grammar, or sentence
> structure. Problems interfere with meaning or distract the reader.
>
> Developing. Contains some errors in mechanics, usage, grammar, or sentence struc-
> ture. Problems may, on occasion, compromise meaning or distract the reader.
>
> Competent. Is generally free of errors in mechanics, usage, grammar, or sentence
> structure. Reads smoothly. Problems do not compromise meaning.
>
> Advanced. Demonstrates mastery of spelling, punctuation, usage, and mechanics.
> May use language and punctuation to enhance meaning. (James Madison University
> Writing Rubric, 2008)

"Mastery" used thus can evoke control, and grammar and punctuation can
be seen as rhetorical devices. At the same time, mastery as a metaphor is problematic. Mastery may simply evoke writing without error, as might be implied
by this rubric's focus on the number of errors ("pervasive," "some," "generally
free," progressing to "mastery," presumably meaning none), although the concept of error is complicated by its relation to meaning. Much, then, depends
on how we interpret "May use language and punctuation to enhance meaning."

The Sacramento State University Writing Rubric (2008) directly addresses
the issue of multicultural writers while also using "control" as a measure: An
"A" paper "displays evidence of careful editing with superior control of
grammar and mechanics appropriate to the assignment" (Appendix, rubric
#13). An additional postscript provides "Guideline for multilingual writers":

"Grammatical errors are rare and do not interfere with overall effectiveness of paper; occasional imprecision in word choice and usage may occur" (Sacramento State University Writing Rubric, 2008). As I read this, multilingual writers are expected to have an "accent." This rubric casts the control of error/convention as a matter of editing and rhetorical choice more than as a sign of intelligence or a willingness to conform. However, once again at the lower levels, writers are hampered by the need to master the dominant standard. The lower level states the "D" paper "Needs significant editing for grammar and mechanics; errors impede understanding" and focuses in the advice for multilingual writers on error only rather than on accent or rhetorical experimentation with non-standard forms: "serious and frequent errors in grammar, word choice, or usage seriously hinder communication" (Sacramento State University Writing Rubric, 2008).

A rhetorically based rubric used at Washington State University (2008) to assess the communication of critical thinking introduces another feature of multilingual rubrics, consistency: the emerging writer's "style is inconsistent or inappropriate" (Appendix, rubric #10). However, it is not clear how consistency is to be achieved or understood; like "appropriateness," which asks us to envision a white reader, it might be a red flag to the code switcher: stay consistent within one language variety and don be doin what Kermit and Geneva do, usin slang like "We Is Who We Was" (Campbell, 2005) or "the thangs we usta do, we ain't do no mo" (Smitherman, 2004). On the criterion of language, the Washington State rubric leaves more room for the code switcher or the writer using colloquial language purposefully, as the highly rated essay "clearly and effectively communicates ideas. May at times be nuanced and eloquent" (Washington State University, 2008). Presumably, consistency means a unified ethos, in which case language variety would not be precluded.

Also promising is the rubric used at St. Mary's University of Minnesota (2008), which relies on both consistency and appropriateness and subsumes them under "style": "Phrasing and word choice are consistent and appropriate to audience and purpose" (Appendix, rubric #11). At the mid-range levels, the writer is enjoined not to be "predictable," "generic," or "inappropriate," which could encourage the use of a variety of languages or styles. In the criterion of grammar and mechanics, the highly rated essay contains: "Few, if any, minor errors in sentence construction, usage, grammar, or mechanics [...] Handling of grammar and mechanics enhances the reader's understanding of the writer's purpose" (Saint Mary's University of Minnesota, 2008). There is a sense that the writer is manipulating grammar for rhetorical purposes rather than to simply conform to an expected standard. The reader is pleased because the writer is achieving his or her rhetorical purpose.

In summary, the multicultural rubric takes a rhetorical approach, especially toward error and convention. Although error is an undeniable feature of weaker writing, it is understood as deviation from a set of conventions appropriate in a specific context. Appropriateness, in turn, is nuanced so that it does not represent a monolithic white academic audience (a fiction at any rate) or any single standard. This rubric avoids the terms "error" (especially as to quantity), "standard," and "rules." Error, or lack of adherence to convention, is related to ethos (as in damage to ethos or inconsistent ethos) or readability, rather than to comprehensibility. Grammar is judged for its rhetorical effectiveness or effect on style rather than for adherence to a standard. Writerly control and judgment in creating a unified and consistent ethos are expected, and thoughtful experimentation is encouraged. Both audience and purpose are considered in judging writing quality.

Rescuing Rubrics And Teaching Practices

Even if rubrics will always be imperfect instruments, they can be improved and have an important impact on writing instruction, simply because they are influential texts that shape attitudes and articulate values. However, if the prevailing philosophy of learning is accommodationist, nothing will shift—rhetorically-based will merely mean conformity to the same white academic reader. From the way we train writing teachers for public education to the way we run programs in higher education, we have neglected professional development in the area of language variety. We do not educate our educators about language varieties at syntactical, phonological, lexical, and discourse style/function levels (Ball & Lardner, 2005; Delpit, 2006, pp. 95–96). Neglecting this topic results in attitudes that reify our notions of correctness; so, for example, we hear students who believe, as Jordan in this volume discovers, that attitudes that devalue language variety are alive and well among both students and professors. As much as we resist linguistics, we must work from knowledge of the linguistic details of students' language—we cannot simply teach the standard (as elusive as it is) or confine ourselves to converting outward signs of language difference into academic English. Composition researchers have an obligation to study language attitudes as they impact assessment and instruction, as we see Jordan, Inoue, and Fowler and Ochsner do in this volume and as Kinloch (2010) does. Their findings provide important insight into how students negotiate the demands placed upon them by the pressure to conform and demonstrate how teacher attitudes affect assessment.

A multicultural approach provides more linguistic opportunities for more students: "The teacher's job is to provide access to the national standard as well as to understand the language the children speak sufficiently to celebrate its beauty" (Delpit, 2006, p. 100). García and Menken (2006) advocate crafting a "third space" for language learning, where careful description of language and linguistic understanding are cultivated (p. 177); where pedagogies include serious consideration of non-literary text by masters of oral and written discourse from other language variety traditions (Ampadu, 2004); and where the literacy narratives of our students are invited as texts that can provide a learning experience for both teacher and student (Richardson, 2004). Jordan's informant "Shanika" (this volume) shows what students may achieve when they can use their own language.

Trimbur (2006, p. 584) argues that our *de facto* national language policy recognizes only the Anglophone tradition. In spite of the CCCC's language policy that Smitherman (1987, 2003, 2004) and many others have promoted, we too often unwittingly perpetuate assessment practices that penalize students who employ language variety. The policies we enact must include professional development, encouragement of multiculturalism, and tolerance of all varieties and types of World Englishes. Designing multilingual writing rubrics may not by itself solve the problem, but it will be an important step in the process.

Appendix

To access rubrics that may no longer be available, try Wayback machine, an Internet archive at <http://www.archive.org/web/web.php>. Some of the rubrics below use this archive address.

Acculturationist Rubrics

1. *Fordham University General Evaluation Rubric for College Papers.* 5 May 2009. Retrieved at http://www.fordham.edu/halsall/med/ rubric.html.
2. *Northeast Community College Writing Rubric.* Northeast Community College. 1 Dec. 2008. Retrieved at http://web.archive.org/web/20081203145150/ http://northeastcollege.com/AN/Assessment/PDF/FACS_Rubrics/Writi ng_Rubric.pdf.
3. *Writer's Choice Grammar and Composition Writing Assessment and Evaluation Rubrics Grade 12.* Glencoe/McGraw Hill. 1 Dec. 2008. Retrieved at http://www.glencoe.com/sec/writerschoice/teacher_resources/grade12/ G12WAER.PDF.
4. *College Essay Writing Assignment Scoring Rubric.* 5 May 2009. Retrieved at http://eureka.mhsl.uab.edu/lp/CollegeWritingRubric.html.

Accommodationist Rubrics

5. *College-Level Writing Rubric.* Saint Mary's College. 5 May 2009. Retrieved at http://www2.bc.cc.ca.us/jfulks/basicSkills%20course_coding/Example_ Writing_Rubric.pdf.
6. University of Central Florida Writing Center, *Rubric for Holistic Scoring of Analysis of an Argument.* 24 Sept. 2011. Retrieved at http://pegasus.cc.ucf. edu/~uwc/Faculty_Resources/fac_assessing_writing_pages/fac_rubric_an alysis.htm.
7. *Texas Education Agency Score Points.* Texas Education Agency. 1 Dec. 2008. Retrieved at http://web.archive.org/web/20080822074948/http://www. tea.state.tx.us/student.assessment/taks/rubrics/writing.pdf .
8. *State University of New York Report of the Writing-Discipline Committee.* State University of New York. 1 Dec. 2008. Retrieved at http://www.suny.edu/ provost/academic_affairs/SUNYWritingRubric.cfm.
9. *Goucher College English Writing Program Assessment Report, Fall 2006 and Spring 2007.* 1 Dec. 2008. Retrieved at http://www.goucher.edu/ documents/IR/PaperWritingProg.pdf.

Multicultural Rubrics

10. *Washington State University Critical & Integrative Thinking Rubric.* Washington State University. 1 Dec. 2008. Retrieved at http://wsuct project.wsu.edu/CIT_d7.html.
11. *St. Mary's University of Minnesota Writing Assessment Rubric.* Aug. 2005. St. Mary's University of Minnesota. 1 Dec. 2008. Retrieved at http://web. archive.org/web/20060920082447/http://www.smumn.edu/OCA/Cont ent_Areas/Writing/Evidence/Writing_Assessment_Instrument.pdf.
12. *James Madison University Writing Rubric.* 1 Dec. 2008. Retrieved at http: //www.jmu.edu/assessment/resources/JMU_Final_Writing_Rubric_f08. pdf.
13. *Sacramento State University Writing Rubric.* 1 Dec. 2008. Retrieved at www. csus.edu/wac/WAC/Teachers/rubric.doc.

Grading Contracts: Assessing Their Effectiveness on Different Racial Formations

Asao B. Inoue

I've used grading contracts for several years now. I initially chose to adopt contracts because they solve at least three problems I have with grading writing. One, grades are deceptive; not only do they replace real feedback on student writing with a one-dimensional, somewhat arbitrary symbol, but that symbol often is perceived by the student to stand in for how well he or she is doing. Two, grades create false hierarchies that are counterproductive to a collaborative and educative learning environment, making some students feel bad about themselves as writers when they should not and prematurely halting revision in other students (Bleich, 1997; Elbow, 1993). Three, grades tend to create a need in students for more grades, often at the expense of formative and more authentic response (Elbow, 1993; Kohn, 1993). The presence and expectation of grades tend to construct an ill-fitting kind of motivation for the writing classroom, one based on extrinsic rewards that keep students from learning. I prefer to encourage intrinsic rewards for writing.

These grade-related problems are not new. They and other issues have been identified in the writing assessment literature. Beyond the literature on portfolios (Belanoff & Dickson, 1991; Black et al., 1994), which often discusses the delaying of grades (Hamp-Lyons & Condon, 2000, p. 34), Huot, for instance, advocates for a distinction from grading in our reading and evaluation practices, calling for "instructive evaluation" (2002a, p. 69). Similarly, Bleich (1997) argues against grading from a historical perspective and for "descriptive evaluation" (pp. 29–31). And, of course, there's the literature that questions the reliability of grades. In one famous study, 300 papers were given to 53 judges (roughly half were from academia and half held non-academic positions, such as editors, lawyers, and writers). The researchers found very low reliability—a median correlation of .31—in the grades given to the papers (Diederich, 1974, p. 6). Bowman (1973) found similar results on assessment in business writing courses, with the same piece of writing receiving a wide range of grades from senior and junior teachers (pp. 28–29).

In a summary of the research on grading, O'Hagan explains that while grading emerged in the U.S. around 1850, "studies as early as 1912 questioned the validity of grading, suggesting that in writing instruction [...] grades were far too subjective" (1997, p. 4). While O'Hagan claims the subjectivity of grading is an issue of validity, I would say it falls under the category of reliability, or the consistency of grades. The common complaint that grades are too "subjective" to be useful seems equally an issue of reliability or consistency as it does in validity. Regardless, classroom grading practices have had many critics, and I consider myself one of them.

In attempting to solve these grading problems, I moved to a grading contract, but after several years, I wondered: how effective has my grading contract been for my students? Does it work better for some students than others? Like Kelly-Riley in this collection, I wanted to know how various racial formations were faring on our assessments. In this chapter, I assess the effectiveness of grading contracts on three racial formations, Asian Pacific Islanders (APIs), African Americans, and whites, in Fresno State's First Year Writing (FYW) program.

I ask about grading contract effectiveness not just to understand its impact on various racial formations in classrooms but to illustrate the way any assessment technology may have differential effects on various students. As Hanson (1993) has argued convincingly about testing generally, grading technologies are never neutral systems. Like any other "test," grading produces the very traits, characteristics, and categories it claims to measure in students and their writing (Hanson, 1993, pp. 284, 287–288). So in part, I wonder what biases my grading contract has. Furthermore, grading contracts, like all grading technologies, make obvious that we form agreements with students to produce evaluations of their writing and course grades, agreements that have governing criteria, criteria that may have biases unknown to teachers (or students), and potentially differential effectiveness for various students. In short, the effectiveness of our grading technologies, whatever they may be, may not be evenly distributed among all students.

Elements Of Effectiveness In Grading Contracts

In many ways, it is unfair to measure the effectiveness of grading contracts against conventional grading systems. Contracts are so different to teachers and students that their "effectiveness" may look quite different from conventional grading technologies. However, according to the literature on contracts in composition, contracts do possess at least three features of effectiveness. In 1973, Mandel offered a contract system in which the more written projects a student completed, the higher the course grade that student received. Mandel explained that his contract allowed him not to grade student writing through judgments of quality, which he found detrimental to student learning (p. 623); instead, he graded on quantity (p. 628). A few years later, Knapp (1976) discussed a similar contract system, one also based on quantity. Papers were given a simple binary judgment: acceptable or unacceptable. If unacceptable, the student took her feedback and revised for submission the next week. Each successive paper demanded more of the student, and the more papers the student completed, the higher her grade in the course. Knapp distinguishes an important feature not present in Mandel's contract: every essay gets a binary decision, which is unlike Mandel's system in which "faith in students" to achieve and challenge themselves drives drafting and writing efforts (Mandel, 1973, p. 629). Despite this important difference in how drafts are judged, both share one important feature in their contracts. Grades are calculated primarily by the quantity of work produced, which I argue is crucial to how effective both contracts can be. And so, grading contract effectiveness can be measured in part by the quantity of work produced by students.

Of course a focus on quantity is not paramount to disregarding quality. Mandel lets quality organically spring from the cycle of drafting and conferences, while Knapp uses that binary judgment, a judgment mainly about quality, to ensure that students are ready to move to the next writing assignment. Additionally, many who believe grading contracts are a better choice often voice the opinion that the more a student practices writing, the better she will get, arguing that quality is a function of quantity.

The focus on quantity of work over quality of work to determine grades is a hallmark of most grading contract systems. Bauman's grading contract (1997, pp. 164–165) is a good example. Bauman's main concern, however, is with the contract's ability to motivate students in the right ways. She argues that grades motivate students toward the wrong ends in a writing class, toward extrinsic rewards (p. 166), something that Danielewicz and Elbow mention about Elbow's contract (2009, p. 247). Drawing on Paris and Turner (1994), Bauman explains that motivation is not simply a "characteristic of people or a property of events"; it is "derived from contextual transactions" (Bauman, 1997, p. 167). People and their contexts create motivation (p. 167). Grading contracts' emphasis on quantity (and not grades), Bauman argues, creates an environment for such intrinsic motivation. Motivation as a measure of effectiveness of contracts, however, is difficult to assess. Motivation may show up in a variety ways, but most agree that it is a reaction to the learning environment.

Spidell and Thelin's (2006) study of student resistance to grading contracts offers some insight on motivation. While Spidell and Thelin's methods did not allow them to separate data by racial formation, they found several general trends in student surveys and interviews about contracts in their mostly white student population: (1) many students resented contracts because they were used to working in point systems (p. 40), which quantified efforts (p.

41); (2) a "perception of increased responsibility led to anxiety and resistance" to contracts (p. 42)—i.e., it felt like too much work; (3) some students felt that the contract leveled the grading curve too much (p. 44); (4) "students felt the contract made the course more difficult than necessary" (p. 48); and (5) while some students found that the contract made expectations clearer and motivated them to do work, others felt it may have offered clear objectives for grades but did not motivate students to write better (p. 50). Spidell and Thelin's study helps us see a third feature of the effectiveness of any grading technology: effectiveness can be measured by students' reactions to the grading contract.

In sum, the effectiveness of grading contracts, if judged on their own terms, has three features, which I'll use in this study. Effectiveness is a measure of (1) the quantity of work produced, (2) the quality of writing produced in class, and (3) student reactions to and acceptance of the contract itself. I'd like to note two things about the literature on grading contracts reviewed above. First, there is no discussion of differential impact or effectiveness of contracts on different racial formations. Second, there is no quantitative research published on the effectiveness of contracts. This chapter attempts to fill both of these gaps.

Fresno State's Grading Contract

Fresno State's FYW program uses a grading contract that is adopted from Shor (1996) and Danielewicz and Elbow (2009). These versions of grading contracts were chosen because they seemed to offer the best chances for our diverse populations to succeed as writers. Shor's and Danielewicz and Elbow's contracts both use the main elements of contracts mentioned above. In addition to focusing on quantity of work to produce course grades and cultivating intrinsic motivation for doing work in the class by grading less or not at all in the semester, Shor's contract is negotiated with students, and attempts to do the things that Shiffman is looking for in a grading system: share power and redistribute authority self-consciously (Shor, 1996, p. 20; Danielewicz & Elbow, 2009, p. 245).

Danielewicz and Elbow offer an instructive way to compare the similarities between Shor's contract and theirs. They explain that Shor's contract's emphasis on resisting the "culture of capitalism" is similar to their contract's focus on resisting a "culture of grading and assessment" (Danielewicz & Elbow, 2009, p. 248). The two cultures function similarly on the individual: conventional grading "helps induce student compliance by obscuring analogous structures of unfairness" (p. 248). Finally, Danielewicz and Elbow explain that their contract encourages extrinsic motivation, in the form of doing a certain amount of work to get a course grade of "B," but this extrinsic motivation leads to intrinsic motivation (p. 257). They argue that contracts motivate students in the opposite direction from what Bauman promotes, but intrinsic motivation is the goal, just as Bauman argues. Thus by doing the work, students become more interested and engaged. Practice makes for engagement and interest, for motivation, and thus better writing. The contract's direct critique of conventional grading's tendency to obscure "structures of unfairness" seemed a perfect solution for the difficulties that two particular racial formations—Asian Pacific Islanders (who are mostly Hmong), and African Americans—historically have had in the FYW program.

In a nutshell, all contracts in Fresno State's FYW program are negotiated in the first week or two of classes. Our contracts justify grades, typically a "B," by the amount of work done, with little attention to the quality of writing, except in the crudest sense of judging whether basic requirements are met, which is akin to Knapp's binary distinction (acceptable or not). Our contract language describes meeting the contract's expectations as turning in writing "in the manner and spirit it is asked" of students. The contract also attempts to limit the teacher's power over student writing and revising by limiting the range and potency of judgments possible that affect student course grades. The logic is that fewer teacher judgments of quality and fewer distinctions of quality in writing will allow students to have opportunities to make and articulate decisions as writers, even ones teachers do not agree with, then discuss those decisions in portfolio reflection letters. Thus, all assignments are typically acceptable or not acceptable, meaning they either have met basic assignment requirements or they have not (e.g., due time and date, word count, addressing particular texts or questions, etc.).

Methods And Data

To address the effectiveness of grading contracts, I gathered data from three sources: (1) anonymous exit surveys of FYW students in the writing program; (2) final portfolio ratings from the same group of students; and (3) course grade distributions of the same students. All three data sources come from English 5B students from the Spring 2009 and Spring 2010 semesters in Fresno State's FYW program. English 5B is the second and final course in the stretch option, one option students may choose to fulfill their university writing requirement. A student's 5A and 5B teachers are typically the same instructor, and 5A uses a mandatory grading contract and is a credit/no credit course. Additionally, the FYW program is a Directed Self-Placement (DSP) program similar to the one discussed by Royer and Gilles (1998, 2003) at Grand Valley State University. Roughly 69% of all incoming first-year students chose the stretch option in the 2008–09 AY, while 56.5% choose it in 2009–10 AY. I've written more about Fresno State's DSP, stretch courses, curricula, program portfolio, students, and our program assessment efforts elsewhere (Inoue, 2009a).

Surveys

The anonymous surveys were conducted online, and asked students to answer the following questions about grading contracts in their classes: (1) "How effective overall did you find the grading contract to be in your writing class?" (2) "How happy are you with the grading contract as a student in the class?" and (3) "Do you prefer a grading contract over traditional grading systems (where grades are placed on each assignment) in courses like this one?" Additionally, two open-ended responses were solicited: (1) "Please explain below what you like about the grading contract in courses like writing courses, or how the contract helped you as a student or writer," and (2) "Please explain below what you do not like about grading contracts in courses like writing courses." I later grouped similar open-ended responses into themes. This allowed me to both quantify the kinds of open-ended responses received and consider qualitatively their content.

As seen in Table 1, when student enrollment statistics for Fall 2008 and Fall 2009 (only fall enrollment is published by the university) are compared to students who completed the spring 5B exit surveys, students of color are somewhat overrepresented in the survey. In both years, white students are underrepresented when compared to overall university enrollment figures.

	Spring 2009 survey		Spring 2010 survey	
	N	%	N	%
African American	27	6.25%	43	8.69%
Native American	1	0.23%	3	0.61%
Asian Pacific Is.	100	23.15%	126	25.45%
Hispanic	186	43.06%	209	42.22%
White	118	27.31%	113	22.83%
unknown	0	0%	2	0.020%
Total	432	100.0%	496	100.0%

Table 1. English 5B FYW Exit Survey Participants By Race

Portfolio Ratings

The program portfolio consists of 10 pages of polished work (often 2–3 pieces), usually coming from the main projects dictated by the program's curriculum, one previous draft of each document included, and a letter of reflection (not counted in the 10 pages). Portfolio ratings are generated by blind readings conducted in the summer by teachers in the program. The only portfolio ratings we collect for the stretch program are from the English 5A midterm and English 5B final portfolios; thus these are the ratings reported in this study, constituting a semester and half of instruction using a grading contract. Each portfolio is rated on a linear scale from 1 to 6 on five of the program's eight outcomes (with 1–2 being inadequate quality, 3–4 being proficient quality, and 5–6 superior quality):

- READING/WRITING STRATEGIES: Demonstrate or articulate an understanding of reading strategies and assumptions that guide effective reading, and how to read actively, purposefully, and rhetorically;
- REFLECTION: Make meaningful generalizations/reflections about reading and writing practices and processes;
- SUMMARY/CONVERSATION: Demonstrate summarizing purposefully, integrate "they say" into writing effectively or self-consciously, appropriately incorporate quotes into writing (punctuation, attributions, relevance), and discuss and use texts as "conversations" (writing, then, demonstrates entering a conversation);
- RHETORICALITY: Articulate or demonstrate an awareness of the rhetorical features of texts, such as purpose, audience, context, rhetorical appeals, and elements, and write rhetorically, discussing similar features in texts;
- LANGUAGE COHERENCE: Have developed, unified, and coherent paragraphs and sentences that have clarity and some variety. (California State Fresno, 2009, n.p.)

Grade Distributions

The grade distributions were gathered and processed by the university's Office of Institutional Research, Assessment, and Planning, the same office that completed the statistical work on the portfolio ratings and enrollments.[1]

Participants

Asian Pacific Islanders (API) at Fresno State consist mostly of Hmong students, of which about half speak Hmong at home and half English.[2] In this same formation, just less than 50% identify their parents as having "less than a high school education." Approximately 26% reported that their parents have a high school diploma or GED. Fewer than 15% reported that their parents have some college or an Associates degree, and about 5% say their parents have a Bachelor's degree. In Fall 2009, 86.1% of all regularly admitted, first-year API students were designated as needing remediation.[3]

African American students in the FYW program report that they speak English at home (97.78% of the time), with Spanish as the only other language spoken at home (2.22% of the time). Their parents are generally more educated than the Hmong population, identifying 6.82% with less than a high school education, 27.27% with a high school diploma, 34.09% with an Associates degree, 22.73% with a Bachelor's, and 9.09% with a Master's. In Fall 2009, 78.3% of all regularly admitted, first-year African Americans were designated as needing remediation by the university, a marginally better rate than APIs.

Finally, white students primarily speak English at home (92.11% of the time), with Spanish (2.63%) and other languages (5.26%) also spoken. Most of their parents have more than a high school diploma (24.3%), with 28.04% identifying an Associates, 21.50% a Bachelor's, 17.76% a Master's, and 4.67% a PhD, EdD, or MD degree as the highest level of parental education. This racial formation comes from the most educated households, and has the lowest remediation rates in Fall 2009, at 59.8% needing remediation.

Results: Effectiveness As Quantity, Student Acceptance, And Quality

Effectiveness of grading contracts in English 5B is measured in this study by considering three data sources: (1) exit surveys, which help determine student acceptance and response to the contract; (2) English 5A midterm and English 5B final portfolio ratings, which help determine quality of writing and development or growth in writing;[4] and (3) English 5B grade distributions, which help determine the quantity of work done, since all contracts are for "B" grades.

Asian Pacific Islanders (API)

In English 5A midterm and 5B final portfolios, API students performed better than the mean of all students in every category in both years (Tables 2 and 3). They did not have the biggest difference in ratings, but like all students, they moved from just above "poor" (overall average 2.97 and 2.52) to "acceptable" quality (overall average 3.68 and 3.54) in most dimensions in both years. Interestingly, the one dimension in which Hmong students did receive statistically significantly higher average ratings than all other racial formations on the final portfolio in both years is a critical program outcome, "summary and conversation" (difference of .81 and 1.25). Focusing on quantity of work done may be helping API students engage better with academic texts and incorporate them appropriately in their own writing. More writing seems to equate to better summary and engagement with texts in their writing. API students also met the contract's workload obligations at about the same level as all students, 79.1% receiving "As" and "Bs" in 2009 and 80.1% receiving the same grades in 2010; however, in the year that fewer of all categories of students met contract obligations (2010), more API students met their obligations. Whatever changes occurred in classrooms in 2010, they did not affect API students negatively. In fact, those changes seemed to help them. The quantity of work our contracts demanded could have been a factor in APIs' abilities to engage appropriately with academic texts in their writing and show significant improvement along this dimension in both years.

Additionally, APIs were the most consistently accepting of the contract (Table 4). APIs found the grading contract about as effective as all students in both years (81.48% and 77.78%), and were "happy" or "very happy" with the contract in about the same rates as all students (73.75% and 71.56%). However, it is their preference for the contract, higher than any other formation in both years (81.48% and 70.64%), that stands out. While APIs' preference rates dropped at a similar rate as all other groups in 2010, they did not seem to match how many API students met their contracts, since more met their contracts in 2010 than 2009. So the changes that occurred in 2010 did not adversely affect APIs' ability to meet their contract obligations (the quantity of work).

In their open-ended responses on surveys, APIs had mostly positive comments, with 129 positive and 116 negative comments entered. They had the most positive comments in three related themes, "expectations and clarity," "motivation and staying on track," and the most interesting one, "freedom to write without grades." There were 34 comments made concerning "expectations and clarity." Similar to Spidell and Thelin's (2006) findings, most respondents explained that the contract allowed them to know the expectations for a grade in the class: "I like how the grading contract gives us certain days to miss a class and how many assignments we can miss to receive a certain grade." There were 22 "motivation and staying on track" comments, which praised the contract for keeping them on task throughout the semester: "this grading contract helped me to be on task about doing my homework and essays."

Race and Writing Assessment

	All Students (n=130)			Asian Pacific Islander (n=21)			African American (n=14)			Latino/a (n=52)			White (n=32)		
	5A mid	5B fin	diff.*	5A mid	5B fin	diff.*	5A mid	5B fin	diff.*	5A mid	5B fin	diff.*	5A mid	5B fin	diff.*
overall	2.88	3.53	.65	2.97	3.68	.70	2.83	3.73	.90	2.75	3.51	.76	3.01	3.41	.40
strategies	2.62	3.35	.72	2.81	3.48	.67	2.64	3.64	1.00	2.48	3.37	.88	2.63	3.16	.53
reflection	2.73	3.54	.81	2.90	3.81	.90	2.71	3.79	1.07	2.56	3.48	.92	2.81	3.44	.63
summary	2.98	3.61	.62	2.90	3.71	.81	2.93	3.64	.71	2.88	3.56	.67	3.19	3.47	.28
rhetoric	2.98	3.50	.52	3.14	3.57	.43	2.93	3.57	.64	2.85	3.50	.65	3.16	3.44	.28
lang co	3.08	3.67	.59	3.10	3.81	.71	2.93	4.00	1.07	3.00	3.65	.65	3.25	3.53	.28

TABLE 2. FALL 2008 5A MIDTERM AND SPRING 2009 5B FINAL PORTFOLIO MEAN RATINGS (1-6 SCALE)

* Results are based on Paired Samples T Tests (N>=20) or Wilcoxon Signed Rank Test (N<20) with significance level 0.05. Significant differences are in bold.

	All Students (n=156)			Asian Pacific Islander (n=36)			African American (n=15)			Latino/a (n=60)			White (n=31)		
	5A mid	5B fin	diff.**	5A mid	5B fin	diff.**	5A mid	5B fin	diff.**	5A mid	5B fin	diff.**	5A mid	5B fin	diff.**
overall	2.47	3.49	1.02	2.52	3.54	1.02	2.28	3.27	.99	2.39	3.42	1.03	2.67	3.63	.96
strategies	2.24	3.36	1.12	2.36	3.47	1.11	1.80	2.87	1.07	2.20	3.30	1.10	2.39	3.55	1.16
reflection	2.22	3.44	1.22	2.47	3.47	1.00	2.00	2.93	.93	2.08	3.42	1.33	2.32	3.65	1.32
summary	2.50	3.54	1.04	2.53	3.78	**1.25**	2.33	3.67	**1.33**	2.40	3.35	.95	2.81	3.48	.68
rhetoric	2.21	3.38	1.17	2.28	3.36	1.08	2.20	3.20	1.00	2.13	3.37	1.23	2.35	3.52	1.16
lang co	3.17	3.72	.55	2.94	3.61	.67	3.07	3.67	.60	3.12	3.65	.53	3.48	3.97	.48

TABLE 3. FALL 2009 5A MIDTERM AND SPRING 2010 5B FINAL PORTFOLIO MEAN RATINGS (1-6 SCALE)

** Regular ANOVA is used to test if there are significant differences in students' improvement among racial groups. The reference group is White students. The level of significance is 0.05. Significant differences are in bold.

	All Students		Asian Pacific Islander		African American		Latino/a		White	
	(n=343)	(n=415)	(n=81)	(n=108)	(n=22)	(n=40)	(n=140)	(n=174)	(n=99)	(n=90)
	Sp 09	Sp 10	Sp 09	Sp 10	Sp 09	Sp 10	Sp 09	Sp 10	Sp 09	Sp 10
effectiveness	79.24%	77.83%	81.48%	77.78%	72.73%	92.50%	81.43%	76.44%	74.75%	76.67%
happiness	72.51%	71.88%	73.75%	71.56%	57.14%	75.00%	75.54%	72.51%	70.30%	70.97%
preference	73.76%	63.46%	81.48%	70.64%	72.73%	62.50%	73.19%	63.01%	68.32%	58.24%

TABLE 4. ENGL 5B EXIT SURVEY ON GRADING CONTRACTS

Finally, there were 22 comments under the "freedom to write without grades" theme, which, unlike Spidell and Thelin's (2006) findings, tended to express appreciation and praise for the contract's ability to keep grades off their writing and assignments. The comments in this theme tended to be longer than those in any other theme, and longer than comments by any other racial formation. Typical comments were as follows:

> It allows me to write and not be afraid that my thoughts or perspective will be marked down if I do not meet the writing standards. The contract helps me concentrate more on my ideas and purpose rather than on grammar errors. It makes me feel like a real and independent writer.

For API students, it seems clear: the emphasis on quantity instead of quality gave them confidence and motivation to write, which they preferred. Contracts produced quality writing that was deemed proficient in their portfolios, as well as marked differences (growth) along all dimensions measured in portfolios, most significantly the key program outcome, "summary and conversation." And since most APIs met their contract obligations and found that the contracts freed them to write without grades, the focus on quantity over quality in order to produce intrinsic motivation to write and write better appears to be most effective for APIs. In these ways, grading contracts were most effective for APIs at Fresno State.

African Americans

In 2009, African Americans' English 5A midterm ratings on most dimensions (overall rating 2.83) were similar to the mean ratings of all students (overall rating 2.88), but their English 5B final ratings were among the highest (overall rating 3.73) (Table 2). Meanwhile in 2010 portfolios, they received some of the lowest mean ratings in many dimensions of all groups at both English 5A midterm (overall rating 2.28) and English 5B final (overall rating 3.27) (Table 3). Still, African Americans in both years moved from generally poor quality to proficient quality, and like their Hmong counterparts in 2009, African Americans in 2010 showed the most growth among all formations along "summary and conversation" (statistically significant growth in 2010, with a difference of 1.33). In fact, in 5B final portfolios, both racial formations were rated higher in this dimension than any other racial formation (APIs at 3.78 and African Americans at 3.67).

Interestingly, African Americans' grade distributions achieve fewer "As" and "Bs" than any other group in both years, suggesting that they had trouble meeting the quantity required by the contract and getting the work done. Only 73.1% (2009) and 62.8% (2010) of African Americans completed their contracts (or received an "A" or a "B"). The fact that more African Americans did not meet the workload (quantity) requirement of their grading contracts may account for their generally lower portfolio scores (quality) in 2010. As mentioned earlier, 2010 appeared to have stricter contract obligations for everyone. Regardless of what affected writing quality or fewer African Americans meeting their contract obligations, the ubiquitous use of grading contracts in our FYW program suggests one thing about our African American racial formation: they have a harder time generally meeting the workload expectations of the contracts. Despite this difficulty, their writing ends up being of proficient quality, and like the API formation, African Americans do best in the key outcome of "summary and conversation," showing statistically significant change in 2010, the stricter year. Ultimately, for African Americans more work did seem to equate to higher quality and more growth in writing, but at the cost of more African Americans not meeting the workload requirements.

African Americans' open-ended responses were mostly positive, with 42 positive and 37 negative comments. The positive comments contained three strong themes, with 11 concerning "expectations and clarity," 8 concerning "relieves pressure," and 12 concerning "effort over quality." Like APIs, comments in the "expectations and clarity" theme praised the contract's ability to make "it more clear on what we were expected to do throughout the class." The comments themed as "relieves pressure" were similar to the API comments themed as "motivation and staying on track," except the focus in African American comments tended toward the contract's way of relieving the pressure created by constantly anticipating grades: "it puts less strain on my grades, and I can just focus on the content of my work, and not whether or not it'll effect my grades." African American comments in the "effort over quality" category focused on how the emphasis on effort makes a writer feel less like a bad writer: "you never feel like you totally failed something, but instead you can see your strengths or weaknesses more."

African Americans found contracts effective and had some of the highest rates (92.5% in 2010) of satisfaction. In 2010, they were also happiest with contracts, with 75% approving of contracts, but least happy of all formations in 2009 at only 57% (Table 4). Perhaps the somewhat erratic findings can be explained by the fewer number of responses from African Americans, which is due to Fresno State's low enrollment of African American students.

Whites

In 2009, white students' portfolio ratings showed little growth (overall difference .40), but averaged in the "acceptable" range of ratings at both English

5A midterm and 5B final (Table 2). They generally started higher in the quality of their work (overall 3.01) than any other formation, but ended lower than all other racial formations (overall 3.41). In this same year, 89.2% of all whites met their contract obligations, which is noticeably higher than all students (80.1%), and a higher percentage than any other racial formation achieved. In 2010, they also generally started with higher 5A midterm ratings (overall 2.67) and ended with generally higher 5B final ratings (overall 3.63) than any other formation; however, whites achieved the least amount of growth in quality (.96) between 5A midterm and 5B final, just as in the previous year (.40). In 2010, they also completed their contract obligations at again one of the highest levels, with 79.6% getting "As" and "Bs." The only group in 2010 who did more work was their API counterparts.

Interestingly, for the white formation, it is unclear as to whether quantity equated to quality, or much growth in quality. In 2009, they received lower English 5B final portfolio ratings (overall 3.41) than all other formations and achieved less growth than all others (overall difference .40), but more whites completed their contracts' workload expectations that year than any other formation (89.2%). Meanwhile in 2010, whites had higher English 5B final ratings than any other formation (overall 3.63), stronger growth (but still less than all other racial formations, with overall difference .96), yet fewer white students met the workload expectations of the contract than had the previous year (79.6%). These findings suggest that there may not be nearly as strong of a connection between the contract's focus on quantity of work producing higher quality of work, or producing intrinsic motivation for writing.

White students found the contract as effective as most other racial formations in both years (74.75% and 76.67%), although the rates are generally a little lower. Their happiness with the contract was also on par with all other racial formations (70.30% and 70.97%). However, white students' preferences for grading contracts were the lowest of all racial formations in both years (68.32% and 58.24%).

White students' open-ended comments included 117 positive and 109 negative comments. The two strongest positive themes were "relieves pressure" (29 comments) and "expectations and clarity" (21 comments). Most comments in the "relieves pressure" theme focused on allowing more time to develop writing without the pressure of grades and taking risks without being penalized by grades: "it alleviates the pressure to do well on each assignment. I think there is some flexibility to try to take risks with writing strategies [...] without being penalized." The positive comments by white students in the theme of "expectations and clarity" were similar to those expressed by APIs and African American students.

The biggest difference in comments was in negative comments by white students in the themes "no grades/how well am I doing?" and "unfair to those who traditionally do well already." The following was typical of whites' negative comments and fits in both themes, which matches findings by Spidell and Thelin (2006):

> I do not like knowing whether I stood in an A or B range for both english 5a and 5b throughout the semesters, I believe that the teacher should be more accurate and grade with the normal system, this way I would know where I stand [...] I feel like it is a lot easier for students to cheat their way to an A, it should be something that you have to work for, which should not be solely depend on a person's quality of portfolio, it should be based off of the work throughout the semester.

The seeming contradiction in the student's response refers to not receiving grades on individual assignments and the dependence on the final portfolio to determine an "A" grade. The source of many white students' negative comments seemed to be frustration centered on the ambiguity of grades.

White students' comments on the theme of "unfair to those who traditionally do well already" further suggested a deep attachment to traditional grading systems. Perhaps whites' higher rates of "As" and "Bs" are one indication that many in this formation expected those grades, and expected them to be given out less frequently to others.

In the end, all three measures of effectiveness (portfolio ratings, exit surveys, and grade distributions) were inconsistent. Grading contracts did seem to be marginally effective in producing growth in white students' writing quality but least effective in generating student acceptance. Despite the higher rates of completing the contract's workload obligations, and high rates of perceived effectiveness and happiness with the contract, white students did not prefer the contract at as high a rate as any other racial formation. Contracts did not seem to harm white students, however, as they produced sufficient quality of writing and growth with respect to the FYW program's outcomes.

Conclusions

Based on the findings of this study, grading contracts at Fresno State are most effective for APIs, somewhat effective for African Americans, and marginally effective for whites. By far, contracts were most effective for our Asian Pacific Islanders, who are mostly Hmong with low parental education levels, often speak Hmong in their homes, and are mostly identified as remedial. Contracts produced similar quality and development, even along the same dimensions in their writing, for African Americans, who have higher levels of parental education, speak English at home, and have high rates of remedial status. African Americans, however, had more difficulty meeting all the contract obligations. The quantity of work expected in contracts appeared to be more difficult to complete for more African American students than any other racial formation, which may account for their lower preference rates in 2010. Finally, for the white student formation, who speak mostly English at home, have high levels of parental education, and the lowest remedial rates, the contract proved to be least effective. While they still met program expectations in terms of the quality of their writing, they rated lower than all others in final portfolios, and had smaller differences in growth in their writing over a semester and a half of instruction with the contract. Additionally, while they had the highest rates of completing the contract, they preferred it at the lowest rates, and had more (relatively speaking) negative responses in surveys.

These conclusions suggest that grading contracts like the ones used at Fresno State, and those promoted by Shor (1996) and Danielewicz and Elbow (2009), tend to be more effective for students who are predisposed to seeing—or can be convinced to view—grades as unhelpful, destructive, or harmful to their learning. At Fresno State, these students tend to be of color, have other languages spoken in their homes, and come from homes with parents who tend to have not gone to college. The majority are identified as needing remediation. Finally, the students for whom grading contracts were most effective were those who either see grades as punishment, as limiting their choices and decisions in writing, as producing pressure to get things right, as reducing freedom to write, or as de-motivating in some way, or those who see themselves as not being good writers already. The API formation at Fresno State best fit this profile.

My findings about the effectiveness of grading contracts for API, African American, and white students suggest that any grading technology may very well affect various racial formations differently. The effectiveness of any grading technology often hinges on the assumptions that the technology makes about the nature of quality writing, the relationship of quality to the workload of the course, the assumptions students must accept in order for the grading technology to function properly, and with whom that technology is interacting (about whom it makes decisions and who makes decisions). What I have not been able to inquire about in this study is teachers' identities, which surely influenced the effectiveness of the grading contracts. The gendered and racialized ethos of teachers may have affected how some students responded to the contract. For instance, most of our FYW teachers are white, middle-class female teaching associates (TAs) in their early to mid-twenties.

In the end, the present study clearly suggests that the effectiveness of grading contracts in classrooms is unevenly distributed among racial formations, and it sheds light on potential biases within Fresno State's grading contract approach. The most important, I think, is a bias toward student effort rather than quality of writing. While quality is a measure of effectiveness, it is not *the only measure of effectiveness* in our contract grading system. In fact, when quality is the primary bias in a grading technology, then I think we doom many students to failure or near failure. Grading technologies with quality biases tend to oppress many students, but especially poorer students and students of color. So maybe it's not simply that grades harm students by placing them into hierarchies, but they harm them by restricting their freedom to write, or taking their sense of self-worth away, because their writing just will not be judged "high quality." Fairer grading technologies would seem to be those with biases that allow all students the ability to achieve the full range of grades. Contracts do this by rewarding effort and labor, and these biases seem more fitting for a truly democratic and diverse society.

Notes

---

[1] I want to thank Tina Leimer, the Director of IRAP, and two of her Research Analysts, Hongtao Yue and Dmitri Rogulkin, for their statistical help.

[2] All information on languages spoken at home and parents' education level comes from anonymous entry surveys in English 5A for Fall 2009. Student demographic numbers, GPAs, SAT Comp scores, and remediation numbers come from CSUF's Office of Institutional Research, Assessment, and Planning office.

[3] While CSU, Fresno uses a DSP model, all CSU students must take the EPT before enrolling, which the university uses to determine remedial status (still). The EPT is administered by ETS and consists of one 45-minute essay section and two 30-minute multiple-choice sections. All remediation statistics by race were obtained from California State University, 2009, n. d.

[4] Most students take English 5A and 5B with the same instructor. English 5A uses a grading contract to determine the credit/no credit grade in the course. Student survey responses suggest that approximately 80% of all English 5B classes in both Spring 2009 and Spring 2010 also used grading contracts.

SECTION THREE
Responding to Racial and Linguistic Variation

I n 1974 a special issue of *College Composition and Communication* was dedicated to *Students' Right to Their Own Language*. In that special issue, the
Committee on CCCC Language wrote in the background statement to the
resolution:

> American schools and colleges have, in the last decade, been forced to take a stand on
> a basic educational question: what should the schools do about the language habits of
> students who come from a wide variety of social, economic, and cultural back-
> grounds? The question is not new. Differences in language have always existed, and
> the schools have always wrestled with them, but the social upheavals of the 1960's,
> and the insistence of submerged minorities on a greater share in American society,
> have posed the question more insistently and have suggested the need for a shift in
> emphasis in providing answers. Should the schools try to uphold language variety, or
> to modify it, or to eradicate it? (p. 1)

Almost 40 years later, the question about what schools should do about the
language habits of diverse students still resonates. The authors in this section
work very much within the tradition of SRTOL, but instead of asking what
schools *should do*, they explore what *is being done* in writing classrooms and in
the ways that we assess student writing. Their research shows the persistence of
negative attitudes toward African American English and other dialects, but
they also show the creative, rich ways that teachers continue to respond to
those attitudes in their teaching and teacher-training. Their work inspires us to
find new ways to understand and change language attitudes.

Zandra L. Jordan shows in "*Students' Right*, African American English, and
Classroom Writing Assessment: Considering the HBCU" that African American students are highly attuned to the cultural devaluation of African American English. Jordan brings the perspective of a teacher who does not see code
meshing and academic writing success as antithetical and who understands the
intimate relationship between writing and identity. She writes that she
"wanted students to learn the ways of writing that would garner academic success [without becoming] so beleaguered in the process that they lost all pleasure in writing, confidence in themselves, and pride in their own languages."

Jordan offers the story of Shanika, a student in her Grammar and Style
class at Spelman College. Shanika, a top-ranked student in her high school,
struggled with college-level writing. Although Shanika identified her greatest
writing difficulty as subject-verb agreement, Jordan recognized that Shanika

needed greater exposure to reading with attention to writing conventions. As she explains, "Exposing Shanika to texts modeling the writing rules with which she is unfamiliar, helping her identify those rules, and giving her opportunities to practice them could better position her for success than simply marking errors and penalizing her for them."

In "Evaluating Essays Across Institutional Boundaries: Teacher Attitudes Toward Dialect, Race, and Writing," Judy Fowler and Robert Ochsner provide the results of a quasi-experimental study in which they compared teacher responses to AAVE and Spanish-influenced writing styles in student writing. Their study asked if teachers at an institution whose student body is made up of mostly a particular racial formation with particular language markers (AAVE at Fayetteville State University and Spanish-speaking markers at the University of California, Merced) would find those markers normative. They hypothesized that teachers who were most familiar with a particular set of racialized language markers would not penalize student writing that contained those markers. Fowler and Ochsner explain their mixed findings:

> FSU readers generally validated the hypothesis in scoring both the AAVE-influenced papers from FSU and the Spanish-influenced papers from UCM: *FSU raters generally penalized the AAVE–the familiar dialect–less than they penalized the unfamiliar Hispanic dialect.* The scoring of the essays at UCM, however, did not validate the hypothesis, nearly ignoring both AAVE and Hispanic speech forms transferred to academic writing in English: *UCM raters did not penalize the relatively unfamiliar AAVE or favor the more familiar Hispanic dialect.*

For possible answers to the differences in ratings, Fowler and Ochsner look to the context in which each set of readers work and the expectations those teachers have of their students.

Finally, in "Challenging the Frameworks of Color-blind Racism: Why We Need a Fourth Wave of Writing Assessment Scholarship," Nicholas Behm and Keith D. Miller argue that writing assessment must "refashion the racial politics of assessment" by considering Bonilla-Silva's (2001, 2006) theoretical framework for identifying color-blind racism. Behm and Miller focus on whiteness and the "white *habitus*" that is pervasive in the academy, classroom, and our language practices and values. They introduce this framework to classroom assessment practices, showing how teachers might interrogate their own practices. Invoking Bonilla-Silva's framework, they conclude with a call to teachers and writing assessment scholars to "challenge entrenched 'white' linguistic patterns lionized as normal, natural, and rational; and to repudiate racialized standards reinforced by rubrics and other classroom assessment practices that reify the discursive practices of whiteness and privilege."

CHAPTER SIX

Students' Right, African American English, and Writing Assessment: Considering the HBCU

Zandra L. Jordan

The 1974 Conference on College Composition and Communication's resolution *Students' Right to Their Own Language* calls for both the acceptance of students' right to use the language of their heritage, as well as educators' responsibility to preserve language diversity:

> A nation proud of its diverse heritage and its cultural and racial variety will preserve its heritage of dialects. We affirm strongly that teachers must have the experiences and training that will enable them to respect diversity and uphold the right of students to their own language. (Committee on CCCC Language, p. 3)

For its radical departure from normative views about language and literacy, the resolution sparked much controversy, inciting harsh criticism and grave concern. Some scholars accused the resolution of "excus[ing]" "poor writing" (Ruble, 1975); "distracting [the field] from the real issues" through "sermonizing" and "sloganeering" (Berthoff & Clark, 1975); and promoting illiteracy, ignorance, and the destruction of American education (Pixton, 1975). Others specifically questioned what "students' right" meant, arguing, for example, that "competent copyreading" does not preclude expression of students' own language (Kelly, 1974) and cautioning educators not to "propagate" the "underdeveloped" resolution without considering its pedagogical "implications" (Baxter, 1976).

The initial criticisms of the resolution reflect the historic debate over honoring, altering, or erasing non-standard English and, in the most ill-conceived cases, proclaim the intellectual inferiority of non-standard English speakers. Reaffirmed by the 2003 CCCC Executive Committee, the *Students' Right* resolution has ostensibly won the debate. The spirit of the resolution is more widely accepted today, bolstered by legal victory (See Ball & Lardner, 1997, on the Ann Arbor Black English case) and linguistic scholarship (e.g., Labov, 1972; Rickford, 1999; Smitherman, 1977, 2000) that firmly establish African American English (AAE) as a dialect or distinct language.[1] The resolution is arguably "one of the most important documents ever published by

CCCC" (Gilyard, 1999b, p. 44). Yet, some pertinent questions regarding implementation of its ideals remain. What is "their language"? What does "uphold[ing] the right of students to their own language" mean for classroom writing assessment and pedagogy? While scholars consider related questions in the context of predominantly white institutions, historically black colleges and universities (HBCUs) have received little attention.

This chapter considers the implications of *Students' Right* for classroom writing assessment at HBCUs. Through the eyes of my former student, an AAE speaker who successfully negotiated the demands of college writing, I call for increased consideration of HBCUs as informative sites for examining the complex issues surrounding writing assessment and language diversity.

Writing Assessment And Language Diversity

Significant scholarship in composition studies addressing writing assessment and language diversity has emerged since the *Students' Right* resolution. For example, in their guide for teachers, *Language Diversity and Writing Instruction*, Farr and Daniels (1986) review research on linguistic variation to assert the "linguistic competence" of all students and advocate best practices for instruction, regardless of the student's dialect. They argue that overemphasizing grammatical errors can lead teachers to the erroneous conclusion that non-standard dialects interfere with learning to write (p. 44). Recommendations for writing instruction and assessment include having high expectations for student performance; focusing on writing processes; providing regular opportunities to read deeply and write for real purposes and a variety of audiences; and emphasizing revision and "flexible [...] cumulative evaluation of student writing" (p. 81).

Like Farr and Daniels, Smitherman (1993), a member of the 1972 *Students' Right* Committee, calls for less emphasis on grammatical correctness and greater appreciation for "Black discourse style." Her analysis of 867 NAEP essays revealed higher scoring for essays exhibiting a "Black discourse style," regardless of the frequency of Black English Vernacular (BEV) grammar. Smitherman urges teachers to "capitalize" on students' strengths by incorporating their successful writing styles (p. 21). Additionally, Smitherman's (1992) analysis of 2,764 NAEP essays produced by 17-year-old African Americans showed that while holistic scoring was lower for essays with more BEV, BEV did not negatively impact primary trait scoring on particular writing tasks (p. 54). Smitherman attributed this difference to teachers' growing sensitivity to dialects and participation in language diversity training.

Balester (1993) agrees that learning about the rhetorics and languages of diverse cultures can "bridg[e] the cultural divide between composition teachers and their students," thereby enabling better understanding of student writing (p. 1). In her study of eight successful African American college writers attending the University of Texas at Austin, Balester juxtaposes rhetorical analysis of the students' writings and personal stories with African American rhetorical traditions, noting that her own analyses of students' texts would have been impossible without knowledge of African American rhetorical conventions and the thought processes behind students' rhetorical choices (p. 157).

While acknowledging Balester's contribution, Holmes (1999) argues that Balester mistakenly essentializes African American students' experiences, overlooking the reality that not all African American students will identify with Black dialect (p. 60). He asks, "How do we get some of our African American students to remain proud of the ways Black Dialect can be used to construct their personal and cultural identity without depreciating other African Americans who don't bear the same relationship to it?" The threat of essentialism reminds us not to delimit students' language experiences because of race. Fulfilling the spirit of *Students' Right* must include recognition that "their language" is not necessarily one or the same language for all African American students and does not automatically exclude Edited American English (EAE).

To help composition studies "realize" the goals of *Students' Right*, Kamusikiri (1996) recommends a "process-based Afrocentric assessment model." This approach promotes equity in writing assessment by recognizing AAE as "a rule-governed language system" and AAE speakers as bi-dialectical writers able to consciously and skillfully code switch (pp. 191–194). Along with changing their attitudes about AAE writers, writing instructors must change their language to describe the writing process. Terms like "influence" rather than "dialect interference" and "translation" instead of "correction" denote the recursivity central to a process-oriented approach (p. 198). Using a process-based Afrocentric assessment model in her classroom, Kamusikiri observed a significant decline in AAE features from students' first to final draft. However, she was careful to note that code switching or "the transference of AAE to Standard English" is more than an editorial exercise; it is "a political choice" (p. 199). Kamusikiri advocates portfolio assessment—evaluation of multiple samples of student writing, over writing-sample tests and timed essay exams, both of which may prevent "dialect transfer" and thereby disadvantage AAE speakers (pp. 200–201).

While Kamusikiri's approach is notable, she seems to overlook students who do not employ code switching easily. That omission raises the question, How should we respond to AAE speakers who have difficulty accessing an EAE discourse? Some scholars, like Young (2009) and Canagarajah (2006a) advocate code meshing over code switching. Comparing arguments in favor of code switching to "Jim Crow legislation," Young (2011) contends that code switching "belies the claim of linguistic equality" and, in effect, reproduces the same racist rationale behind legalized segregation (p. 53; see also Graff, 2003; Prendergast, 2003). Young (2011) recommends code meshing as a "better alternative" (p. 50), arguing that "it allows minoritized people to become more effective communicators by doing what we all do best, what comes naturally: blending, merging, meshing dialects" (p. 72).

Whereas code switching calls for the "translation" of one language variety into another, typically less prestigious varieties (e.g., Spanglish, AAE) into "standard English" (Young, 2009, p. 50), code meshing merges "divergent varieties of English" into "a hybrid text" (Canagarajah, 2006a, p. 598). Like Young, Canagarajah prefers code meshing, a multidialectal approach, over code switching, which often relegates diverse English varieties to informal contexts (p. 594). Code meshing, Canagarajah posits, allows students "to see their own variety of English written in academic texts," admittedly a "small" yet important step towards linguistic plurality (2006a, p. 599).

Young's and Canagarajah's compelling arguments for code meshing underscore the need to consider writing assessment: How do we assess multiple degrees of EAE and AAE integration that often call for fluency in EAE? Such difficult assessment questions are relevant for HBCUs, sites where racial homogeneity may be assumed and language diversity may be mistaken as "bad grammar."

Not Just For Predominantly White Institutions: Language Diversity And HBCUs

As I write this chapter, I am in the early phases of my own study of AAE and college writers at HBCUs. As an alumna of Spelman College where I now teach, I am knowledgeable of HBCUs' goals and of the challenges they face as they admit promising students who might be denied access elsewhere. This is not to say that HBCUs are always a last resort. For many students, they are a first choice because African American students expect to receive more personal care at HBCUs than at predominantly white institutions. Additionally, HBCUs are top producers of students who go on to earn advanced degrees and excel in environments where they are often in the minority.[2] For some students, HBCUs are the place where they know they will be accepted, nurtured, and challenged; they are a home away from home where students experience the "tough love" of professors who know how to reprove without demoralizing. In their mission and in their approach, these institutions expect their students to succeed.

Even though HBCUs appeal to the rich cultural experiences of black students, they still encounter the challenges of assessing linguistically diverse students. Like their white counterparts, HBCUs want their students to produce in speech and writing the Edited American English valued in academe and business settings. Both faculty and students are aware of this goal and bring to the composition classroom varied attitudes about African American English. The HBCU composition classroom with its mixture of Black southern, midwestern, and northern dialects, as well as Afro-Latino, Jamaican, West African, and other influences, is undeniably diverse, but largely overlooked in the scholarship on language diversity and writing assessment.[3]

One exception is Redd's (2001) "'How I Got Ovah': Success Stories of African American Composition Students." In her study of 40 first-year composition students at Howard University she identified several strategies distinguishing "successful" students—those whose command of Edited American English had significantly improved by semester's end, from "struggling" students. Among others things, successful students were better able to identify their own grammatical and spelling errors; they gained their primary motivation from a source other than their teacher; they depended heavily on friends and family for help; and they viewed EAE as a universal language that everyone should know (pp. 10–11). Redd's study reminds us of the value in understanding the attitudes, practices, and motivations of successful students, as well as the importance of broadening our conceptions of what "their language" means.

As part of my ongoing research, I began surveying students at a historically Black liberal arts college for women in 2009. At the time of this chapter I have collected 108 surveys, mostly from first-year composition students.[4] Looking across the surveys, I noted the most variance in students' responses to four questions. While it is not my intent to make generalizable claims here, student responses do reveal a spectrum of attitudes about AAE that bear on writing assessment. Using a constant comparative method, the emerging patterns indicate that some students (and faculty) conditionally accept AAE; they believe that it is acceptable in certain contexts. Some express what might be called a standard view—the general perception that AAE is just bad English. Others demonstrate absolute disapproval of AAE; to them, AAE is never appropriate. I share below responses that illustrate this range and further underscore the importance of considering writing assessment and language diversity at HBCUs.

What Is Black English, Ebonics, Or African American English?

"Incorrect or improper English"

"The type of vernacular African Americans use among each other in an informal setting"

"Ignorance that plagues the African American community and allows other races to believe 'we' are less intelligent"

Do You Or Your Peers Ever Speak African American English In Class? Why Or Why Not?

"Yes, this is sometimes comfortable."

"I do m [sic] very best not to use the language in class."

"No, never! It is not professional and it does not show my academic ability or intelligence."

In Your Experience, How Do Professors Respond To Students Whose Speech Or Writing Includes African American English?

"Well for the most part, they are familiar with the language and able to partake in it when need be."

"They are asked to submit to the standard English language."

"Most of the time the professor are [sic] very aggressive when students use such language."

What Do You Think College Professors Need To Know Or Understand About Students Who Write And/Or Speak African American English?

"While speaking 'African American English' in an academic setting is not appropriate, I do believe that professors should realize that students come from different walks of life."

"Although we as students do have the ability to speak and write correctly, some may need a bit more teaching than others. Furthermore, speaking 'African American English' is a cultural thing, not meant to harm anyone."

"That they as teachers are wrong for not trying to correct it because in the real world Ebonics is not going to get you a great job."

These sample survey responses signify important considerations for writing assessment and pedagogy at HBCUs. As students' perceptions of AAE (e.g., "informal," "incorrect," "ignorance") and of their professors' behaviors (e.g., "partake in," "asked to submit," "very aggressive") indicate, we cannot assume that all HBCU students or their professors share the same understanding of, appreciation for, or relationship with AAE (Holmes, 1999). Nor can we afford to ignore the likely influence of dispositions towards AAE and "Black discourse style" on our assessment practices (Ball, 1997; Smitherman, 1992, 1993). Doing so could lead to devaluing, rather than capitalizing on, the linguistic resources of students who may come to HBCUs in need of acceptance and positive identity formation. Classroom writing assessment that honors language diversity must emerge from classroom pedagogies that acknowledge, accept, and honor language diversity.

Exploring "African American Female Literacies"

How do we create a classroom atmosphere that promotes acceptance of language diversity and honors students' right to their own languages? Kinloch (2005) provides a good starting point; she posits, "[a] renewed commitment to the [*Students' Right*] resolution is a commitment to having conversations with students about linguistic systems and democratic values established in communities, classrooms, and other spaces of public participation" (p. 90). I took up this call in my Grammar and Style course.

When I joined the Spelman College faculty in 2005, I was asked to teach English 150, Grammar and Style—a writing workshop course focusing on problem solving and revision, with a detailed analysis of prose style and grammar in the context of editorial and stylistic choices.[5] While open to any student desiring supplementary writing experiences, English 150 is required for those who resubmit and still do not pass the First-year Writing Portfolio.[6]

For two hours once a week in English 150, students majoring in a variety of disciplines discuss assigned chapters and exercises in Kolln's (2007) *Rhetorical Grammar: Grammatical Choices, Rhetorical Effects*. They learn the seven sentence patterns and begin employing them as they peer-review personal statements and revised papers. Over time, as I listened to the students' ruminations about writing, I realized that many were traumatized by their "bad grammar." They recognized that they did not write "proper" English and desperately wanted to know how to "correct" the problem.

I wanted students to learn the ways of writing that would garner academic success, but I did not want them to become so beleaguered in the process that they lost all pleasure in writing, confidence in themselves, and pride in their own languages. To acknowledge students' right to their own languages and generate discussion about language differences, I introduced two articles: Richardson's (2002) "'To Protect and Serve': African American Female Literacies" and Brandt's (1995) "Accumulating Literacy: Writing and Learning to Write in the Twentieth Century." To make studying grammar more engaging, I added O'Conner's (2003) lighthearted *Woe Is I: The Grammarphobe's Guide to Better English in Plain English.*

Juxtaposition of these texts produced lively discussions about the students' literacies and the language stereotypes that they were struggling to overcome. In turn, the students came to see themselves as part of a linguistically diverse learning community. Some had entered college looking for acceptance, noting that in their predominantly white high schools they were often the only black student in honors classes. Non-honors-track black students ostracized them for "talking white." On the other hand, high achieving students from predominantly black high schools entered college expecting to find acceptance among equally motivated peers. While their experience had been largely positive, in this context they were sometimes painfully aware of their "country" accent and "bad grammar." The students united around the shared goal of becoming more successful academic writers, heeding my admonitions that a judgment-free, supportive atmosphere was an essential part of effective peer review.

Students were asked to write a three- to four-page response to Elaine Richardson's article, taking for inspiration aspects that they found provocative. Required elements included a clear thesis, supporting evidence, specific references to concepts in Richardson's article, citations as appropriate, and editing across drafts. Submission of an introduction and thesis, a one- to two-page draft, and a revised two-page draft preceded submission of the final draft. I did not expect students to produce flawless essays, but hoped to see evidence of thoughtful engagement with the topic and application of course concepts.

The essay that follows is an excerpt from the final draft of an English 150 student's response essay. The student, whom I will call Shanika, was required to enroll in the course in 2007. With the exception of her name,[7] the excerpt below matches exactly the original document and is reprinted here with the student's permission.

Living Through Language

> "N-I-K-A take yo bath so that yo mama can hurry up and comb dat hair of yours so we won't be late for church. Yall make me late every Sunday [...] HURRY UP!!" These were the words that my grandmother would always say on Sunday morning while I was still sitting at the table trying to finish my third homemade buiscuits she cooked every Sunday morning. However, when she yelled for me to get my bath there was something about her tone of voice that informed me that she wasn't playing with me, and that I was to get up from the table that very exstinct. It was

something about that "mother tongue" tone in my grandmother's voice, when she got upset, that put deep fear in my heart.

My grandmother is a woman who many respect because her tone of voice, body language, and facial expressions was like no other. She was a true mother that emphasized the values of discipline children and by doing so she was an avacant of sharing with others about her experiences in life. Mother tongue and storytelling is indeed traditions in the African American community that has connected several families to values, history, and discipline that has contributed to individuals current lifestyles as they go through their own life's journey.

These two points sparked my interest the most because I could actually visualize what the author was referring to with storytelling. My up brings has made my "mother tongue" differ from that of the author. You see, my mother had me at a very young age. Therefore, my grandmother was like my mother. So, my grandmother told most of the stories that were handled down from her mother and so on. This is how I became informed of my family history, and I am sure this is how other families were informed also. Storytelling came from so many of the women from my neighborhood and church members. Many African American women made sure they took good care of their community and went to church. The "mothers" in my life made up for anything that my younger mother couldn't accomplish or provide for me. The old saying that "it takes a village to raise a child" was indeed true in my childhood.

Living in the down south my mother and grandmothers language was quite different from others. My grandmother received a high school diploma and my mother became very successful after having a baby in high school, which many people said that she had destroyed her life. The fact of the matter was that she had the ability and determination to not let, what many called, one particular mistake ruin all of her life's dreams. Just as the author in the article started off with a ruff lifestyle; she was able to raise above some bad life decisions and become successful by obtaining a PhD.

The recurring subject-verb agreement errors in Shanika's essay might lead one to assume that AAE is the most significant barrier to her mastery of EAE. On the contrary, many of the errors in Shanika's final edited draft, like misspelled words and awkward sentence structures, can be attributed to unfamiliarity with certain writing rules. As Redd and Webb (2005) explain, according to the print-code hypothesis, students rely on their "oral resources" when writing rules are unknown (p. 63). According to this view, focusing on errors in our assessment of student writing might not be as helpful to students like Shanika as greater exposure to reading with attention to writing conventions. Exposing Shanika to texts modeling the writing rules with which she is unfamiliar, helping her identify those rules, and giving her opportunities to practice them could better position her for success than simply marking errors and penalizing her for them.

"Living Through Language": What One Student Interview Reveals

Shanika's own insights about her journey bring greater clarity to the complex issues surrounding writing assessment and language diversity. The interview that follows was conducted during Shanika's senior year, two years after her enrollment in English 150.

At her predominantly black high school in South Carolina, Shanika was in the top of her class and was considered a strong public speaker. Upon entering college, her confidence in her speech and writing was challenged:

> When I was back at home, I was considered one of the most smartest girls, you know, and then when I got here its more so like oh, uh uh, you know, let me take a back seat as opposed to back at home in high school I was always on the front of things. So, I came here and had to kind of take a back seat because I found that I was lacking a little bit...So that's the different thing that I had to kind of get to myself and say it's okay to be lacking but you have to push harder to get up to speed where everybody else is.

Hearing for the first time that she had a "country" accent also made Shanika more reserved than is her nature. Peers remarked, "I know you must be from down south."

Regarding writing, Shanika soon learned that AP English "was a different set of writing than first-year composition." In addition to the challenge of "writing all these papers back to back to back," Shanika said all of her professors noted her problem with subject-verb agreement. Although she knew she had improved since her first year, she identified subject-verb agreement as her greatest writing vice. Shanika continued to overcome the challenge by working hard:

> I ended up getting a B in the class, but that was because I worked and worked and worked. I got "most improved student" or something like that [...] cause I knew I was a step behind, but the writing portfolio, that kind of showed my lack, my lack of writing. That's how I ended up in Grammar and Style. To pass the writing portfolio, they said I had to take Grammar and Style and it would help me along the way. I've gotten a lot better, but I realize that I still struggle. I don't wanna say it's going to be a lifelong thing, but if I don't practice it will be.

Recognizing some differences in how she reads in comparison to other students, Shanika was initially reluctant to read aloud in class. She noted:

I used to pride myself on public speaking prior to me coming here. I thought I was to-tally comfortable with it, other than hearing some of my [college] sisters, you know, read, just like, you know scan and just picking it up automatically. It's like I read, you know, like two words before to kind of hear it you know before it actually comes out my mouth [...] So that's what kind of gave me a sense of, kind of, you know, a little shy back from reading out loud. Not that I can't read, but it's just more so that I'm not picking it up as well, like it don't seem like they scanning it, you know.

Shanika acknowledged that writing in her major courses was also a challenge. The EAE errors apparent in her first-year composition essays were also present in her Economics papers. Despite the challenges, she remained positive, even when certain comments were hurtful. Shanika recounts her teacher's response to the group portion of her Economics thesis. Although the students did not distinguish who authored particular sections, Shanika said her portion was evident. The teacher questioned, "Who wrote this part? This is not up to par with the rest." Reflecting upon the experience, she added:

In the back of my mind I was like oh that kind of hurt me. I need to jump on it some more. We laughed it off at first, but you still got that kind of feeling in the back-ground that that was kind of crazy.

Although tempted at times to give up, Shanika was determined to get what she came to college for—an education. In our interview, she offered this advice to other college students struggling to meet the demands of college writ-ing:

Don't let that discourage you from getting an education, because sometimes it can be so overwhelming. Like, you just sick of people saying something about your "country accent" or you sick of seeing the same comment on your paper. You know, I wanna say don't let it disturb you, but don't let it, don't ignore it, but don't let it be such, such a big idea where you just totally stress over it [...] School is already enough, you know, and to keep having to say you struggle, you just have to realize that that's an area that you struggle in and try to keep going back over your writing, and try to do as much as you can and keep on going. I mean, this is a lifetime. I grew up with this the whole time, like my whole life I grew up in it [...] You ain't gone be perfect at every-thing. So, it'll eventually get better, but you can't let that totally distract you from get-ting an education.

Considerations For Classroom Writing Assessment

Despite her EAE errors, Shanika successfully navigated college writing demands by being resilient and focusing on the larger goal—receiving an edu-cation. Perhaps we should focus on the larger goal, too. "Don't ignore it," as Shanika said, "but don't make errors the biggest issue." Ball and Lardner

(2005) agree, positing that when teachers are able to distinguish common errors from AAE discourse styles, they can "accept and celebrate" the oral and cultural characteristics in student texts, particularly early on. Later, when students have experienced sufficient instruction and a variety of writing tasks, they should be held accountable for employing an array of writing styles (pp. 171–172).

It seems that some of Shanika's professors recognized the greater goal, too, focusing on her tone and the logical development of ideas, instead of errors. Recalling other teachers' comments on her papers, Shanika declared:

> It was all about rewording and how can the words, you know, not make it so, I guess, aggressive. So, that's like the biggest thing I always heard with my professors or not really going in depth as I need to, but just like hitting little small points and going to the next one. I never really went in depth, or really kind of express my feelings all the way.

Focusing less on errors does not mean that we should hold AAE speakers to a different standard (a belief articulated throughout this collection by contributors such as Valerie Balester as well as Anne Herrington and Sarah Stanley). As Shanika told me, "I never suggested a professor just give out grades [...] If that's the case, [the student] would never develop her writing. You know, so, understand that this is the reason why she might be struggling. So, what can we do to maybe help her become a little bit more better at it?"

We can help students by understanding their attitudes towards AAE and our own; engaging them in dialogue about language diversity through readings and writing; helping them identify unfamiliar EAE conventions and then modeling those conventions, while also honoring the language of their heritage; and bringing these new approaches into the way we assess student writing in the classroom. To college composition instructors wondering how to respond to African American English speakers, Shanika offers these words:

> Don't just knock 'em down. Give 'em something that they can change. They can develop greatly over a semester but the opportunity of just changing completely over a semester is just slim. So, just understand, maybe, where that person is coming from.

Notes

---

[1] As Redd and Webb (2005) explain, social and political theories, more so than linguistics, typically undergird distinctions made between AAE as a dialect or a language. The terms "African American English" (AAE), "Black English Vernacular" (BEV), and "Black dialect" are used interchangeably in this chapter, according to the term preferred by the scholars quoted.

[2] According to Secretary of Education Arne Duncan, in remarks to the National Historically Black Colleges and Universities Conference, "roughly half of all African American professionals and public school teachers" and more than "70 percent of [African American] doctors and dentists" earn undergraduate degrees from an HBCU (2009, para. 14). The United Negro College Fund reports the same numbers.

[3] This assertion about classroom demographics at HBCUs is based on my own composition classrooms. Unfortunately, HBCU enrollment statistics often do not disaggregate racial/ethnic categories. The College Board (2010) indicates that 91% of Spelman College students are Black/non-Hispanic, 4% Non-resident Alien, less than 1% Asian/Pacific Islander, less than 1% Hispanic and 3% did not report race.

[4] The survey data were collected from January to October of 2009. Convenience sampling in dorms and campus spaces included students regardless of classification. Purposive sampling focused on first-year composition students.

[5] English 150, Grammar and Style, has no prerequisites and is open to students of any major and classification. Sophomores and seniors typically take the course, the former by recommendation or requirement and the latter for graduate or professional programs requiring two semesters of writing. Students required to take the course may consider it remedial. English and Writing faculty largely consider it supplementary.

[6] "Common reasons for Writing Portfolios to be evaluated 'Resubmit' have included the following: insufficient citation (in-text and/or on the Works Cited/ References page); lack of central argument or thesis; lack of demonstrated ability to use references in service of the author's own argument (rather than simply 'pasting in' quotations or paraphrases); lack of correct grammar and mechanics; and failure to include one or more required items" (Writing Center, 2009, "What Does 'Resubmit' Mean," para. 2).

[7] A shortened version of the student's name appears in the original essay with hyphens between the letters. I model that stylistic choice with a shortened version of the pseudonym Shanika.

CHAPTER SEVEN
Evaluating Essays Across Institutional Boundaries: Teacher Attitudes Toward Dialect, Race, and Writing

Judy Fowler and Robert Ochsner

In 2005 the University of California, Merced (UCM), a new research campus in the ethnically diverse San Joaquin Valley, and Fayetteville State University (FSU) of North Carolina, a historically black university with a long and distinguished tradition of teacher education, established an informal partnership of writing programs. That partnership enabled us, as directors of those programs, to share pedagogical strategies and refine instructional services in order to better serve the writing needs of academically at-risk students, especially those from historically underserved, low-income populations.

This partnership grew out of our common interest in rhetoric and composition studies when both authors taught in the English Department at the University of Maryland Baltimore County (UMBC) during the late 1980s and throughout most of the 1990s. Later, when Fowler taught at a historically black college/university (HBCU) and Ochsner taught at a Hispanic-serving institution (HSI), we recognized the distinctive opportunity to collaborate on a study examining varieties of English. We agreed to look at teachers' attitudes toward second or home languages in students' writing. Specifically, we wanted to determine empirically how a student's home language might influence final course grades in writing classes, and if unfamiliarity with a home dialect would negatively affect an instructor's grading.

Our partnership between dissimilar universities embraces Kenneth Burke's adage that any way of looking at one thing is necessarily a way of not looking at something else. This paradox fundamentally determines how our scholarship on teacher response to student writing has been conducted. Our initial research project, which is reported in this chapter, was to determine whether experienced writing teachers would differ significantly in the way they evaluated writing samples from students with various "dialect"[1] markers. Although this was not an original approach, we were surprised to discover relatively few *comparative* studies of teacher bias in evaluating student writing that are not reductively focused on black/white dualities in language use. As Jordan notes in this volume, this duality typically excludes the broad range of AAVE that could potentially include "Afro-Latino, Jamaican, West African, and other influences." We discovered even fewer examples of scholarship that specifically attend to multiple levels of dialects within groups or that consider dialect features of three (or more) categories of diverse college students (e.g., African American, Spanish heritage, and Asian American).[2] In our own study of teacher bias in the evaluation of writing, we have focused on linguistic markers in the writing of African American students and Latino/a students. We hypothesized that when scoring students' papers, (1) teachers accustomed to one group's linguistic markers in writing would ignore those markers, and (2) conversely, teachers *not* accustomed to a group's linguistic markers in writing would penalize papers with those markers. Stated another way, frequent exposure to certain dialect markers can render those markers normative, a phenomenon consistent with the principles of language change (Wolfram & Thomas, 2002; Klein, 2003).

According to our hypothesis, because FSU has a student body that is 73% African American and a first-year class containing an even higher percentage of African American students, faculty would not penalize African American linguistic markers in writing. However, FSU faculty would penalize the *unfamiliar* Spanish-language markers. Similarly, faculty at UCM, having normalized Spanish-language markers, would not significantly penalize writing with such markers but would penalize essays with African American markers.

We have not artificially constructed a study that would have asked students at FSU and UCM to write the same type(s) of essays or required faculty to use the same system(s) of essay evaluation. Instead, we have identified standard practices at each program and compared them, an approach that allows us to maintain the authenticity of each academic context. The design of our study also enables us to ask how the local setting at each campus affects the assessment of writing.

To analyze our assessment results beyond scores, we looked to contextual factors. For example, FSU has until recently admitted anyone who had a desire to learn; and the university has often accepted and encouraged students who have not fared so well academically as those recruited by North Carolina's three state research universities (UNC-Chapel Hill, UNC-Greensboro, and NC State University). In contrast to FSU, UCM restricts admission to applicants in the upper 12.5% of their high school class.

Methods And Procedures For The Research

To test our hypothesis, we collected both empirical and qualitative evidence. Toward those ends, both of us supervised double-blind scoring sessions of essays from first-year composition classes with department members who taught those classes serving as scorers. Selected essays from the other school (selected because they contained home-language features transferred from speech to writing) were included in each school's scoring batches. We functioned as participant observers.

Preparation Of Student Papers For Scoring

Determining teacher bias required that essays with Spanish-influenced markers be embedded in the batches scored by FSU raters and that essays with features of African American Vernacular English (AAVE) be embedded in the batches scored by UCM raters. Five essays from each university selected for this study were chosen specifically because they contained numerous dialect markers. Many of these markers have also appeared on prior lists of "bothersome" or most common grammatical "errors" (Hairston, 1981; Redd & Webb, 2005).

At FSU, essays were selected from a collection of multiphase essays written for first-year composition courses, a collection begun in 2003, for programmatic purposes. The papers originated in one of the two required first-year composition courses, English 110 (exposition) and English 120 (researched argument).

At UCM, essays were selected that had been written during AY 2005–2006, essays originally collected for ongoing programmatic assessment. All papers selected were produced in a developmental composition course, Writing 1. More than 600 writing samples were generated in writing classes near the end of the semester, as a timed (one hour) impromptu writing exercise used for programmatic assessment of writing. From these 600 essays, 200 were randomly selected for evaluation, and five were chosen for this study as clear examples of home-language (Spanish-influenced) writing. This selection was informed by a UC system-wide test of writing called the Analytic Writing Placement Exam (AWPE), a two-hour, impromptu, high-stakes writing test completed by prospective first-year students the spring before they enroll at a UC campus. In May of each year, about 200 composition instructors convene in Oakland, California, to read more than 200,000 AWPE essays, with each essay scored on a six-point scale by at least two readers. If both readers mark an essay with an "E," the essay is designated as an example of second-language-influenced writing. Noting E-designated AWPE essays and cross-checking for demographic information about each E student's language background, the UCM director identified a subset of more than 100 Spanish-speaking first-year students. It should be stressed that this study did not use examples of AWPE essays; rather, that test keyed the random selection of other writing samples generated at UCM.

At UCM, timed, impromptu writing samples were chosen from Writing 1 because they are more likely to produce unedited discourse, thus providing examples of dialect features that would not be as likely to appear in traditional essays with ample opportunity for editing and revision. These impromptu writing samples are not incorporated in course grades except as examples of class participation; instead, they are included with course portfolios as one of many indicators that inform program (not individual student) assessment. Using these writing samples for programmatic purposes simply extends their assessment function: to note, in this case, the reaction of teachers to dialect features in student writing.

Another reason for using impromptu writing was to control the length of UCM texts without setting artificial page limits just for this study. In Writing 1, the typical length of an essay assignment written out of class is at least 1,000 words. At FSU, a comparable writing assignment would result in text half that length, or even less. The temporal challenges of an impromptu writing assignment also offset some of the differences in academic preparation that characterize FSU and UCM first-year students.

After selecting essays, each director then created a normalized copy of the five selected essays from each institution, converting home-language traces of AAVE or Spanish into Edited American English. These changes were almost entirely at the word and sentence levels. For example, "she go" would be changed to "she goes," "he be talking this summer" would be changed to "he talked all summer long," and "she talked on the car" would be changed to "she talked in the car." In addition, minor changes in content were made to obscure from the readers the provenance of the writer. For example, in a paper from a UCM student headed for FSU readers, "here at UCM" might be changed to "at this university" or, content permitting, "here at FSU." This provided a total of 10 essays from each institution and a total of 20 essays overall for research purposes.

Both writing program administrators kept an original and a normalized copy of their school's selected essays and also sent an original and a normalized copy of each to the writing program director at the partner university. Both writing program administrators then coded papers to indicate whether they were the original or a normalized version of the essays. One cohort of UCM graders examined the matched sets of essays (20 total essays), and a separate cohort of FSU graders also examined them.

Scoring Of Student Essays

At FSU, the total number of FSU essays used in this study was 35, with 20 of those essays collected for this research and 15 others serving as decoys. At

FSU, there were 13 scorers: three associate professors, one visiting distinguished professor, five assistant professors, two instructors who have full-time university jobs for which teaching is part of their workload, and two regular part-time instructors. One scorer was African American, one Euro-African, one Eastern European, and 10 Euro-Americans.

At FSU, the course number and a two- to four-sentence description of the writing assignment were provided. Inclusion of these modifying circumstances recognizes the claims of recent scholarship that writing should be judged not on positivist-inspired immutable traits but on adjustments to and compatibility with the purpose and circumstances for writing (Huot, 2002a). To avoid any FSU scorers' suspicions that the embedded UCM papers were something other than papers collected from FSU students in first-year classes, papers were given an English 110 course designation, a short assignment description, and a date.[3]

Further caution to preclude FSU graders' discovery of the embedded UCM papers was undertaken with the organization of the folders of essays to be scored: the same scorer could not be allowed to evaluate both the original and the normalized copies of the same essay. Color-coding of the FSU folders of essays precluded a scorer's viewing of both original and normalized copies. Because no more than six people had signed up for each of the three scoring sessions, the essays were divided into six groups of six essays each and placed in the color-coded folders. Original and normalized sets were separated and put into same-color folders, and a single scorer would then receive a folder of a given color only once. Each essay was scored by five graders, and their sheets were collected after each scoring to ensure the double blind.

During the UCM scoring sessions, 12 writing faculty evaluated the essays selected for this study, with six faculty evaluating the normalized versions and six faculty evaluating the original texts. The faculty did not know that these essays were paired as original and normalized texts or intended for use in a separate study of teacher reactions to dialect. Subsequently, on different days, UCM writing faculty scored the remaining 200 essays.

Because the research was designed to measure the *difference* between scores given to the original and the normalized copies from both cohorts of readers, each director devised a way to hide the before-and-after nature of the papers. The identity of the writer and the instructor was thus removed. FSU papers were coded so that the pre-tests that the FSU faculty had administered at the beginning of the term as well as the post-tests could be identified (by the leaders of the sessions but not by the graders) and the differences between the two sets of scores could thus be measured (as an indication of program success).

As a new campus, UCM had no firmly established procedures for programmatic assessment, allowing the director to align most features of scoring at UCM with those at FSU. Nevertheless, some differences remained. One difference involved the number of essays being read and then discussed. By using the 10 FSU samples (five originals and five revisions) during a norming session and by including them with the 10 UCM samples (five originals and five normalized essays), the UCM readers examined 20 essays total, compared to the 35 essays evaluated at FSU. Another difference, already noted, was that UCM essays were in-class, timed writings. Even so, some UCM essays were lengthy compared to the FSU essays which had been identified by the professors contributing them as examples of "low" (as opposed to "middle" or "high") quality, and one UCM essay, transcribed at four typed pages, exceeded the length of many other multiphase FSU essays. A final difference occurred in the awarding of a final rating point. At UCM, the raters met in pairs, then in groups of three, to resolve discrepancies of one rating point or more in scores and, whenever possible, to agree on a single score. All discrepancies in scoring at UCM were eventually negotiated so that one original score was accepted rather than an average of two scores. At FSU, discrepancies were discussed at the end of the scoring session but only after all the essays had been scored and handed in.

The Scoring Sessions At FSU

So that the FSU scorers of the essays in Spring 2006 would view the scoring as normal business, it had to follow at least some local traditions set during previous scoring sessions. Some incremental variations had been added over the years, so introducing a few changes, especially when accompanied by logical explanations, was not expected to—and did not—appear either to cause consternation or to sully the research design.

FSU's original purpose in collecting sample multiphase essays, as specifically stated by the department chair at the time, was to satisfy regional investigating accreditation teams, who expect to see evidence of student work and teacher reaction to it. These teams also like to see evidence that instructors have discussed standards and their applications, thereby encouraging the local control recommended by recent commentators on the appropriate scope of writing assessments (Hillocks, 2002; Huot, 2002b; Broad, 2003). Widely understood by department members, the desires of the accreditation team rendered sensible the discussion and scoring of actual multiphase essays instead of batches of pre/post tests, which are typically extemporaneous and may eliminate reading material in favor of personal observation as source material and knowledge from prior reading. Even though some instructors have some affection for the controlled nature of pre/post procedures, they recognize its limitations, especially for English 120 (researched argument). As in-class timed writings, the pre/post tests neither reveal students' command of true process nor create conditions encouraging the kinds of supporting evidence or "substance" (Hillocks, 2002) that characterize academic papers (see also Ball et al., 2005). Timed writing also elicits students' weakest performance as writers, a relevant consideration for this study, particularly at UCM, since we are, for this research, concerned foremost with faculty reaction to dialect features that may not appear in multiphase writing.

During the three three-hour scoring sessions at FSU, the first hour was spent discussing what the group values in student essays. Each group reviewed the familiar list of departmental goals for English 110 and 120. They also looked at a document defining the "C Standard" that standardizes first-year composition across institutions in the University of Maryland System (Shapiro et al., 2006). Following that, scorers articulated their standards and integrated them with the other documents as appropriate to their consensus. This hour-long discussion brought the individual scorers to a consciousness of what they value in an essay, given a knowledge of the assignment, the programmatic goals, the course for which it was written, and the part of the semester in which it was composed. Each faculty member scored three trial essays, and a discussion of the appropriate score ensued. Once the discussion ended, the faculty were asked to consider these things when they scored papers individually.

The Scoring Session At UCM

The 12 UCM readers who scored the FSU essays were all full-time faculty with lecturer appointments in the UCM Writing Program, and none had previously been employed at a HBCU or school with a majority enrollment of African American students. Averaging 10 years of teaching experience, most of the scorers were from California, and several others were from the Midwest and Southwest. Ten of the 12 scorers were white; none were African American; just two of the 12 had previously taught at campuses with a Hispanic population of 25% or more.

During the fall and spring semesters of UCM's inaugural year, the scorers all had participated in several group evaluations of student writing, nearly always achieving a high degree of consistency as raters of essays. As previously noted, in the UCM Writing Program the results of pre/post tests are restricted to program evaluation and apply to students' individual grades only as an indicator of class participation. Course portfolios are used to assign individual grades for courses.

As part of a 90-minute norming session for pre/post test review, the UCM scorers evaluated five FSU essays, not knowing that they were rating normalized samples and the other six scorers were reading the original papers with errors. These 12 UCM evaluators worked initially in pairs, then in groups of three, to read and exchange "range finder" samples of student writing; they subsequently compared their evaluations with other groups, and among the four groups, no substantial differences of more than one rating point emerged. The same procedure was followed for evaluation of the masked FSU essays, all of which were read during a 75-minute scoring session. Each reader could have submitted a separate score if irresolvable differences had arisen in a group.

Scores On Original, Dialect-Marked Essays

Results of our research were mixed. FSU readers generally validated the hypothesis in scoring both the AAVE-influenced papers from FSU and the Spanish-influenced papers from UCM: *FSU raters generally penalized the AAVE– the familiar dialect–less than they penalized the unfamiliar Hispanic dialect.*[4] The scoring of the essays at UCM, however, did not validate the hypothesis, nearly ignoring both AAVE and Hispanic speech forms transferred to academic writing in English: *UCM raters did not penalize the relatively unfamiliar AAVE or favor the more familiar Hispanic dialect.*

FSU raters awarded FSU original essays an average score of 1.54, and they awarded the UCM originals an average score of only 1.30. The FSU readers thus seemed to find the familiar AAVE dialect of their own students *less* bothersome though only by .24 points. It should not be surprising that both FSU papers and UCM papers prejudged as flawed in formal written English were scored poorly by raters at both universities. Such scoring from both cohorts of raters indicates a consistent evaluation of what constitutes either a generally poor paper or a paper that has sufficient dialect features to interfere with reader understanding.

In response to essays with AAVE or Spanish markers, FSU readers scored both at low levels, but they rated the Spanish ones somewhat lower, presumably because of their unfamiliarity with Spanish-influenced writing. As a group, FSU readers did not value essays with nonstandard vocabulary, usage, and syntax, regardless of their familiarity with a nonstandard feature. In this respect, the hypothesis of preference for the familiar dialect is only marginally valid for FSU readers.

In response to FSU originals, UCM raters assigned an average score of 1.63. With this small difference of .09 points (1.63 versus 1.54), both groups of readers would seem to have similar standards for what constitutes a poor paper as well as how much nonstandard grammar and usage interfere with meaning.

UCM readers gave their own students' original essays an average score of 1.87 as opposed to the 1.63 given to FSU originals. This .24 contrast does not suggest much difference in their reaction to nonstandard grammar and usage or presence of dialect markers. As a group, UCM readers tended to give lower average scores than FSU readers, also suggesting UCM readers' indifference to unfamiliar dialect features. Instead, they apparently assigned scores according to the text's global features of organization, development, and logic.

Original Vs. Normalized Essay Scores

As shown in Figures 1 and 3, FSU readers' positive reactions to the UCM *normalized* essays suggests that they found the *original* Spanish-influenced texts bothersome. Once these dialect markers had been removed from the UCM essays and replaced with Edited American English, FSU readers awarded an average score of 2.74, a considerable gain of 1.44. Because these essays remained the same except for the changes in dialect features, the alteration in these word- and sentence-level factors could be regarded as the probable reason for the higher score. Considering that the same FSU readers awarded their own students' normalized essays an average score of 2.31, only .77 higher than the originals, the nearly doubled difference between the originals with *unfamiliar* dialect (the UCM ones) and the normalized ones in *standard* dialect strongly suggests that an unfamiliar dialect earns *less* favor from a reader or teacher than those of familiar dialect. Looked at another way, *removal of the unfamiliar dialect allowed the FSU readers to see higher-order traits.*

The difference between the *normalized* FSU papers and the *normalized* UCM papers also suggests that the FSU faculty scorers saw the UCM students as having submitted superior writing samples. The FSU scorers did not know that the UCM original and normalized versions had been written by students whose home language is Spanish, yet they found the UCM originals of poor quality, presumably because the dialect markers masked assets of the texts. This negative reaction should also be noted in the social context of a relatively selective university that admits only the top 12.5 percent of California's high school graduates. In other words, UCM students are more likely than students from a nearly open-admissions university like FSU to exhibit academic strengths in their writing, yet FSU readers do not "see" those strengths because of the masking effects of dialect.

As shown in Figures 2 and 4, although the UCM raters awarded a slightly higher rating to 5 of the 10 *normalized* essays, this difference is never more than .17 of a rating, and given our small sample size, not a statistically significant result. Also attesting to the UCM readers' neutrality toward dialect markers are the following: The remaining normalized FSU papers received the same score from UCM readers, and one UCM paper received the same score and one other only a slightly lower score on the normalized version. Thus, UCM readers seem virtually indifferent to dialect, including forms they do not routinely see.

While our small sample size does not provide enough evidence for reliable statistical claims supporting firm conclusions, we are nevertheless intrigued by the sharp contrast in reader responses at each school. For instance, where the UCM readers noted improvement in normalized texts, they regarded that command of Edited American English as a relatively minor feature of overall writing ability. These raters were essentially "blind" to evidence of dialect regardless of its provenance. The readers at UCM maintained a high level of inter-rater reliability, ranging from .82 to .91. The average score was .87. A similarly high level of consistency was sustained throughout the scoring of the UCM and FSU original and normalized writing samples.

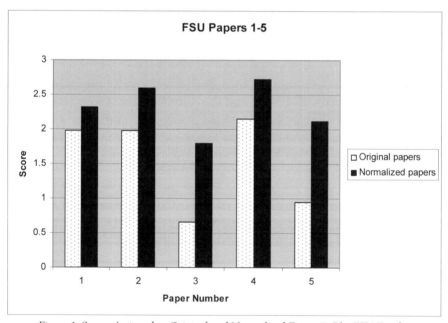

Figure 1. Scores Assigned to Original and Normalized Essays 1–5 by FSU Faculty

In contrast, the FSU scorers awarded an average gain of .67 to texts written by their own FSU students, a considerably higher gain than the average assigned by UCM readers. This improvement, however, is quite modest in comparison to the average gain of 1.5 that the FSU scorers awarded to UCM writers, a gain more than twice what they assigned to FSU writers. When FSU raters evaluated texts exhibiting an unfamiliar dialect, they evidently penalized the writers even though the quality of writing was relatively high, as indicated by the much higher scores they awarded the normalized UCM texts.

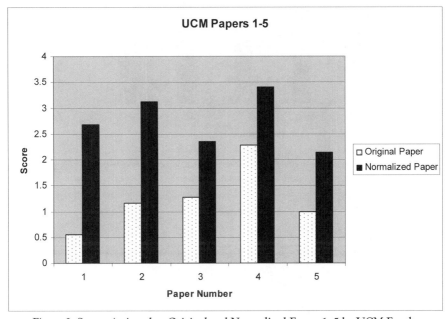

Figure 2. Scores Assigned to Original and Normalized Essays 1–5 by UCM Faculty

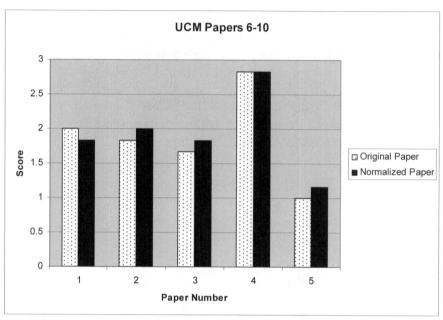

Figure 3. Scores Assigned to Original and Normalized Essays 6–10 by FSU Faculty

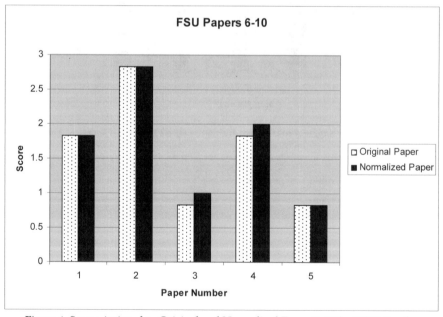

Figure 4. Scores Assigned to Original and Normalized Essays 6–10 by UCM Faculty

Discussion

The scores awarded the student essays in the two comparable end-of-semester scoring sessions—one at FSU and one at UCM—indicate that our initial research question about readers' responses to unfamiliar dialect features cannot be clearly answered as we had mixed results. We predicted that faculty accustomed to a specific kind of dialect in writing would not penalize those familiar dialect markers but would penalize dialect markers to which they were not accustomed. In fact, FSU readers, though accustomed to seeing AAVE in academic papers, nearly always penalized papers employing it, even when the content and paragraph structure were otherwise strong. By contrast, UCM readers, accustomed to seeing Hispanic dialect in written form, did not penalize any papers for Spanish-based errors in English and apparently ignored AAVE errors in the FSU papers. Presumably, UCM readers allowed the higher-order concerns of content, organization, and audience receptivity to dictate ratings.

To explain the two radically different approaches to scoring texts with dialect markers, we looked to local conditions. FSU faculty outside English often voice concerns that their own majors' copious grammar "errors" both hinder the communication of meaning in their school writing and put these majors at risk in the job market and later in the workplace. Moreover, several English faculty have loudly vocalized their belief that the department should make teaching usage and convention a priority; the African American department members generally favor teaching grammar because they see good grammar as a way of enfranchising students (Delpit, 1995a, 1995b), and the university's upper administration—mostly African American—has weighed in by purchasing *Criterion* for students in English 110 and English 120, both university requirements, and, formerly for English 108, a developmental grammar and writing course. In another move to help students improve, the FSU administration has also purchased *SmartThinking*, an online tutoring service for writing in a number of courses, including English Composition.

Those concerns are also shaped, in part, by entrenched concepts of writing proficiency. Despite the vital role FSU serves in educating underprepared students, the university's public image is probably shaped more by perceptions of low academic performance than by otherwise compelling evidence of student success. As one example, up until recently when the state abolished the requirement that FSU students planning to teach had to pass the PRAXIS exam (an Educational Testing Service exam), FSU's prospective teachers failed that test at a significantly high rate their first time, and because the official pass rate for the university is based entirely on those first results, FSU as an institution did not compare well to other institutions with teacher education programs.

However, when FSU students retook the PRAXIS exam, often after a period of study in the PRAXIS lab run by the School of Education, they performed quite well, a result that is fraught with implications for high-stakes testing and the challenges that underprepared students must overcome in a relatively short time during their college studies.

At UCM, by contrast, while almost no writing faculty (so far) expresses concern about students' grammatical correctness, concern about plagiarism is widespread, especially in first-year writing courses. Since UCM faculty often see student texts that are grammatically impeccable, the evidence of plagiarism is more likely to be found in contextual or stylistic features rather than correctness itself. This perspective suggests that dialect features, as evidence of genuine authorship, are a sign of student engagement with readings and ideas.

While at first blush the UCM readers seem sympathetic to prevailing but perhaps unexamined attitudes inside the composition community that grammar should be minimized in favor of other emphases such as discussion, reading, invention exercises, even sentence composing (Connors, 2000), the difference in reaction might be attributed to other factors, including the assumption that students admitted to UCM are well prepared for college. That expectation could influence how UCM readers respond to timed writing samples, especially if they attribute word- and sentence-level "errors" to the greater pressure of in-class timed writing and presume that students would edit most of these features in multiphase essays that are written out of class.

Broader social considerations may also affect attitudes at UCM about correctness in writing. A majority of UCM students are pursuing degrees in the sciences and engineering, disciplines in which the research faculty might be more concerned about students' mathematical abilities than their writing abilities. Gender and ethnicity could be related factors too. Distinct from national enrollment trends for undergraduates, during UCM's first four years the university enrolled a majority of males who were taught by a majority male faculty. Particularly in science and engineering disciplines, these faculty often work with colleagues throughout the world whose fluency in English varies considerably. One outcome of this professional experience with international varieties of English could be greater tolerance for varieties of English manifested in their students' writing. Unlike the faculty attitudes at FSU, these matters of academic context at UCM might also engender an academic climate of tolerance for "Englishes" that extends to scoring of writing samples. Obviously, further research is needed to address these points.

The scores given by the individual FSU faculty on individual student papers varied more than those given by the UCM graders. We can attribute this phenomenon to the instructions given to each group. Though the FSU scorers reviewed departmental goals prior to scoring, they also discussed what they valued. FSU readers were told to assign the score that they individually would assign under the specified conditions. The UCM readers, in contrast, were told to discuss each paper with others during each step of the scoring and to come to a consensus. While it is not surprising that the two groups attended to the directive provided by the WPA leader, it would be interesting to see if the instructions or the personal attitudes of the scorers account for agreement and variation. Further, as members of a new campus, the UCM scorers might have been more amenable to reaching consensus because they had no long-term experience working with their colleagues. At FSU, many colleagues in the English department had been together for several decades, a shared experience that adds a diachronic dimension to consensus building. For that reason alone, replicating this study at UCM five years later could produce quite different results.

Conclusion

Based on the results of this study, we plan to examine future scoring sessions for similar purposes, supplemented with retrospective interviews of scorers. As composition researchers, we welcome complexity in our research because it foregrounds points that would not otherwise be apparent. In that sense, each study is a new pilot study, one that enriches our understanding of a complex phenomenon such as reader bias. The interplay of cultural, social, racial, linguistic, and individual factors that shape a reader's response cannot be segmented into discrete parts without distorting the rhetorical and political context. By accepting rather than controlling differences between our schools, our research is almost certain to generate conflicting or mixed results, yet those results nevertheless have more value than the term "pilot study" implies. We are, instead, conducting embedded studies that are attuned to cultural and contextual nuance.

In this broader social and cultural context, we do not discount Rhymes and Anderson's (2004) belief that American teachers may have a tendency to attribute a higher status to Spanish and thus by extension to Hispanic dialect transferred to writing than they do to AAVE and its speech and transference to writing. While our research did not support such a hypothesis, we do not dispute it. Additional research could further examine the spectrum of differing regional attitudes of teachers.

Given the complexities of grammar as a social and academic term (Hartwell, 1985; Noguchi, 1991), our embedded research on dialect is the first step in a multiphase project that plans to attend next to partnership issues of teaching and learning, specifically to examine the racial and sociopolitical issues of teaching "white" academic English at each campus. Our research could also lead to additional study demonstrating any differences in the expectations for student writing held by instructors of different ranks and types of employ-ment—with significant implications for race, gender, and academic politics.

Notes

[1] We use the term "dialect" in a non-hierarchical linguistic sense of language varieties, none of which are inherently superior as a system of verbal expression.

[2] Our point about research that examines several different language groups could also ap-ply to "generation 1.5 students" (Harklau, Losey, & Siegel, 1999), who face significant linguistic and cultural challenges in understanding and using the written conventions of Edited American English in academic discourse. At UCM, for instance, about 40% of entering first-year students are from bilingual or multilingual households, and 18% are from families that do not speak English at home (University of California, "Merced," 2010).

[3] This research design was submitted to the Institutional Research Board (IRB) at each campus. The IRBs independently approved the project's design.

[4] There are many varieties of Spanish-influenced English. Over 40 years ago Stockwell, Bo-wen, and Martin (1965) wrote *The Grammatical Structures of Spanish and English*, a two-volume contrastive analysis of sound systems and grammatical systems of both languages. That founda-tional study did not attend to all varieties of Spanish or English, but it did establish that these languages differ linguistically in ways that are systematic, predictable and relatively uniform.

CHAPTER EIGHT

Challenging the Frameworks of Color-blind Racism: Why We Need a Fourth Wave of Writing Assessment Scholarship

Nicholas Behm and Keith D. Miller

As white, middle-class males, we work and live in classed, gendered, and racialized environments in which we materially benefit from systemic and structurally inequitable power relations. In regards to structural white supremacy, for instance, we often question whether our teaching practices actually contest whiteness since we interpret and analyze the world through white-colored lenses. Indeed, our participation in this conversation and classroom assessment practices may be exercises of race privilege made possible by mechanisms that maintain racial inequality. However, conscious of our racial positioning and committed to challenging the diffusion of "color-blind racism" (Bonilla-Silva, 2006, p. 25) in the classroom and on our respective campuses, we strive to practice anti-racism in our personal and professional lives.

Our work to practice anti-racism and to challenge structural white supremacy in our courses often involves the study of writing assessment, since as an inherently ideological practice, writing assessment often involves what Trimbur (1996) calls "conflicts of interest, asymmetrical relations of power, hidden motives and unforeseen consequences" (p. 45). It reinforces value systems and defines, positions, and excludes groups of students, possibly limiting access to resources that facilitate learning and that improve students' life chances. Although recent scholarship in composition studies integrates post-colonial theories and critical race studies, that scholarship often neglects to examine how race "function[s] as an absent presence" and how, particularly in assessment practices, racism functions as an "absent absence," ensuring that the racialized landscape of writing assessment remains uncontested (Prendergast, 1998, p. 36).

We contend that the discipline needs to interrogate and refashion the racial politics of assessment. While we acknowledge that social scientists have long debated the relationship between race and scores on achievement tests (Freedle, 2003; Breland et al., 2004; AERA, APA, & NCME, 1999), we examine writing assessment by presenting a theoretical framework for understanding race relations and white cultural hegemony, a framework that is salient to

composition studies and to the study of writing assessment in general and
classroom assessment in particular. First, relying on the work of Bonilla-Silva
(2001, 2006), we offer a theory for unpacking racialized discourse and suggest
how such discourse pervades classroom assessment. Second, we discuss an activity that we use in training teachers of writing to challenge their racial pre-
suppositions when assessing the writing produced by students whose discourse
differs from or challenges academic discourse and Edited American English.
We also outline the concepts of a critical race pedagogy and advance critical
race narratives as a way to develop racially conscious classroom assessment
practices. Finally, in an effort to address the racial politics of writing assessment, we propose a Fourth Wave of writing assessment, a move that foregrounds race and racism in writing assessment scholarship and that
encourages teachers of writing, writing program administrators, and other
stakeholders to think critically about the racial implications of writing assessment.

Color-blind Racism And Its Diffusion Into Four Frameworks

Often intertwined with relations of power and dominance, race functions
as a chief element in American life (West, 1993). For instance, in *Playing in the
Dark*, Nobel Prize winning novelist Morrison (1992) argues that American fiction creates white identity by establishing white characters' parasitic relationship to an Africanist other. She contends that the presence of an Africanist
other functions to enshrine the privilege and power of what she terms a widespread, "impenetrable whiteness" (p. 32). Thus, to comprehend the work of
fiction, the reader must take on the subjectivity of the *"new white man,"* participating in a reflexive fabrication through which an enduring Africanist presence serves as a touchstone against which whiteness is constituted, privileged,
and perpetuated. Morrison succinctly comments:

> Africanism is the vehicle by which the American self knows itself as not enslaved, but
> free; not repulsive, but desirable; not helpless, but licensed and powerful; not history-
> less, but historical; not damned, but innocent; not a blind accident of evolution, but
> a progressive fulfillment of destiny. (1992, p. 52)

The culture of whiteness that prevails in canonical American novels continu-
ally, in her words, marks "others" as alien in order "to assert privilege and
power" (1992, p. 52).

Recently, Bonilla-Silva (2006) has proposed four conceptual frameworks
that illuminate the dominance of whiteness in American culture, a dominance
that, as Goldberg explains, is "manifest [...] in the microexpressions of daily
life" (1997, p. 20) and that, we argue, also manifests in the assessment of writ-

ing. Consisting of inconspicuous mechanisms that reinforce racial inequality, a new racial framework has emerged.[1] An essential component of the "new racism" is what Bonilla-Silva (2006) calls "color-blind racism," a racial ideology that rationalizes endemic economic, political, and social disparities among racial groups as nonracial (p. 2).[2] To explain "color-blind racism" and its diffusion, Bonilla-Silva (2006) argues that whites are socialized within a "white *habitus*," consisting of historically and culturally constructed dispositions and discourses, which "*conditions* and *creates* whites' racial taste, perceptions, feelings, and emotions and their views on racial matters" (p. 104, emphasis in original; Bourdieu, 1997). In essence, a white *habitus* is actualized by and actualizes whiteness and its identities, dispositions, and privileges. One consequence of the white *habitus* is to construct "a white culture of solidarity" that naturalizes whiteness and fashions a white lens that many whites use to interpret systemic racial disparities as nonracial (Bonilla-Silva, 2006, pp. 104, 123–125). A white *habitus* and whiteness work in a dialectical fashion to denigrate aggrieved racial groups, constructing the ostensible neutrality, objectivity, and naturalness of white ways of knowing and privileging white identity while simultaneously imposing subordinated positions onto people of other races (Keating, 1995; Ratcliffe, 2000; Barnett, 2000; Frankenberg, 1997).

Whiteness and white privilege are fundamental components of "color-blind racism," serving to mask the "constructedness, specificity, and localness" of whiteness (Frankenberg, 1997, p. 16). Bonilla-Silva (2001) characterizes "color-blind racism" as the "central ideological formation that has emerged to support and reproduce the new racial structure of the United States" (p. 137). He (2006) explains "color-blind racism" by proposing that whites use four frameworks to rationalize racial inequality: *abstract liberalism, naturalization, cultural racism,* and *minimization of racism* (pp. 28–47). These four frameworks are the product of the dialectical relationship between a white *habitus* and whiteness, and the frameworks function to legitimate and condition white dispositions and constructions of lived experience (Bourdieu, 1997, p. 145).

Bonilla-Silva (2001) remarks that his first framework, *abstract liberalism,* accounts for the tendency to embrace tenets of political and economic liberalism (equal opportunity, meritocracy, free market, and individual choice) in a "decontextualized manner" to justify and rationalize racial inequities (p. 141). In a composition course, this frame may be exhibited by a teacher's uniform application of rubrics to student essays, an application based on the assumption that all students benefit from an equal opportunity to learn within the classroom environment, disregarding the possible inequitable racial relations that subtly segregate students of aggrieved racial groups and that possibly inhibit their opportunity to learn course content. *Abstract liberalism,* according to

Bonilla-Silva (2001), is the most powerful framework because citizens of the U.S. routinely valorize the fundamental tenets of liberalism, rendering those tenets so natural, normal, and moral that they seem unassailable. Because these precepts are fundamental to an American *habitus*, they enable those who employ them to sound "reasonable" (2001, p. 141).

The second framework, *naturalization*, explains the process through which white Americans often rationalize racial inequity by suggesting that residential and school segregation and racial preferences in friends and partners are all perfectly normal and natural. *Naturalization* enables some to designate residential and school segregation as either a choice or as a biological tendency. According to Bonilla-Silva (2006), naturalization promotes an attitude of "that's just the way things are" while suggesting that preference in associating with one's race is "almost biologically driven and typical" human behavior, rendering segregation as a bland, unobjectionable practice (p. 28). Teachers of writing may invoke this framework to explain students' racial preferences in establishing writing groups, peer response groups, or other group formative assessment activities. That students segregate themselves along racial lines during group activities may seem like a "natural" phenomenon to some teachers who are unaware of this framework.

The third framework, *cultural racism*, explains racial inequities as resulting from supposed group characteristics. This framework is a dubious revision of the framework of biological inferiority that segregationists used during the era of Jim Crow, which ascribed pejorative characteristics to particular groups and treated them as biological (Bonilla-Silva, 2006, pp. 39-40; 2001, pp. 147-151). Before and during the civil rights movement of the 1950s and 1960s, Southern segregationists justified racial inequalities by claiming that African Americans were less intelligent and biologically inferior. Today, however, some whites adjust their racism by arguing that Latino/as, African Americans, Native Americans, and/or other aggrieved racial groups are inferior as a result of culture, rather than biology. Some whites claim that members of one or another aggrieved racial group are typically lazy, irresponsible, violent, and/or that they do not value education and do not embrace family values.

Conditioned by color-blind racism, many whites do not recognize the racism entrenched within discourses of cultural deficiency. Whiteness and racism are learned, as van Dijk (2002) notes, through racist representations embedded within and reinforced by the negative characterizations of cultures. Such representations privilege and "affirm the validity and power of 'whiteness'" while simultaneously subordinating people of other races (Keating, 1995, p. 906; King, 1991). As Bonilla-Silva (2001) explains, the framework of cultural racism is dangerous because it is "as extensive as biological racism used to be" in the Jim Crow era and because it enables whites to safely articulate "resentment and hostility" by falsely claiming that minority groups "are where they are [...] because they do not want to get ahead" (p. 148).

Although many teachers of writing may vehemently deny that this frame manifests itself in their assignments, lesson plans, constructive feedback, and other aspects of their teaching, they may not realize how this frame actually constitutes conceptualizations of "good students," strong writing, active participation, and other parameters of student behavior that may reinforce—and be reinforced by—whiteness. For instance, in response to an essay authored by an African American student, a white teacher may characterize the student's ostensible failure to reproduce Edited American English and academic discourse as a lack of effort or laziness, instead of thinking critically about how these discourses are informed by and reinforce whiteness (Behm, 2008; see also Jordan in this collection). The conventions of academic discourse and Edited American English generate a linguistic architecture that cloaks whiteness while reinforcing what Morrison (1992) calls "racial unconsciousness" (p. xii). Indeed, the criteria of clear language, careful organization, and grammatical correctness constitute what Morrison (1992) terms a "vocabulary designed to disguise" the process of "othering" (p. 50). Much like the American literature that Morrison (1992) critiques, we maintain that Standard English exists, in part, because it contrasts with—and is parasitic toward—other forms of discourse, such as African American English and various World Englishes, which white teachers frequently and pejoratively code as "other," that is, as irrational, chaotic, illogical, and abnormal (Dyer, 1993; Horner & Trimbur, 2002). We further claim that many writing teachers' standards of good writing exist because they contrast with other kinds of writing practiced by students of color (Haymes, 1995). Coded white, rational, logical, orderly, and in control, Edited American English hides the coercive force of whiteness by seeming so ostensibly neutral, normal, and commonsensical as to deracialize whiteness while simultaneously highlighting and defining "others" as abnormal and inferior (Mercer, 1990; MacCannell, 1989).

Bonilla-Silva's fourth framework, *minimization of racism*, accounts for the widespread view that racism no longer plays a significant role in the United States and advances the assumption that racism only involves the aberrant acts committed by people who are easily codified as racist (Bonilla-Silva, 2006, p. 29). Thus, as West (1997) contends, some whites minimize racism by exteriorizing it, conveniently repudiating racial prejudice by assuming that they remain "outside of society, outside of ideology, outside of rhetoric, outside of responsibility and accountability" (p. 221). This framework enables the opportune attribution of racism to the white, working poor, displacing critical attention away from the more complex mechanisms of whiteness and allowing "middle-class and elite whites to ignore their own racism" (Beech, 2004, p. 173). This frame, too, could be invoked by writing teachers. While attempting to understand a disproportionate grade distribution along racial lines, teachers could apply the minimization of racism frame to evade critical reflection on how their evaluation criteria may be racially coded. As Ball (2009) and Kamusikiri (1996) demonstrate, racialized evaluation criteria and conventions pervade classroom assessment practices, constructing—and constructed by—a white *habitus* distilled into a white discourse that denigrates those who do not replicate its conventions.

All four frameworks protect white hegemony by deflecting attention away from how racism is systemic and by forming an "impregnable yet elastic wall that barricades whites from [...] racial reality" (Bonilla-Silva, 2006, p. 47). Moreover, the frameworks are products of a white *habitus*, ensuring a "predictable" white interpretation of "racial phenomen[a]" (Bonilla-Silva, 2006, p. 26). Many whites narrate and interpret the sociopolitical power of whiteness convincingly, diffusing their interpretations widely and reifying them as common sense (van Dijk, 2002; Bonilla-Silva, 2001, pp. 62–65). Scholars and practitioners of writing assessment may employ—or witness colleagues employ—one or a combination of these frameworks to explain why students from minority groups perform poorly on placement tests; to rationalize the disproportionate enrollment of minority students in developmental writing courses; or to deflect attention away from how a writing program and its various assessment practices may work unwittingly to maintain white privilege by reducing the opportunities of students of color.

Classroom Assessment And Teacher Training

In graduate classes aimed at training teachers of writing (many of whom are white and middle class), we advocate using non-fictional argumentative speeches and essays by speakers and writers whose language challenges "color-blind racism," a white *habitus*, and the criteria of whiteness. Particularly, we favor the writing of Fannie Lou Hamer (2010), a sharecropper from the Mississippi Delta who, with little formal education, became a nationally recognized, nonviolent crusader in the civil rights movement of the 1960s. We share portions of Hamer's inspirational speeches, such as the following:

> Some of the white people will tell us, "Well, I just don't believe in integration." But he been integrating at night a long time! If he hadn't been, it wouldn't be as many light-skinned Negroes as it is in here. The seventeenth chapter of Acts and twenty-sixth verse said: "[God] has made of one blood all nations." So whether you black as a

skillet or white as a sheet, we are made from the same blood and we are on our way! (p. 49)

> And then how can they say, "In ten years' time, we will have forced every Negro out of the state of Mississippi"? But I want these people to take a good look at themselves, and after they've sent the Chinese back to China, the Jews back to Jerusalem, and give the Indians their land back, and they take the *Mayflower* from which they came, the Negro will still be in Mississippi. (pp. 52–53)

While asking students to assess Hamer's language, we explain that her editors describe her idiom as "southern black vernacular" (Brooks & Houck, 2010, p. xxiii). We also explain that, albeit tortured for her activism, Hamer incited thousands of oppressed and disenfranchised African Americans to risk their jobs and their lives by attempting to register to vote. As students in our classes note, whatever label one might apply to Hamer's idiom, one cannot doubt her persuasiveness in strongly and effectively overturning white supremacist rule in the South and making possible civil rights laws that outlawed de jure racial segregation. We also ask students to read the writing of Geneva Smitherman (2000), who often intermingles Standard English and what she calls Black English or BE (and what others call African American Vernacular English or AAVE):

> Ain nothing in a long time lit up the English-teaching profession like the current hassle over Black English. One finds beaucoup sociolinguistic research studies and language projects for the "disadvantaged" on the scene in nearly every sizable black community in the country [...] And we black folks is not gon take all that weight, for no one has empirically demonstrated that linguistic/stylistic features of BE impede educational progress in communication skills, or any other area of cognitive learning. Take reading. It's done been charged, but not actually verified, that BE interferes with mastery of reading skills. Yet beyond pointing out the gap between the young brother/sistuh's phonological and syntactical patterns and those of the usually-middle-class-WE-speaking teacher, this claim has not been validated. (2000, p. 57)

As part of our conversations about Hamer and Smitherman, we ask students to consider how they think English teachers should assess and grade student essays written in African American dialects and other non-standard dialects. We discuss how Hamer's and Smitherman's texts challenge the racialized ideologies that reinforce whiteness and narrate racial oppression. Reading both of these passages, for instance, helps our students confront the four frameworks that Bonilla-Silva (2006) outlines. Since Hamer's writing was authored in a historical context of de jure systemic, sociopolitical racism, it encourages our students to think critically about the historical articulations of racial relations and the diffusion of those racial relations into central components of human life, like language and writing when compared to Smitherman's writing and the writing of critical race scholars. From this exercise, students can come to understand the centrality of race and racism in determining the life chances of students who identify with aggrieved racial formations. Smitherman's writing prods our students to question the possible hasty application of the cultural racism framework when teachers of writing assess writing that refuses to conform to the conventions of Standard English and academic discourse. We build on this discussion by distributing several student essays written in a variety of discourses, including—but not limited to—Edited American English and African American Vernacular English.[3] During this discussion, we draw on the research of Labov (1970, 2010), Smitherman (2000), Young (2007, 2011), and others to explain, in much greater detail, the lexical structures and rhetorical features of disparate discourses, pointing—for example—to the many varieties of African American Vernacular English, such as that of Charles Chesnutt's (2011) late nineteenth-century reconstruction of Southern slave dialect, Hurston's (2006) very different 1930s presentation of rural Florida dialect, and Vershawn Ashanti Young's (2007, 2011) analysis of teenage street dialect in contemporary Detroit. Through this discussion, our graduate students come to understand how even if students of color successfully replicate Standard English, they may never be truly heard or have their hybrid voices respected (Villanueva, 1993, 1997, 2003; Royster, 1996). Rather, because of their alternative linguistic patterns, they may be branded as "troublesome, not worth listening to, and lacking in potential for success" (Feagin, Vera, & Imani, 1996, p. 15).

Because a majority of our graduate students have been socialized within a white *habitus*, they often initially resist our interrogation of Standard English, purposely failing to read the material or strongly objecting to the material during class discussion. Some students, for example, say the following: "Shouldn't all students know the grammatical rules of Standard English before they are allowed to break those conventions?" Other students say that, "by allowing students of color to write in their 'ghetto discourses,' we are setting them up for failure in their professional lives." Another typical objection that some students raise is that "this material is another example of misguided multiculturalism." We consider the raising of these objections as teachable moments, instances when we can engage students in directly questioning the myths and fabrications of whiteness (Feagin & Vera, 1995; Feagin, 2010). Since we, too, were socialized within a white *habitus*, we understand how disorienting and difficult this necessary critical interrogation of whiteness can be. In interrogating Standard English, the frameworks of "color-blind racism," and a white *habitus*, we do not necessarily seek to transform our graduate students into anti-racists, for such a project would probably be impossible in a semester course. Rather, we hope that, because of the preparation that they receive in our teacher-training courses, our graduate students will recognize the application of the frameworks of "color-blind racism," understand how the four frameworks manifest in their teaching materials and assessment practices, and work against racially charged phenomena in their own classes.

Critical Race Pedagogy And Narratives

In our writing and teaching, we also encourage our graduate students and writing assessment scholars to develop a critical race pedagogy in their classrooms, a pedagogy consisting of many interrelated practices that are informed by critical race theory (Yosso, 2002, p. 95; Yosso et al., 2004, pp. 3-4). Such a pedagogy complements Bonilla-Silva's (2006) theory of "color-blind racism" because it acknowledges that race, although a social construct, plays a central role in how society is structured to advantage whites at the expense of aggrieved racial groups, and it foregrounds critical analyses of race to highlight and subsequently remedy racial disparities, as well as all forms of subordination. To advance critical analyses of race and to challenge the application of the four frameworks outlined by Bonilla-Silva, a critical race pedagogy marshals a variety of discourses, frameworks, and theories from an array of disciplines, making it an inherently transdisciplinary praxis (Yosso et al., 2004, p. 4). Such a pedagogy also works to identify and clarify the intersectionality among race, gender, class, sexual orientation, disability, and other cultural markers; pursues social justice tenaciously and tirelessly; and valorizes the lived experiences, cultural knowledge, and discourses of students of color (Yosso, 2002, p. 95; Yosso et al., 2004, pp. 3-4). It is a formidable activist pedagogy determined to challenge all inequitable power relations, particularly those that sustain structural white supremacy. Using a variety of genres and rhetorical strategies, critical race theorists construct critical race narratives that celebrate experiential bodies of knowledge, strengthen group solidarity, reveal the ubiquity of racism and the hidden power relations that perpetuate it, and interrogate majoritarian frameworks that rationalize "color-blind racism" (Solorzano & Yosso, 2002; Delgado, 1989).

To apply a critical race pedagogy as part of enacting a fourth wave of assessment and constructing racially conscious assessment practices, instructors could help students construct portfolios consisting of critical race narratives. As Prendergast (1998) notes, critical race narratives blur genres, integrating allegory, fantasy, fiction, satire, etc.; relate intense personal experiences with racism; critique dominant discourse conventions, such as those that sustain Standard English; textualize double-consciousness; and develop discourses that reveal systemic racism (pp. 39–45). We argue that the frameworks of "color-blind racism," reinforcing and propagating whiteness, work analogously to sustain both micro- and macro-mechanisms of assessment and lionize assessment—especially practices that yield quantitative data—as essential to education. Critical race narratives, then, work against these frameworks, demonstrating that writing and the practice of assessing writing are never objective, race-neutral, or a-historical.

Race And A Fourth Wave Of Writing Assessment

In "Looking Back as We Look Forward: Historicizing Writing Assessment," Yancey (1999) outlines the history of writing assessment into three distinct waves: the first wave encompassed the early years of the discipline and revolved around ostensibly "objective" testing; the second wave (roughly 1970–1986) focused on holistic essay scoring; and the third wave (1986–present) has emphasized portfolio and programmatic assessment measures. As Yancey (1999) articulates, writing pedagogy facilitates self-formation, and "writing assessment, because it wields so much power, plays a crucial role in what self, or selves, will be permitted—in our classrooms; in our tests; ultimately, in our culture" (p. 498). Since assessment practices can possibly exclude groups of students and inhibit individual self-formation, practitioners must develop assessment practices that resist the possession and proliferation of white cultural capital and that reject "color-blind racism."

To that end, we propose that composition scholars pursue a Fourth Wave of writing assessment scholarship that accounts for the intersection of race and writing assessment and how writing assessment practices are constructed within and reinforce a white *habitus*. A Fourth Wave of scholarship would develop out of the rich tradition of writing assessment scholarship, and critique that tradition, revealing how theories and practices of assessment are racialized and identifying how writing assessments construct and are constructed by inequitable racial relations that have exploited and excluded students of color. Additionally, a Fourth Wave would place whiteness and "color-blind racism" at the center of scholarly discussions of classroom and programmatic writing assessment, analyzing the ways in which assessment practices and interpretations of data constitute and are constitutive of a white *habitus*. For example, Ball (2009) maintains that "writing assessment is a part of the power culture," suggesting that racial differences between teachers and students cause gross forms of misunderstanding about appropriate behaviors, conventions, and languages (p. 358). Observing white faculty as they teach students from non-European racial and ethnic backgrounds, she confirms Smitherman's (2000) argument that white teachers lack the knowledge to accurately assess the linguistic practices of students of color. Reading alternative discourses that stray from valorized academic English, composition faculty, according to Kamusikiri (1996), may jettison process-oriented pedagogies and assign "outmoded, de-contextualized grammar and usage exercises" (p. 188). As a result, teachers may emphasize the "eradication of deviant language patterns," functioning as a "gatekeeper, a destructive force," negatively assessing the competency of students of color (Kamusikiri, 1996, p. 188). As Ball (2009), Kamusikiri (1996), and other scholars mount these arguments, they implicitly claim that Bonilla-Silva's (2001) framework of *cultural racism* appears in our classrooms and in our assessment practices.

In relation to classroom assessment, practitioners can heed Morrison's analysis and exercise a Fourth Wave of writing assessment by interrogating the supremacy of rubrics and by contesting racialized ideologies embedded within rubrics that enforce monolingualism. As Balester notes in this collection, rubrics—because they impose Edited American English and present writing as a-rhetorical and a-historical—often summarily exclude students from multilingual backgrounds. What are needed, then, are rhetorically based, theoretically informed rubrics that are co-constructed with students, respect students' right to their own languages, and encourage multilingualism. This collection, we believe, nicely exemplifies a Fourth Wave of writing assessment scholarship. For example, Kelly-Riley in this collection invokes a race-conscious approach to writing assessment when she urges WPAs to consider race when they evaluate the validity of their assessments. Inoue notes how grading contracts perform differently for disparate racial formations at Fresno State and offer a more effective classroom environment for Asian Pacific American (Hmong) students. Lewis Ketai undertakes a textual analysis of placement guides to discern if they reinforce Bonilla-Silva's definition of "color-blind racism."

We hope that this collection will empower Fourth Wave scholars of writing assessment to contest racialized explanations of achievement gaps; to challenge entrenched "white" linguistic patterns lionized as normal, natural, and rational; and to repudiate racialized standards reinforced by rubrics and other classroom assessment practices that reify the discursive practices of whiteness and privilege those white students who, in Shor's (1997) words, "speak and look like those already in power" (p. 98). We also hope that, as part of a Fourth Wave, scholars will rebuke public policy makers and accrediting agencies who attempt to prescribe Standard English—the language of whiteness—as the ultimate template and touchstone for evaluating all student writing and who egregiously misuse assessment practices—like practices dictated by No Child Left Behind—for political gain. Scholars of the Fourth Wave will certainly incorporate Ball's (2009) suggestion that faculty from a rich variety of cultural backgrounds should work together to design, administer, and inter-pret assessment programs and practices. When that happens, scholars and teachers of writing may no longer measure all student essays within the frameworks of "color-blind racism" or according to criteria of whiteness. In-stead, scholars of the Fourth Wave may generate multifaceted criteria for as-sessing student essays that follow appropriate standards, including the standards of AAVE, Latino/a Englishes, and World Englishes (Canagarajah, 2006a; Horner & Trimbur, 2002).

Notes

---

[1] What Bonilla-Silva (2001, 2006) terms "color-blind racism" is a post-civil rights phe-nomenon. Prior to the civil rights movement, Jim Crow racism enforced racial inequality explic-itly through "white only" signs, literacy ordinances, school segregation, voter intimidation, and a variety of other means to perpetuate white supremacy and to prohibit African American mobili-zation. As civil rights legislation criminalized explicit racism, the ideologies buttressing and maintaining white supremacy rearticulated to include liberalism and cultural tropes to justify and rationalize racial inequality—a rearticulation that allows whites to blame racial minorities for their subjugated position in the United States (Bonilla-Silva 2006, p. 7). According to Crenshaw (1995) and Bonilla-Silva (2006), "color-blind racism" became a master framework, permeating all social and political systems, during the vehement neoconservative backlash to the civil rights movement in the1970s and 1980s. For example, according to Crenshaw (1995), the Reagan administration launched a full-scale assault on civil rights policies and legislation by arguing that race-specific policies were anti-democratic (p. 103). The argument advanced by the Reagan ad-ministration rested on color-blind ideology that positioned race consciousness as inherently racist; therefore, affirmative action and other race-based remedies to discrimination were charac-terized as leftist politics gone awry. Color-blind ideology has been reinforced and propagated by neoconservative politicians; pundits, such as Rush Limbaugh, Glenn Beck, and Bill O'Reilly; and analysts, such as Lawrence Mead (1986), Shelby Steele (1991), and Dinesh D'Souza (1995).

[2] Bonilla-Silva (2006) developed his understanding of "color-blind racism" by analyzing data generated from two studies: the 1997 Survey of Social Attitudes of College Students, a study in which 627 college students from three universities were surveyed about their perspec-tives regarding racial relations. Of the 627 students, forty-one white students were randomly selected for follow-up interviews (2006, p. 12). The second study that Bonilla-Silva (2006) credits is the 1998 Detroit Area Study (DAS), "a probabilistic survey of 400 black and white Detroit metropolitan area residents" (pp. 12–13). Eighty-four subjects (66 white and 17 African Ameri-can) were randomly selected for interviews (2006, p. 13). Both studies, of course, possess limita-tions. The 1997 Survey of Social Attitudes of College Students, for instance, only interviewed white students and its sampling was based on convenience. The DAS only surveyed white and African American residents, excluding Detroit residents who may identify with other racial groups.

[3] Not only do many African American students speak EAE, so do some Latino/a and Pa-cific Islander youth in American high schools (Paris, 2009).

Composition Placement Assessment

In "The Opening of the Modern Era of Writing Assessment: A Narrative" White (2001) describes a critical moment in writing assessment history when English faculty in the California State University system defeated the administration's attempt to hand over assessment of student writing to ETS in an externally administered multiple choice exam. Less than two years later, in 1973, English departments in the California State University system administered their own assessment of student writing, a timed, impromptu exam consisting of two 45-minute essays. In wresting control of assessment from the CSU administration, White observes that English faculty developed a test that "embodied current writing theory, writing research, and writing pedagogy" (2001, p. 309). More significantly, they developed a test that made a statement about what was valued in college-level writing (White, 2001, p. 309).

In tracing this critical point in writing assessment history, White offers a portrait of placement assessment that is messy. He writes that assessment is a site of contention and that perspectives of teachers may reside alongside (or be displaced by) the views of legislators and other institutional constituents (see also Yancey, 1999). Assessment, especially placement assessment, is contentious because there are many competing demands on what large-scale writing assessment is supposed to measure and how it should or can measure (not to mention who pays for it and who gets to use the results for what purposes).

White's article is a useful frame for the chapters in this section as our contributors raise important questions about the possibilities and limits of placement assessment when stakeholders' views result in outcomes that have high-impact consequences for students of color and English language learners. In taking up the subject of how assessment may result in unintended outcomes, our contributors echo contemporary notions of validity. Current conceptions of validity insist that assessments are only as good as the accuracy of the interpretations that we make from them. Indeed, as the history of assessment has shown, flawed interpretations of assessment results have had a negative impact on those populations who are often most vulnerable in educational contexts: working-class students, non-native speakers, and students of color.

The chapters in this section show how identity markers of class, race, and language overlap with notions about writing proficiency and its assessment. At the heart of these chapters is an understanding not only that racial formations are socially constructed, but also that technologies such as writing assessment coalesce with other social mechanisms to result in inequitable outcomes.

In "Race, Remediation, and Readiness: Reassessing the 'Self' in Directed Self-Placement," Rachel Lewis Ketai offers a close reading of directed self-placement guides, noting how the language used to describe reading and writing practices is potentially indexed with racialized assumptions. Lewis Ketai writes that race is woven through the fabric of placement testing and through conceptions of literacy and educational identity. She encourages writing programs to consider the messages about identity that they send to students through DSP placement guides and other placement materials, and she offers revised language for DSP guides. In the end, Lewis Ketai is optimistic about the potential of DSP if we provide a fuller accounting of student writing ability in ways that do not draw on racialized assumptions about literacy practices, or that account for the racial formations being placed.

Anthony Lioi and Nicole Merola, in "The Muse of Difference: Race and Writing Placement at Two Elite Art Schools," encourage us to go beyond the "look" test (counting the number of students of color in basic writing and concluding that a test is flawed) in judging writing placement exams. Instead, Lioi and Merola encourage us to interrogate how assessment technologies embedded within institutional contexts can perpetuate erroneous preconceptions about student writing ability. An assessment is flawed if that placement exam is not based on a theoretically sound process for making placement decisions, if the placement has a negative impact on student educational outcomes, if the assessment process creates a hostile relationship between students and the academic unit delivering the test, and if the subsequent curriculum is not aligned to the test. Lioi and Merola show us how writing program administrators at two institutions sought to change the culture of assessment at their institutions and address issues of equity in that process.

CHAPTER NINE

Race, Remediation, and Readiness: Reassessing the "Self" in Directed Self-Placement

Rachel Lewis Ketai

In a *College Composition and Communication* article (1998) and subsequent book (2003), Daniel J. Royer and Roger Gilles introduced *directed self-placement* (DSP), a student-centered method of composition course placement founded on the notion that with guidance from the writing program and a clear sense of first-year composition (FYC) course expectations, students are better equipped than administrators to assess their readiness for college writing. David Blakesley (2002) enriched these early discussions by framing composition course placement as "a fundamentally rhetorical and thus social act" (p. 12) through which entering students learn important lessons about the institutions they are joining and their identity within them. By highlighting the role of composition course placement as messenger of institutional values to entering students, Blakesley also underscores DSP's power to transform those messages and the institutions they represent.

As Sharon Crowley (1998) and Mary Soliday (2002) and, more recently, Kelly Ritter (2009) and Jane Stanley (2010) have noted, assessment practices too often define basic writers according to institutionally articulated, historically racialized conceptions of writing ability and student "need."[1] This body of scholarship builds on the foundational work of Mina Shaughnessy (1977), calling into question the capacity of institutions to define, through traditional placement methods, who basic writers are and what basic writing is in ways that benefit students. DSP, on the other hand, allows students to choose writing classes based on self-assessments of their writing histories and their confidence to succeed in particular writing courses. For Royer and Gilles, DSP's student-centered approach to remediation can "upset the status quo of our programs and curricula" by encouraging writing programs to listen and respond to students' "perceived needs" rather than defining those needs for them (2003, p. 10). For Blakesley, the potential of DSP extends even further: "The simple act of providing students some stake in exercising personal agency in such an explicit way can begin the process of achieving that more noble goal of higher education: to prepare a citizenry to write its own future by deliberating on its past" (2002, p. 29). For those of us interested in issues of racial identity and writing assessment, DSP offers the potential to address the racialization of basic writing that too often occurs through traditional placement practices.

However, to recognize the potential of DSP for diverse learners, more work on DSP needs to take issues of race and racism into account. As Carole Center (2007) has noted, basic writing scholarship has a tendency to "screen out race" (p. 23) despite the significant and persistent implications race holds for our work as teachers and researchers. She suggests basic writing teachers enrich their contributions to the field by "making race visible in scholarly writing" (p. 36). Likewise, Kelly-Riley concludes her chapter in this collection by encouraging administrators to attend to issues of race and racism when examining the validity of their programmatic assessments. Both of these suggestions have much to offer studies of DSP. For example, a recent study by Gere et al. (2010) of the University of Michigan's DSP program shares the results of a multi-dimensional validity inquiry and raises questions about the validity of DSP at that institution. Though the study responds to calls for attention to local contexts and consequences of programmatic assessment (Lewicki-Wilson, Sommers, & Tassoni, 2000), it could be enriched through further considerations of race and, potentially, the unaccounted effects of racism. For, as Susan Latta and Janice Lauer (2000) point out, self-assessment is not immune to the inequities typically associated with more traditional writing assessments. They end their postmodern and feminist critique of self-assessment with a question that DSP advocates would be wise to consider: "By asking students to assess themselves, are we asking them to internalize the strictures and guidelines of a system that may be discriminatory?" (p. 32).

It is worth asking, then, whether DSP helps address inequities in composition course placement or simply rearranges them. In order to address any potential racial inequities associated with DSP, validity studies will need to examine what Inoue (2009b) calls the "racial validity" of DSP–"the entire racialized and hegemonic environment that dialectically produces and is produced by the writing assessment" (p. 111). Through the publication of his assessment results from California State University, Fresno (CSUF) (2009a), which I will summarize below, Inoue initiates a conversation regarding the potential racial consequences of DSP–a conversation Inoue points out in which racial "validation is not concerned just with consequences of assessment decisions [but] with the entire environment in which those decisions are produced and situated" (2009b, p. 112).

This environment includes what Inoue calls the "technological artifacts" of our writing assessments, a term he adopts from Feenberg's critical theory of technology to mean "the sum of all objects and processes involved" in a technological structure (as cited in Inoue, 2009b, p. 105). Artifacts are the smaller parts of a larger system, and they can be mined to uncover the ways racial biases are built into the internal structures of a hegemonic environment. Inoue (2009b) names these biases "racialized rationalities" (p. 111)–(a phrase adapted from Marcuse's concept of "technological rationality")–to illustrate how the racial order of the status quo comes to *seem* reasonable when it is reinforced at both the macro and the micro levels.

After outlining the potential racialized implications of DSP, I turn to one of the most visible artifacts of DSP–placement guides. Placement guides are typically brochures that administrators distribute to students to help guide them through the placement decision. Undertaking a textual analysis, I ask, do these texts contain any "racialized rationalities" and, if so, how might they be reformed? Through this analysis, I call into question the rhetorical construction of the "self" on DSP placement guides and then propose solutions reflective of Howard's (2000) model of dialogic self-assessment. My critique operates with the basic assumption that DSP is a major advancement in programmatic writing assessment with unprecedented potential for social justice along racial lines.[2] With this analysis, I hope to uncover ways that DSP can more fully realize its potential to promote racial equity in our writing programs.

The Racial Consequences Of DSP

An inquiry into the racial consequences of DSP should begin by asking the following questions: Do students of color place themselves into preparatory courses at roughly the same rate as white students? Are the effects of composition course placement better, worse, or the same for students of color with DSP than they are with other means of placement?

In his recently published program article (2009a), Inoue begins to answer these questions by providing data from the CSUF DSP program that takes issues of race into account. CSUF's DSP program works in conjunction with exit portfolio assessments and a stretch sequence of FYC courses. Thus, its results reflect not only the influence of DSP, but also innovations in classroom assessment and the restructuring of a first-year-writing sequence that does not include a traditional "basic writing" course. CSUF students place themselves on one of three course paths, all designed to achieve the same course outcomes but over different periods of time: a one-semester accelerated course, a yearlong stretch sequence, or an ELL course in preparation for the yearlong sequence. To guide students through their placement decisions, the CSUF writing program provides students with information regarding course outcomes as well as prompts that help students assess their own readiness for each course path.

The CSUF program report from the 2007–2008 academic year found that, under DSP, both the accelerated and the stretch options "have very similar racial and gender formations as those that occur in the university at large, which is complex" (Inoue, 2008, p. 17). In other words, students of color were not placing themselves disproportionately into any particular course path. Even more encouraging, "By the end of the year, most students felt their DSPs were accurate (80%)." Inoue's article (2009a) also suggests that DSP raised retention and passing rates for students who were designated remedial writers under the more traditional composition course placement model used previously at CSUF, the English Placement Test.

Though his data are admittedly complex, especially with regard to race, Inoue (2009a) expresses optimism about DSP's potential to empower students once designated remedial by administrators and the English Placement Test (EPT). He concludes, "When students do well in our writing program, one that gives them choice and agency through the DSP, they stay in the university longer, especially when choosing [the yearlong supplemental stretch option]" ("Assessment Research Findings, para. 15). However, despite designing the program to help students of color, Inoue hesitates when it comes to praising the benefits of DSP for all students. He writes, "we also have evidence from just about every source that shows Blacks are most at risk, least satisfied, and fail most often" (2009a, "Assessment Research Findings, para. 17). In "The Technology of Writing Assessment and Racial Validity" (2009b), he points out, "If we separate the English 5A passing final portfolios from the failing ones, we have just separated students primarily by race [...] 81.6% of all failing portfolios are from students of color, yet they make up 70% of the current sample" (p. 103–104). Inoue's data suggest that CSUF's DSP program disproportionately benefited white students who had previously been designated remedial. Thus, despite some of the promising results at CSUF, it is far too soon to state with any confidence that DSP has positive racial consequences for students of color. The question remains, does DSP sidestep racialization simply by shifting the placement decision from administrators to students?

DSP As Racial Project

Those most optimistic about DSP typically praise its emphasis on student agency for empowering students, especially for "remedial" students. Royer and Gilles make this point in "Basic Writing and Directed Self-Placement" (2000), likening DSP to liberatory and progressive pedagogies because it promotes what they call the "basic educational values of agency, choice, and self-determination" (para. 2). Advocates maintain that this emphasis on student agency can motivate even the most marginalized first-year writers to take charge of their education as they transition into the role of a college writer.

However, if we are going to consider DSP's impact on students of color, it is worth noting that a narrative about agency, choice, and self-determination can perpetuate racism in the post–Civil Rights era. Since the end of legally sponsored racism in the 1960s, racial inequality has persisted despite legislative bans on the most visible forms of segregation and prejudice. In *Racism without Racists: Color-Blind Racism and the Persistence of Racial Inequality in the United States* (2006), Eduardo Bonilla-Silva describes how "color-blind racism" acts as a rationalizing tool for whites to continue racial inequalities after the Jim Crow period as the products of nonracial dynamics (p. 2). Rather than pointing to a "No Negroes" sign on the front door of a business, for instance, whites can explain that individuals simply choose to stick together. Instead of claiming that blacks are intellectually inferior, whites can suggest certain students or families just do not place a high value on education. And before acknowledging any social privileges of their own, whites are likely to defend their personal work ethics. These claims of color blindness could not resonate so powerfully without what Bonilla-Silva calls the racial story line of "abstract liberalism," a rhetorical frame that allows whites to "appear reasonable and even moral, while opposing almost all practical approaches to deal with de facto racial inequality" (2006, p. 28). Racism still saturates this rhetorical landscape of denials, justifications, and historical re-visioning, but color blindness avoids the public outcries and political solutions of the Civil Rights era by disguising the racial inequalities as a matter of individual choice. For a more extensive treatment of Bonilla-Silva's racial frames, Behm and Miller in this volume discuss it in terms of the "white *habitus*" it engenders.

In composition course placement, it is impossible to detangle the role of race from any given variable of the placement process—the race of administrators doing the placement, the race of the students being placed, and perhaps most important, the racialized history and impact of socially constructed concepts like "writing ability" and "readiness for college writing" that guide those assessments. Race is woven throughout the fabric of placement testing and through conceptions of literacy and educational identity. As Catherine Prendergast illustrates in *Literacy and Racial Justice: The Politics of Learning after Brown v. Board of Education* (2003), "literacy has often been regarded as a White trait, something that whites possess naturally, rather than as a White privilege" (p. 8). Indeed, color-blind narratives about readiness for college writing have too often deemed students of color "unprepared" for not performing literacy practices historically associated with white, middle-class males. When these narratives rely on the rhetorical frame of individual choice, determination, and agency, they also imply that "unpreparedness" results from an individual student's poor choices or lack of determination.

In *Rhetorical Listening: Identification, Gender, Whiteness*, Krista Ratcliffe (2005) explains the consequences of what she calls "the reduced *ethos* of the rugged white male individualist" (p. 124): "Within this reduced concept of *ethos*, which celebrates individual will and toil, 'falling outside' can be interpreted in only one way: as failure of individual will and toil" (p. 125). In turn, the racist assumption that white students are naturally more prepared for college writing than students of color persists today through the color blind version of that claim—that individuals have the agency to determine their own readiness for college writing regardless of social circumstance.

These rhetorical maneuvers constitute a part of what Philomena Essed (2002) calls "everyday racism"—the daily, often invisible, practices of individuals that create and confirm structures and ideologies of racism (p. 185). Michael Omi and Howard Winant (1994) argue that racism permeates a culture of individualism that frequently denies the reality of racial difference. Although racial categories may be socially constructed, they exist through "racial projects" that make racial differences between groups meaningful. They explain, "Racial projects connect what race *means* in a particular discursive practice and the ways in which both social structures and everyday experiences are racially *organized*, based upon that meaning" (p. 56). As the introduction of this book points out, writing assessment is indeed a racial project, and the self-assessment that DSP requires is no exception.

Racialized Rationalities: Placing Skills, Placing Selves

Because narratives about self-determination and agency coexist with narratives about writing deficiencies and other racial formations, DSP advocates would be wise to consider the messages their programs communicate via placement guides about the agency of individual students to prepare themselves for college writing. Questions to ask of such materials include: Do DSP materials define readiness for college writing through a frame of color blindness? In their focus on student choice, do they promote ideologies of individualism that rationalize racial hierarchies?

Traditional DSP programs provide students with self-inventory guides that resemble Tables 1 and 2. Table 1 offers the original versions Royer and Gilles used at Grand Valley State University (GVSU) (2003, pp. 233–234), and Table 2 shows the more recent version currently used in Inoue's program at CSUF (2008, p. 110). Though these samples may not be representative of all DSP guides, they were chosen as readily accessible examples from published scholarship.

GVSU's guide reflects the foundational DSP program that served as a model to subsequent programs, while CSUF's guide illuminates a more recent iteration of DSP program design. Both guides present checklists of characteristics that reflect students' general readiness for college-level writing. Students are asked to assess which list of characteristics best describes them and then choose a course path accordingly.

Though both of these programs use DSP to place students into writing courses, some of the language they put forth in their respective guides reflects individualistic definitions of writing readiness. In their focus on past behaviors, both guides define unpreparedness for college writing as a set of personal behavior patterns through first-person admissions ("I do not read"; "I did not do much writing") that isolate all of these activities to the individual student. The difference between a student who can boast reading newspapers and magazines or reading for one's own enjoyment, for instance, and a student who must confess that she does not, often comes down to much more than the student's individual behavior patterns. These behaviors reflect certain sociocultural and economic influences that shape behavior (Heath, 1983; Taylor, 1997). However, the language on the guides does not reflect these social influences; quite to the contrary, the guides focus exclusively on the behavior patterns and composing processes of individual students.

This individualistic language encourages students to assess what and how often they read and write as if these behaviors were divorced from any social influences. For instance, CSUF's prompt for the yearlong stretch option, "I am unsure of myself when I plan my writing," does not situate the writing in any specific context. Does "my writing" refer only to school-specific, or English-class essays? Or might it refer to text messages, song lyrics, blog posts, or other writing situations? In what language? Similarly, "reading" could be any reading in any context. GVSU's prompts for the yearlong stretch option, "Generally, I don't read when I don't have to" and "In high school, I did not do much writing," may suggest context (reading out of school and writing in school, respectively), but the questions still remain: What kinds of reading and writing? For what purposes, and in what context? And, how much writing counts as enough to be prepared for college? Of course, the guides imply that these reading and writing behaviors should be those that would prepare a student for college-level courses, but they do not specifically outline how writing outside academic contexts might translate in first-year composition practices. The rhetoric of individual choice suggests that students who fail to meet the requirements of a prepared college writer do so because of a "failure of individual will and toil" (Ratcliffe, 2005, p. 125), not because of a discriminatory social system that defines and distributes literacy unequally across racial, so-

cioeconomic, and educational lines. The guides imply that all students have
equal opportunities to prepare themselves for college writing. In this way, the
guides conform to Bonilla-Silva's rhetorical framework of color blind racism.

Indeed, these guides illustrate how the racialization of literacy occurs
along many axes—not only through conventional assessments like tests and
grades but also through self-assessments that require students to consider their
past experiences with literacy activities that occur within spaces like schools,
families, peer groups, and neighborhoods. Perhaps these students did not read
for fun because they worked full-time or grew up in families who placed little
emphasis on literacy practices that would neatly align with those convention-
ally valued in academic contexts. In fact, many of the behaviors that these
guides attribute to individual students would be more honestly attributed to
the schools those students attended. How many essays a student writes each
year in high school has much less to do with him or her as an individual and
much more to do with the academic culture of the high school.

Option 1: English 098	Option 2: English 150
I read newspapers and magazines regularly.	Generally, I don't read when I don't have to.
In the past year, I have read books for my own enjoyment.	In high school, I did not do much writing.
In high school, I wrote several essays per year.	My high school GPA was about average.
My high school GPA places me in the top third of my class.	I'm unsure about the rules of writing—commas, apostrophes, and so forth.
I have used computers for drafting and revising essays.	I've used computers, but not often for writing and revising.
My ACT-English score was above 20.	My ACT-English score was below 20.
I consider myself a good reader and writer.	I don't think of myself as a strong writer.
	I have been advised to take English 100 following a diagnostic writing.

Table 1. From the placement guide used at Grand Valley State University
(Royer & Gilles, 1998, pp. 56–57).

Surely, when entering students assess their past behaviors via DSP, they do
not just assess themselves. Students evaluate an index of innumerable social
and cultural factors, many of which are both raced and classed—their previous
schools, English teachers, parents, siblings, racial identities, class backgrounds,
languages of origin, and more. They place the social forces that have shaped
their behaviors on a continuum of college preparation (e.g., "My high school

was the best in the state, and I did OK there, so I belong in advanced writing." "No one from my neighborhood has ever attended a four-year institution, so I must belong in basic writing." "Students with my color skin on this campus seem to opt for basic writing, and therefore I won't cut it as a college writer without extra help.") Certainly writing programs do not intend to send the message that students acquire these college-preparatory writing behaviors in a vacuum. Yet implicit in these lists is the message that individual students have acted out isolated behavior patterns that either did or did not prepare them for college writing. This message reinforces the "racialized rationality" that students who are "prepared" for college writing have earned that designation through personal effort alone. Those who are "unprepared" have only themselves to blame.

Of course, administrators do not design DSP guides to be the last word in twenty-first century definitions of writing ability; they are meant to prompt reflection, discussion, and ultimately, a choice. Self-placement guides offer only a small glimpse into the much more complex and contextualized reflective process of DSP overall. Administrators likely expect that students will consider an infinite number of personal and social factors that would be impossible to anticipate and then include on a guide. What's more, when mailing guides to entering students, administrators usually attach letters that urge "students to consult with parents, teachers, and counselors" before deciding on an appropriate first-year writing course (Royer & Gilles, 2003, p. 2). Finally, most DSP programs offer the chance for students to meet with academic advisors to discuss if their previous experiences have prepared them for college writing. Indeed, CSUF's guide is situated in a student-friendly brochure that includes detailed course descriptions and advice from the writing program. Yet neither course descriptions nor advice from the writing program fully accounts for the social contexts of students' self–assessments.

Recent studies support a broader, more contextualized understanding of students' self-assessments. Bedore and Rossen-Knill's (2004) evaluation of the DSP program at University of Rochester indicates that "informing students of their writing choices should involve more than mass communication of college standards of writing" (p. 70). They find that students make more informed and authentic choices when their placement process is enriched with critical dialogue about actual writing either with a counselor during orientation or a writing instructor during the first few weeks of class. Furthermore, Gere et al. (2010) found that "DSP questions guided the decisions of only a small percentage of students" and that interview responses showed students remembering the choices of their peers as one guiding factor in their placement decision (p. 164).

Both of these studies reiterate the importance of context, specifically the complex social lives of students, but neither addresses the racialized nature of these contexts. In order for DSP to confront the "racialized rationalities" of composition course placement, it will need to contextualize the full range of self-assessments required for students to situate themselves in a new landscape of reading and writing expectations. Without adequately contextualizing students' self-assessments, the rhetoric of DSP placement guides risks sending the message that racial inequalities in writing programs are student-generated—reflective of the choices of individual students.

In order to choose your option, read the descriptions below and decide which of the three best describes your reading and writing abilities.		**OPTION 3** *I spoke another language besides English when growing up,* *OR* *a language other than English is used in my home.* **AND** *I am fluent in spoken English but it takes me a long time to read and write in English.*
OPTION 1 *I think of myself as a strong reader and writer.*	**OPTION 2** *I think of myself as an average reader and writer.*	
READING:		**READING AND VOCABULARY:**
I am comfortable reading complex essays and take notes as I read.	I feel reading can be boring and hard and I don't really do much other than just read and put it away.	I often lose the meaning when I read because I get stuck on words I don't understand.
When I read, I make connections to other things I have read or experienced as a means of understanding a reading.	When I read, I am still not sure what the author's point was, and it is difficult to explain how the reading relates to anything.	I find it challenging to follow main point from section to section when I read.
I feel comfortable identifying the structure and organization of the things I read.	I would like to learn more about how writers connect and organize ideas in their writing.	I want to develop my vocabulary for college-level English.
WRITING:		**WRITING:**
I do well finding topics to write about and I can relate my ideas to the ideas of others.	I have trouble coming up with good topics and ideas for my essays.	I have ideas for writing but it's difficult to express my ideas, so I usually don't write very much..
I have effective strategies for outlining and organizing my writing.	I am unsure of myself when I plan my writing and could use tips on planning strategies.	
I feel comfortable doing research, know how to locate and evaluate sources and relate them to my own writing.	I need to improve my research skills and learn how to use outside sources in my writing.	When I make paragraphs, the point isn't always clear and the sentences don't seem to flow.
I am confident about the conventions of grammar, punctuation, and spelling.	I could use some brushing up on grammar and punctuation.	I need help with writing effective sentences and editing grammar mistakes in my writing.
CONCLUSION:		**CONCLUSION:**
I am ready to work at a quick pace, with the instructor as my guide.	*I would prefer to get more practice and help from my instructor as I learn to write college-level assignments.*	*I prefer to take an extra semester to work on my English before taking English 5A and 5B.*
ENGLISH 10	**ENGLISH 5A AND 5B**	**LINGUISTICS 6**

Table 2. From the placement guide used by California State University, Fresno (Inoue, 2008, p. 110).

DSP In Dialogue

Yet, DSP can offer another possibility for students and writing programs. DSP can help writing programs take strides toward racial equity by contextualizing students' assessments of their readiness for college writing within their complicated social histories. This kind of contextualized message about writing readiness would confront rather than rationalize the racial inequities embedded in students' self-assessments, and it would acknowledge that "readiness" for academic discourse is a racialized construct. In "Applications and Assumptions of Student Self-Assessment" (2000), Moore Howard provides the blueprint for a mode of self-assessment that fits these purposes. She suggests administrators provide students with materials that encourage what she calls a "dialogic" self-assessment. These include materials that contextualize the behaviors necessary for successful writing in particular courses, and then ask students to assess their readiness for college writing in relation to those new contexts (p. 53). "One essential component of a dialogic rather than hierarchical self-assessment," she says, "is the provision of local context, so that the student has recourse not just to context-free, 'objective' categories of 'ability,' but to the context-specific exercise of writing" (p. 41). She also suggests that self-assessments focus less on general concepts like "ability" and "self" and more on specific and contextualized "deeds"—"the deeds of past and future writing instruction and experiences" so that students may "imagine the relative difficulty or ease with which they will accomplish those deeds" (p. 53).

To achieve a dialogic model of self-assessment on DSP placement guides, writing program administrators should shift the emphasis away from acontextual questions and toward questions that contextualize students' writing backgrounds. Table 3 proposes ways that several of GVSU's and CSUF's prompts about students' previous literacy behaviors could be revised to contextualize students' self-assessments.

The first two revised prompts add more specificity to students' self-assessments about previous reading and writing behaviors by detailing the genre conventions specific to assignments in college writing classrooms. For example, if a college writing course will assign mostly non-fiction and persuasive essays, this sort of detail should be passed on to the student. Likewise, if students are expected to read long novels, guides should encourage students to reflect on their previous experiences reading and understanding long novels. DSP guides should encourage entering students to consider the number, length, and genre of the essays they wrote in a typical high school semester. This sort of specificity and contextualization helps students better compare their past and future writing behaviors as well as communicate a program's appreciation for the local, contextualized, and often highly varied measures of literacy that are defined across different neighborhoods, schools, and classrooms.

Adding genre-specific information to students' self-assessments also sends the message that reading and writing are context-specific acts. Apart from these additions of genre information, however, my revisions do not change the content of the prompts. For the most part, they simply reframe the language of the prompts to emphasize the local contexts in which students performed their previous literacy activities. Rather than ask students if they have enjoyed or have been successful as readers and writers in general, my revised prompts locate those self-assessments within the most relevant local literacy context for entering college students—high school classes. Even broad measures like grammar and punctuation should be framed within the local context of school, for students' control of grammar and punctuation may have served them just fine in their text messages, song lyrics, or poems, but failed to serve them well in school.

GVSU & CSUF Prompts for Stretch Options	Proposed Revisions
Generally, I don't read when I don't have to.	I have rarely enjoyed or understood complicated non-fiction and persuasive essays assigned in school.
In high school, I did not do much writing.	My high school did not frequently assign writing that: • required me to analyze complex texts. • used quotes from multiple sources. • was 5 pages or longer.
I've used computers, but not often for writing and revising.	My school and/or home gave me plenty of access to computers and the Internet, so I'm confident I can research, write, and revise college essays using the computer.
I need to improve my research skills and learn how to use outside sources in my writing.	My high school classes did not prepare me to conduct research and use outside sources in my writing.
I could use some brushing up on grammar and punctuation.	My teachers often advised me to improve my grammar and punctuation on writing assignments.

Table 3. Proposed revision of placement guide prompts.

While administrators and counselors may resist asking students uncomfortable questions about racial discrimination, parent income, or school ranking when entering students show up for orientation, we can ask students what factors may have influenced their writing activities before college. Why not ask students how they believe their family, previous school, or community has helped prepare them to succeed in the college writing course described in a DSP guide?

The inclusion of contextual questions like these during the placement process may or may not radically alter the ways students place themselves into the hierarchy of first-year courses. However, the rhetoric of DSP placement guides indeed composes a part of the racial project of composition course placement. Though a revision of this rhetoric will never eradicate the racial project of DSP altogether (for all assessments are inherently racial projects of one kind or another), it can help to expose the persistent ways that our assessments operate as racial projects.

Royer and Gilles (2003) argue that the difference between DSP and previous placement methods is that, with DSP, students who place into basic writing "[see] themselves as poor readers and writers. In the past, we had done the seeing for them" (p. 62). The shift toward student agency they mention here will not realize its potential for social and curricular change until those students can see what social forces helped to construct the identity of the "unprepared" reader or writer. DSP should and can ask students to see "preparation for college writing" as a construction that they might reflect on and change.

Notes

---

[1]Critics like Bartholomae (1993), Shor (1997), Crowley (1998), Soliday (2002), and, more recently, Ritter (2009) and Stanley (2010) maintain that institutions construct student need according to shifting, contextual, and self-serving definitions of literacy, not the expressed interests of students.

[2] Issues of race and class always intersect; however, my focus in this essay is specifically on issues of race. Though I do not specifically name other modes of difference and inequality (like class, gender, ethnicity, sexuality, language of origin, disability, etc.), I understand race as an organizing concept that both shapes and is shaped by a complicated web of other social structures.

CHAPTER TEN

The Muse of Difference: Race and Writing Placement at Two Elite Art Schools

Anthony Lioi and Nicole M. Merola

Faculty in the liberal arts at the Juilliard School in New York City and at the Rhode Island School of Design (RISD) in Providence regularly speak about the ways in which their students demand a unique approach to classroom teaching, especially in the teaching of writing. Yet, the issue of difference at elite art schools—in race, nation, gender, sexual orientation, and class—remains to be systematically explored, especially in the arena of writing assessment.[1] In this essay we examine the technology of the writing placement exam at our respective institutions. In offering case studies of placement testing at our institutions, we investigate how inflections of race, class, and nationality resonate in institutional discourses about writing and in the process of placement assessment. In describing our particular situations, we illustrate our agreement with Huot (2002a) regarding validity that the "value of an assessment can only be known and accountable to a specific context" (p. 99). At Juilliard the specific context necessitated a writing test that would place students into an ELL course, a basic writing course, or the beginning of the Liberal Arts core sequence. In the past, placement decisions had been based on assessment of student records rather than assessment of student writing. At RISD the context demanded a revised writing test to place students with no or low SAT, ACT, or TOEFL scores into either a developmental writing course or a college-level writing course. After discussing our local contexts and placement exams, we conclude with practical advice for colleagues facing similar issues so they might draw from our experiences in tailoring their own local placement practices.

The "art school"—a tertiary institution whose mission includes the liberal education of students majoring in the performing, fine, or design arts—has rarely been the subject of inquiry in composition studies. Given that art schools attract a diverse population of students, including English Language Learner populations as high as 40% of the student body, the question of diversity in writing assessment is important. Yet, in part because art schools were not the scene of conflict during the liberation movements of the 1960s, the open admissions policies of the 1960s and '70s, or the culture wars of the 1980s and '90s, discourse about racial and cultural difference in these schools is underdeveloped or absent. Further complicating dialogue about race and writing assessment at art schools is a fundamental tension between the institutional identity of the art school as an engine of professional training and its duty to provide the skills of the liberal arts to a diverse student body. Yet, artists need writing skills to communicate with one another, the public, and funding institutions—what might be called an "esoteric need"—and to participate in white-collar supplemental work, the day job—the "exoteric need."

Moreover, art schools share an increasing vulnerability to market forces in their fields; even graduates of elite art schools cannot count on immediate employment in their major field. As Todd (1989) explains, artists need liberal arts instruction, such as writing, "to ensure the development of their theoretical and analytical skills as well as to help them understand their cultural heritage and to form their personal values" (p. 13). Because of the exoteric and esoteric need for writing in the life of an artist, the processes of writing assessment that track art students into different trajectories within a liberal arts curriculum may shape their professional fate in profound and unpredictable ways.

Because art schools are different from universities in form, function, and history, we take a moment to clarify why the standard narrative scholars tell about the development of assessment technologies, such as the one told in the California State system that Asao B. Inoue details in this collection, does not describe the art school milieu. Yancey (1999) describes the history of assessment as a series of "waves," but this approach implies too much coherence when applied to art schools. Many art schools do not have an English department, writing faculty, or a writing curriculum. Likewise, most art schools lack systematic, reliable recording of student data or any recognizable discourse on assessment. New faculty thus face a partially untraceable history of idiosyncratic local practices that cannot be fitted into the traditional meta-narrative of assessment technologies. As one of our colleagues put it, "It's a real Mom-and-Pop shop around here." In our experience, Juilliard and RISD have approached assessment technologies in piecemeal fashion.[2] For example, until 2008, Juilliard employed no assessment technology. Instead, students were assessed on the basis of SAT scores, or incomplete records if no SAT score was available, by faculty not trained in composition. Likewise, the English Department at RISD has been administering some form of placement exam for at least 15 years. During this time, the exam content has changed numerous times; until 2010, however, the exam generally privileged the assessment of visual texts over the assessment of written texts.

Given that the art school demographic is likely unfamiliar to most of our readers, we describe broadly the significant local institutional trends that directly affect writing assessment and writing instruction at Juilliard and RISD. Both schools similarly manifest a student body best described as an "international artistic elite," even though the extent to which each student body is "international" is different. Our students may already excel in their chosen performing, design, or fine arts field, but they may simultaneously be under-prepared for college-level courses in the liberal arts. Another important factor at our institutions, directly linked to the focused nature of the students who pursue education at Juilliard and RISD, is the primary mode of affiliation through which students form their social groups. The intensity of professional self-identification among art students gives racialization a special shape at art schools. Although at each institution this phenomenon presents differently, students at both institutions tend to identify themselves in artistic rather than racial or national terms. One hears remarks that use "cellist" and "dancer" or "apparel girls" and "architecture kids" as markers of a caste, even a worldview. In suggesting that our students take professional labels taxonomically, we do not mean that race disappears from the picture, only that students want to see a color-blind meritocracy in which their professional skill is paramount. However, as Gilroy (2000) reminds us, this kind of thinking is less innocent than it may seem, having been formed in the larger context of Western systems of race in the last two centuries: "Raciology has saturated the discourses in which it circulates. It cannot be readily re-signified or de-signified, and to imagine that its dangerous meanings can be easily rearticulated into benign, democratic forms would be to exaggerate the power of critical and oppositional interests" (p. 12).

However, as we explain below, while our students might prefer to foreground the post-racial category of profession as their primary marker of identification, the writing placement exam at each institution functions as a location where older forms of identity (race and nation, most significantly) come into contact with the professional identities our students want to privilege. That is, the writing placement exam and its segregating outcomes become a location where professional and racial identities come into conflict. The desire of our students to speak about and affiliate themselves according to professional identity makes visible an interesting tension between the ways they want to position themselves—foremost as a member of a group that coalesces around a particular skill set or vocation—and the ways the technology of the placement exam tends to aggregate them—according to racial and national identity. In the next sections, we describe how the placement technologies used at our respective institutions shape race along familiar lines that are shared by other kinds of institutions and along exceptional lines that make art schools a peculiar environment for assessment.

The Juilliard School: Race And The Art Of Placement

Founded in 1905 to develop an American alternative to European conservatories (Olmstead, 1999, p. 7), Juilliard now attracts a high percentage of "minority" and "international" students. In AY 2008–2009, of approximately 750 students, graduate and undergraduate students, 41.3% were minority students and 36.2% international students. It is important to note that Juilliard follows the racial categories of the U.S. Census and that students are double-counted if they are not American citizens or permanent residents and also not "white"—e.g., Mexican citizen and "minority" (K. Gertson, personal communication, January 5, 2009). Like its host city, Juilliard is at once profoundly cosmopolitan and deeply "islanded," a synthesis of elite tastes, a blue-collar work ethic, and a strong sense of place.

Juilliard supports three divisions—Music, Dance, and Drama—and each of these divisions is "raced" in its own way. Dance and Drama—the youngest divisions—are also the most traditional: their students are mostly white, middle-class U.S. citizens. Though the Music Division is the oldest stratum and began as a European-style conservatory, it now contains the majority of African American students and international students, mostly European and Asian students. A significant number of the white, U.S. students in Music have been home-schooled.

Placement procedures had to consider if students belonged in an English Language Learner class, a basic writing class, or the first semester of the required Liberal Arts core curriculum. Before the introduction of a universal writing placement test in 2008, students were placed in these classes by an assessment of their records (e.g., SAT scores) and educational background, not their writing. This method created a single section of basic writing in which students' skills varied widely, though they were predominately African American, home-schooled, and English Language Learners. As defined by Huot et al. (2010), there was neither content validity—since there was no test that contained writing—nor construct validity—since the assessment of student background could not be standardized to measure ability against the expectations of the Liberal Arts core (pp. 505–506).[3] In sum, the interpretations being drawn about student writing ability could not be defended given current definitions of validity.

Interdivisional Liberal Arts, the academic unit in charge of placement and the writing courses themselves, had constructed through its previous placement mechanisms the category of the "underprepared student." In doing so, it had become stigmatized in a system that valued techniques of audition—such as playing behind a screen—that sought to impede stereotypes of race and gender. This sense that it is possible to compensate for racism and sexism by changing the conditions of artistic judgment reinforces the meritocratic story students rehearse of the artist on a quest for self-expression and world-improvement. In this story, the school was a progressive force, while Liberal Arts was regressive, setting up the "academic" part of the curriculum as a remnant of the old days. By stigmatizing students with inadequate placement technologies, Liberal Arts set itself up to be stigmatized in return, creating a negative feedback loop that compromised the legitimacy of writing instruction. Though they did not, of course, employ a formal academic term to describe this situation, the basic writing students made it clear that Liberal Arts had created a state of constant distrust through its reductive placement process. For the new Director of Writing and Public Speaking—the WPA for a school without a writing program—the responsibility was readily apparent. The first task of any new technology would be to unmake this state of distrust.

Though we were familiar with machine-based placement, self-directed placement, and portfolio review, we chose a timed, impromptu essay test to be taken on the first day of student orientation at the beginning of the year. While this choice may seem regressive relative to the dominant narrative of technological development in writing assessment, we chose a timed, impromptu test because it was both practically and institutionally a better first step than other assessment methods. In comparison, machine-based placement would have seemed both impersonal and pedestrian in the Juilliard arts culture. Some version of self-directed placement may become feasible as the Liberal Arts curriculum stabilizes after a recent round of revision, but it presents its own difficulties: the multinational character of the students and their lack of a common understanding of U.S. college culture; the need to address second language writing issues in the curriculum (Hamp-Lyons, 2009, p. 346); and the paucity of writing courses to choose from posed challenges that we could not initially address. (Lewis Ketai in this collection also addresses potential issues with DSP for students of color.)

The timed essay test, on the other hand, allows for a reading to be distributed in advance of student arrival so that students can read and digest the material. The experience of the common test situation creates a moment of isomorphism with other testing practices that surround admission. Students are required over the summer to read a long piece of journalistic or academic prose related to questions of ethics, the subject of the first Liberal Arts core class. Though the exam prompt is withheld until the moment of the exam, students are instructed to be prepared to accurately summarize the text, respond to the text with a position of their own, and apply their analysis to an ethical case of their own choice. They have 90 minutes to compose. Exams are scored holistically by three faculty members. Based on the results, students are placed in the core course, basic writing, or in an ELL writing course.

Racial Formation in Basic Writing	Fall 2007 placement	Fall 2007 % in basic writing	Fall 2010 placement	Fall 2010 % in basic writing	% Change in basic writing
African American/ Black (U.S. citizen and international)	4	29%	2	5%	-24%
Asian (international)	7	50%	17	41%	-9%
White (U.S. citizen and international)	2	14%	22	52%	+39%
Asian/American Indian/AK Native (U.S. citizen)	1	7%	0	0%	-7%
Hispanic/Latino/a (U.S. citizen and international)	0	0%	1	2%	+2%
Total Enrollment	14	100%	42	100%	

Table 1. Change in Enrollment in Basic Writing by Race:
Before and After Implementation of Placement Exam
(Office of the Registrar, The Juilliard School, personal communication, February 1, 2011).

To date, we believe that the changes made to the assessment process have resulted in a more valid assessment because the content of the new placement test reflects the content of the Liberal Arts core. The conclusions we are making from test results have meaningful consequences for entering Juilliard students. A secondary effect of these changes was an alteration in the racial formations of basic writing, as reflected in Table 1.

As shown in Table 1, with the advent of the placement exam, the racial makeup of the students in the basic writing course changed dramatically. In terms of relative numbers, the percentage of African American students placed in the basic writing course dropped from 29% to 5% of the group, the percentage of Asian students has dropped from 50% to 41%, while the percentage of white students increased from 13% to 52%. There are now four sections of the basic writing course rather than one and a population in those classes more representative of the general racial composition of the student body. Beyond these demographic changes, the final effect of the new assessment has been a change throughout the school in ideas about the purpose and rationale of basic writing instruction.

RISD: What We Fail To Discuss When We Discuss The Writing Placement Exam

From its beginnings in 1877 as a school meant to teach "useful arts as, for example, designing for calico printers, for jewelers' designs, for carriage and furniture making" (McCabe, 1994), the Rhode Island School of Design has grown into one of the premier art and design schools in the world. In alignment with its current mission—"to educate its students and the public in the creation and appreciation of works of art and design, to discover and transmit knowledge and to make lasting contributions to a global society through critical thinking, scholarship and innovation" (RISD, "About RISD," 2012a, para. 1)—RISD has five divisions: Architecture and Design, Fine Arts, Foundation Studies, Graduate Studies, and Liberal Arts. Within the division of Liberal Arts exist three departments: English, History of Art and Visual Culture (HAVC), and History, Philosophy, and Social Sciences (HPSS).

In three ways relevant to our analysis of writing placement technologies, RISD differs from Juilliard. The institution is larger: RISD enrolled approximately 2,300 undergraduates in AY 2008–2009 (*Rhode Island School of Design Catalog*, 2008). The RISD Admissions Committee evaluates both artistic facility and traditional academic preparation (E. Newhall, personal communication, October 10, 2008). And, in terms of racial and national identity, the student body at RISD is significantly different than at Juilliard. For AY 2008–2009 RISD advertised a student body comprised of 24% "students of color" and 16% "international" students, though these statistics mislead. As does Juilliard, RISD double counts many "international" students as "students of color"[4]. Disengaging these numbers from each other makes it apparent that RISD's undergraduate population comprises 8% U.S.-born students of color and 16% international students. Of these international students, approximately half come from South Korea. One factor that contributes to this demographic difference is RISD's limited ability to disburse financial aid to all admitted students who need it. Because of the ways in which class and race overlap, the admitted students who must turn elsewhere for their art and design education are often U.S.-born students of color[5]. While some faculty express concern regarding the ways these demographics impact the classroom, as a whole the institution chronically undertheorizes how the racial, economic, and national backgrounds of its students shape its academic programs. The writing placement exam administered by the English Department represents one microcosm wherein the material effects of such undertheorization become visible.

During the admissions process, the academic records and educational background of all students are scrutinized; "underperforming" students are subject to a second technology—the placement exam. Leaving aside discussion of the problems in using academic records and educational backgrounds to subject a group of students to an additional assessment technology, the following discussion examines RISD's placement exam. Below we highlight the effects of placing a student in the developmental writing course, Fundamentals of Writing, and discuss how we attempted to address the undertheorization of the previous placement exam evaluation process.

Placing a student in Fundamentals has a marked impact on the first-year experience in that it separates students from other students in their cohort; this impact trickles into the second year as well. First, placement into Fundamentals imposes a visibly different rhythm on the schedule of these students. The schedule of Foundation Studies studios, which meet three days a week for at least eight hours a day, dictates the timetable for all first-year courses in Liberal Arts. So, students who share a Foundation Studies section also likely share a section of English and/or Art History. A student in Fundamentals, however, meets for his or her English class in the late afternoon or evening, after most classes have finished for the day. Students in Fundamentals are therefore in class while their peers gather to socialize or work together in the studio, a circumstance that affects their personal and professional bonds. Second, successful completion of the first-year writing course called Literature Seminar: Design in Words (E101) is the gateway for all other English courses and also for the required History, Philosophy, and the Social Sciences (HPSS 101) course most students take during the spring of their freshman year. So, students initially placed into Fundamentals must take E101 in the spring of first year and HPSS 101 during the fall of second year, effectively delaying their entrance into elective English and the HPSS course.

The temporal segregation of the students in Fundamentals is visible to all the first-year students. A further bifurcation, primarily visible within each section of the course, augments this separation in that ELL students and basic writing students often have different instructional needs. The difficulty of contending with two distinctly different sets of instructional needs results, in practice, in the construction of two unofficial tracks within Fundamentals. In order to progress to E101, for example, some basic writing students tend to need more instruction and practice with reading comprehension and analysis, help truly developmental in nature. English Language Learners, on the other hand, might have analytical capabilities that would allow them to succeed in

E101, but they require more instruction in making their written work conform to the conventions of college-level writing in English. Whereas some basic writing students benefit most from spending more time reading, ELL students benefit most from writing exercises. In splitting students according to the instructional need, therefore, Fundamentals has effectively divided into native-speaker and ELL sections.

Although Fundamentals students express concern about temporal separation from their studio cohort more often than anxiety about stereotypes associated with their writing placement, expressions regarding professionalized social bonds may well stand in for their racially and nationally inflected understanding of their placement. Even though students fervently desire to maintain the self-constructed narrative of primary identification with professional identity, the institutional practice of the placement exam makes doing so a difficult prospect.

Given the way placement in Fundamentals correlates with race and nationality and the material effects of such placement on the first and second years, assessing the validity of the placement exam itself was crucial. Prior to fall 2010, the exam focused primarily on visual material. For instance, in one former incarnation of the exam, students were asked to summarize and analyze the visual content of a painting. Another former iteration of the exam asked students to discuss the relationship between a cartoon and three paragraphs of introductory text from the book in which the cartoon appeared. While the inclusion of visual material on the placement exam acknowledged "the visual thinker" and, therefore, conformed to RISD's art and design context, these previous placement exams were suspect in that they included minimal writing. That is, they did not contain "adequate content to measure the desired ability or trait" (Huot et al., 2010, p. 505). And, it was unclear whether asking students to evaluate and analyze visual material would correlate with success in either Fundamentals or E101. Including visual material as an "out" for art school students, we suggest, actually makes it more difficult to determine whether students possess the necessary skills for reading complicated written texts and producing the kinds of argument demanded in compelling college-level writing. Furthermore, given the population of students required to take the placement exam, we found the phrase "visual thinker" to have the pernicious effect that Gilroy (2000) warns against in that it covertly indexed a racialized population[6].

Placement tests given prior to 2010 tended to produce a Fundamentals classroom that was overwhelmingly comprised of students of color and ELL students. Upon investigation, we found the demographics of Fundamentals, and its lack of isomorphism with the demographics in E101 or the school as a whole, were symptomatic of a deeper issue with the placement exam.

Although some members of the English Department saw little reason to change the placement test, other members pushed for implementing a new exam; discussion of whether, and if so how, to change the exam took place at two different department meetings during AY 2009–2010. Taking the content of these discussions under advisement, the head of the department devised a new English Department placement test. Given for the first time in fall 2010, the new exam consisted of a 500-word newspaper article on a contemporary artwork. Students encountered the article for the first time at the exam and were given 90 minutes to read the article, summarize it, comment on elements of the author's style, and offer an evaluation of the artwork using textual evidence from the article. Anecdotally, these slight improvements to the exam made a difference. According to the Head of the English Department, the exam better identified students who would most benefit from taking Fundamentals (P. Barbeito, personal communication, January 8, 2011).

As of writing this chapter, the impact of the new placement test on the demographics of the Fundamentals and E101 classrooms is unknown. In order to help the department assess its placement technologies, we are embarking on a project to track the progress of students placed in Fundamentals to see how they fare during their course of study at RISD. This project will also track those students with low test scores placed in E101 and compare their four-year performance with students from the Fundamentals courses. The results of this project will help us continue to fine-tune the two placement technologies currently in use at RISD: the scores that flag a student for the placement test and the content of the test itself.

Given local institutional conditions, the RISD English Department is unlikely to adopt a placement technology other than the timed, impromptu test.[7] Within this constraint, however, we still have much to improve with respect to the overall validity of our placement process. A universal placement exam would do away with having to decide which test scores flag a student for the exam. Asking all students to perform their facility with reading, writing, and analysis would be familiar to RISD students, all of whom submit as part of their admission materials a drawing of a bicycle. Although no one labels the bicycle drawing a universal drawing test, it effectively functions as such. And, the way in which this drawing registers a student's facility with line, perspective, and "experimental thinking and risk taking" is, in theory, blind to racial, national, and other forms of identity because it does not single out single specific students for additional assessment (RISD, "Apply," 2012b, para. 8). To echo the bicycle drawing with a writing placement test that asks students to read, comprehend, analyze, and write about the kinds of material they will encounter in their courses would democratize the RISD writing classroom. It would also render the technology of placement visible to all students while simultaneously making apparent to them the intellectual and discursive levels at which they would need to function in their English courses. So far, the English Department has resisted the idea of a universal placement test, primarily due to workload, budget, and scheduling issues. Until we can achieve the most democratic scenario, the department would do well to revisit the scores that determine a student's inclusion in placement exam testing and to further refine the validity of the exam, making the material about which students will write more consistent with the kinds of material they will encounter in the Fundamentals or E101 classrooms into which they will be placed.

Conclusions

As we noted in the beginning of this chapter, the dearth of previous writing assessment scholarship on art schools along with the constraints of our local contexts made developing effective writing assessments difficult. Yet, we have been able to make progress at our institutions and, in doing so, are working to make our assessments more valid for all students. Given our experiences, we offer some tentative conclusions that we hope will set the stage for richer inquiry into writing assessment in art school contexts. In order to address issues of race and assessment at art schools, we suggest the following:

- Assess the category of "art school" itself as a meaningful analytic tool for the construction of placement technologies and the history of placement technologies.
- Engage in a heuristic practice of placement, considering all available technologies (portfolio, exam, self-directed placement, etc.) as they potentially operate in the culture of the art school.
- Understand the racial composition of the student body, and, moreover, the categories by which this composition is characterized, using the best data available. It should be noted that racial categories are often inconsistent relative to other schools and to earlier records at the same school. One school may use the categories of the national census, and another may count "white students" versus "students of color" with no further differentiation. Though this will result in incommensurable records, making comparisons difficult, such incommensurability is itself an important datum about the discourse of race at any given institution.
- Understand the various taxonomical regimes used to categorize students into identity groups, not just the regimes of the faculty and administra-

tion, but those of the students themselves, as they relate to placement and other modes of assessment.

- Analyze the local discourse surrounding the liberal arts, and writing in particular, including the "buzz" about assessment practices in the student body, the faculty, and the administration, and how that institutional discourse contributes to or rebukes racial stereotypes. Data to be considered include: mission statements, course catalogue copy, student orientation materials, and oral traditions.

Keeping all of this in mind, we urge colleagues at other art schools to confront the history of race and writing assessment at their own institutions and to communicate the results of their work to the profession through collaborative scholarship and other forms of collegial communication. The muse of difference demands no less. We also believe the art school contexts detailed above have broader implications for all who assess student writing. By providing two institutional examples of the crucial role that race and nation play in writing placement, we illustrate and emphasize the necessity of investigating the particular contours of our institutional contexts. In doing so, we underline how every institutional location will generate specific sets of intersections between race, nation, other forms of identity. Therefore, we encourage all colleagues involved with writing assessment to attend to the intersections most salient to their institutional conditions as they seek to refashion their own placement practices.

Notes

[1] The lack of scholarship in composition studies at art schools stems, in part, from the small pool of tenure-track faculty at these institutions who are trained in rhetoric and composition. Institutional attitudes toward writing, and more generally toward the liberal arts, at art schools also contribute.

[2] At Juilliard, Anthony teaches in the Interdivisional Liberal Arts, a division composed of 12 regular and two adjunct faculty. The two adjunct faculty teach composition exclusively. Of the regular faculty, two teach sections of composition each semester and three teach composition once every three years. At RISD, Nicole teaches in the Department of English, which is housed in the Division of Liberal Arts. Ten tenure-track and 24 adjunct faculty comprise the department. Roughly half the tenure-track faculty teach one or two sections of E101 each year. Adjunct faculty teach the rest of the E101 sections and all the Fundamentals sections each year.

[3] Huot et al. (2010) follow Cronbach and Messick in understanding validity as a unitary concept, arguing that "any claim for validity must address construct validity, which includes issues of content and criterion validity" (p. 507).

[4] Like Juilliard, RISD employs United States Census racial categories on any forms that students complete.

[5] One effect of the relatively low discount rate at RISD is that most of the international students, who are of course ineligible for federal and much private U.S.-based aid, pay full tuition. This sets up interesting class-based distinctions among the students in which there is disparity about the "visibility" of class between the U.S.-born students and the international students. In other words, the U.S.-born students, even if they do not receive assistance, could, and are therefore not assumed to be upper class in the ways the international students are.

[6] In making this argument we do not mean to devalue visual literacy. In fact, such literacy constitutes an essential element of art and design education. Although members of the department do utilize visual materials in our classrooms, helping RISD students develop and refine their acuity vis-à-vis visual material is generally understood as the primary purview of the studio departments.

[7] The reasons RISD uses a timed, impromptu test rather than machine-based placement, self-directed placement, or portfolio review are those Anthony identifies as salient for the Juilliard context.

Beyond Composition Placement Assessment

In his 2011 statement on International Literacy Day, UN Secretary-General Ban Ki-moon proclaims, "Literacy unlocks the capacity of individuals to imagine and create a more fulfilling future. It opens the way to greater justice, equality and progress. Literacy can help societies heal, advance political processes and contribute to the common good" (para. 3). In his book *College Admissions for the 21ˢᵗ Century* (2010), Sternberg echoes this hope, detailing Project Kaleidoscope, a college admissions assessment that attempts to tap potential students' wisdom and ultimately their "capacity for positive leadership" (p. 120). Students at Tufts University, who first took part in Project Kaleidoscope, wrote essays to demonstrate those qualities.

Ban and Sternberg remind us that there is a world beyond composition studies that seeks to tap the promise of writing for peace, development, and leadership. In this spirit, the authors in this section look beyond writing programs to college admissions and international comparative assessments, providing us two very different perspectives on the promises and perils of writing assessment beyond college composition programs and classrooms. They posit that students' experiences are often not accounted for in assessments; because those experiences are often quite different for students of color and poor students, assessments account for only a small segment of the "lived curriculum," often the curriculum of white, middle-class families.

In "College Admissions and the Insight Resume: Writing, Reflection, and Students' Lived Curriculum as a Site of Equitable Assessment," Kathleen Blake Yancey shows how one innovation in college admissions assessment may better account for the diverse experiences that our students bring with them. She describes the Insight Resume (IR), a compelling, new admissions technology developed at Oregon State University. The IR, Yancey writes, was designed to produce "a specific outcome congruent with the [institution's] mission and with the intellectual life of the university." IR questions tap into prospective students' experiences with leadership, creativity, ability to deal with adversity, community service, handling of systemic challenges, and task commitment. In doing so, the IR invites students to bring in the lived curriculum, not simply the delivered or experienced curriculum of schooling. Although Oregon State continues to use SAT scores (along with GPA) for making admissions decisions, the effects of the Insight Resume have been notable—namely increased numbers of students of color admitted and higher graduation rates for all students. Yet, Yancey also gives us a word of caution, noting that technologies such as the IR can easily be co-opted, and while knockoff versions of the IR offer the same promises, they cannot deliver.

We conclude the book with "Assessment in the French Context: Language Socialization, Socioeconomic Status, and the Implications of the Programme for International Student Assessment" by Élisabeth Bautier and Christiane Donahue. Bautier and Donahue take us to France where the PISA exam is administered, as it is in many countries, as part of OECD-sponsored testing. While PISA has been touted as a comparative measure, Bautier and Donahue show us that the exam does not accurately reflect French educational expectations and that it is particularly problematic for students "*en difficulté*." In pointing to the problems of international assessments that pay little attention not only to students' racialized backgrounds but also to the national educational contexts in which students learn to read and write, Bautier and Donahue draw primarily from French scholarship as well as the work of U.S. researchers, such as William Labov. As the field of composition studies grows internationally, we look forward to more scholarship such as this chapter, which, as Donahue has argued recently (2011), positions international contexts as both sites of study and as resources from which we all may learn.

CHAPTER ELEVEN

College Admissions and the Insight Resume: Writing, Reflection, and Students' Lived Curriculum as a Site of Equitable Assessment

Kathleen Blake Yancey

At some level, all writing assessments are about validity, and so it's appropriate to begin at the beginning: with validity. There are both many *definitions* of validity and many *dimensions* of validity, which is not surprising given that, as Murphy (2007) has pointed out, validity is "a complicated and changing theoretical construct that has evolved significantly over the past fifty years" (p. 229). Chief among the definitions, however, are three that work together. First, validity refers to the idea that an assessment measures what it purports to measure. Second, a measure is valid to the extent that it is ecological or consequential: that is, that it contributes to a learner. And third, a measure is valid if the interpretations and inferences it leads to are appropriate:

> [Validity] applies to how the scores are interpreted and to the actions that may be taken based on those interpretations, such as the decisions that are made about individual test-takers or the social policies that are instituted as a result of tests. (Murphy, 2007, p. 229)

Historically, college admissions testing has had a validity problem. Initially, no one pretended it was much more than an exercise in legacies: as Lemann (1999) demonstrates, the SAT was designed to shift American higher education from a legacy-based admissions system to a merit-based one. More recently, the College Board (CB) introduced a writing sample (along with a multiple choice test of editing) for the sake of enhancing its predictive validity and for its ecological effects: high school teachers, the CB claimed, would now teach more writing and the addition of the writing test to the SAT score would do a better job of predicting who would succeed in college. At the same time, however, these *are* the two changes we've seen in college admission testing in the last 80 years. And not surprisingly, we haven't seen much change, either, in the number of students of color admitted to college.[1]

Until now: Oregon State University (OSU) has developed a college admissions exercise called the Insight Resume, which calls on students to demonstrate two abilities or capacities: (1) their ability to learn life's lessons, and (2) their ability to articulate those lessons in a series of succinct reflective texts. In doing so, as we shall see, OSU's Insight Resume has accomplished three goals: (1) it has increased the number of students of color considerably; (2) in the process, it has contributed to a higher graduation rate for all students; and (3) it has demonstrated progress toward the idea that an equitable writing assessment is both feasible and valid—in its ability to measure what it purports to measure; in its effect on students; and in the equitable decisions it participates in.

College Admissions Testing

For students seeking admission to colleges that are not open admissions, being able to write well is critical. Although more than 800 schools have gone SAT optional, many schools still require the SAT impromptu essay accompanying a multiple choice test of editing skills. Most four-year postsecondary schools also require a piece of writing they design, typically an essay or personal statement. At Florida State University (FSU), for example, our requirement is for an essay no longer than 500 words whose topic varies every year. In the 2011 admissions cycle, the writing assignment asked students to consider their relationship to Florida State University's philosophy:

> The Latin words, "Vires, Artes, Mores" have been the guiding philosophy behind Florida State University. Vires signifies strength of all kinds—moral, physical, and intellectual; Artes alludes to the beauty of intellectual pursuits as exemplified in skill, craft, or art; and Mores refers to character, custom, or tradition. Describe how one or more of the values embodied in these concepts are reflected in your life. (para. 3, fourth bullet)

Across the country, students at UCLA are given a very different set of tasks; they are required to submit two personal statements. Everyone submits a general personal statement, and then each student submits a second personal statement depending on their status: first-year student; transfer student; or military veteran. Regardless of genre, these college-specific writing admission tasks offer the same opportunity, according to one former admissions officer: they provide the one "place where [the student gets] to say 'Hey, I'm a human being, let me connect with you on that level, here is my voice, here is who I am.'" (Mason, "Responses to This Entry," 2010, para. 2).

What precisely these writing assignments are measuring isn't entirely clear: put differently, the construct that they are tapping varies. In some cases, it might be a student's ability to speak in a unique voice about her experience in the context of a given college's values; in another to be persuasive about his learning as a solider; and in some others, to be persuasive and voiced while they also "relax," as advised by more than one website addressing potential college applicants. But in each of these rhetorical situations, what these writing assignments require are the writing dimensions, like focus and organization, that we assign to writing. At some level, in other words, these admission genres are measures of writing.

At the end of the twentieth century, however, a new approach was being developed, based in new contexts for testing, one of which is a moral context associated with issues of equity. As educational measurement expert Madaus (1993) puts it, we understand now that no technology is neutral, that "all technology including testing is inextricably embedded in a moral context" (p. 9). As Madaus (1993) explains:

> The equity issues are much more profound than those encapsulated in issues of item and text bias or how we will overcome present disparities in test performance by introducing an alternative form of testing. Nonetheless, [...] I approach the debate over the policy role of authentic assessment [that is, about how policy on assessment can forward educational achievement] from the point of view that testing is a technology and must be evaluated as such (Madaus, 1990). Granted, testing is not widely regarded as a *technology*, a word that usually conjures up images of major artifacts like computers, planes, televisions, and telephones (Pacey, 1989) [...] However, much of present technology is specialized arcane knowledge, hidden algorithms, and technical art; it is a complex of standardized means for attaining a predetermined end in social, economic, administrative, and educational institutions (Ellul, 1990; Lowrance, 1986). Testing, embedded in our system of education with its arcane psychometric underpinnings, clearly fits this definition of technology. (p. 11–12)

What we've learned during the last hundred years, in other words, is that testing constructs what it purports to measure as it serves *a predetermined end in social, economic, administrative, and educational institutions*. It does so largely through a technology embedded in a science that is, oddly enough, foreign to most educators. As critiqued by Madaus (1990), the notion of a bias-free test is (1) based on a false analogy between progress in science and progress in learning and (2) keyed to a culture of efficiency that increases in prominence as education seeks to serve larger numbers of students. In other words, any test is, as Madaus suggests, located inside a system, and in this case, it's a system where the ordinary circuits and circulations point in one primary direction: toward enhancing student performance.

The SAT, The Insight Resume, And New Assessment Outcomes

During the last 10 years particularly, the college admissions process has received a good deal of attention nationally. The SAT, for example, has come under increasing scrutiny and has functioned as something of a lightning rod for students, for colleges, and for assessment experts. For its advocates, the SAT provides a level playing field for students across the country, providing opportunity for all students and not for a select few; for its detractors, the SAT rewards the quick, the rich, the glib, the formulaic, and the a-contextual. More recently, this disagreement has been muted by the successful challenge to the College Board's claim that the SAT predicts collegiate success. Instead, as even the College Board concedes, the current single *best* predictor of success is high school grade point average; what's more, high school GPA predicts both initial collegiate success and later success.

Given questions about the value that the SAT contributes to the collegiate admissions process, as noted earlier, more than 800 colleges have gone SAT-optional (or given it up altogether), including some elite schools like Smith and Wake Forest. As important, without including SAT scores in the admissions process, these colleges are enrolling classes of students more diverse and at least as impressive as when they required the SAT as an admissions device.

Historically, of course, college admissions practices have influenced the collegiate landscape in some disproportionate ways, especially relative to writing, which is one reason to focus on them: they function as a bellwether practice in the assessment landscape. The Harvard admissions test of 1874 is often identified as the moment when postsecondary composition was born, for example. Likewise, the ubiquitous college essay—and possible plagiarism on the part of anxious college parents in assisting their children to author it—is touted as one value of the new so-called SAT writing test, where test authorship of the student is the point of reference despite the fact that the two writing occasions and genres—the SAT and the college essay—vary dramatically. Thus, in this context, any new college admissions practice, especially one located in writing and in authentic experience, is of particular interest.

A new practice, such as the "Insight Resume" at Oregon State University, is noteworthy for three reasons: first, it *intentionally* diversifies the student body; second, it does so by inviting students to articulate other kinds of learning; and third, it creates a new model of assessment to accomplish this aim. In this model, assessment is *designed for effects*. Rather than create an assessment that will produce results under a guise of disinterestedness, Oregon State designed an assessment to produce a specific outcome congruent with its mission and with the intellectual life of the university, and it did so in a way that is both theoretically grounded and empirically motivated.

It's useful to understand why Oregon State, like other institutions, might look for a new admissions measure. Basically, many colleges and universities have found that the SAT's traditional effect of homogenizing college populations was exacerbated once affirmative action, which was intended to provide space for diversity, met insurmountable legal obstacles. Since that time, college classes, especially at public flagship institutions, have become both whiter and richer. Much like Madaus, we might find this homogenizing objectionable on political, ethical, and/or equitable grounds; in fact, such grounds contextualized the widespread adoption of the SAT in the 1930s and 1940s in the first place. But the new argument isn't about the value of merit as an abstract concept so much as about intellectual development in a pluralistic society; it links admissions, the epistemology of the academy, and diversity. As Soares (2008) explains in An Open Letter to Faculty on Wake Forest's New Admissions Policy:

> This [University of California] report, "Does Diversity Matter in the Educational Process? An Exploration of Student Interactions by Wealth, Religion, Politics, Race, Ethnicity and Immigrant Status at the University of California," shows that student diversity is key to getting students to think about things from a social perspective different from their own. This is a very exciting report because it is the first to document and prove, statistically, the educational benefits of diversity. The US Supreme Court, and others, have asserted or assumed the cognitive advantages of diversity; this is the first study to quantify those benefits. (#12)

In other words, for students to develop intellectually, they need diverse perspectives that they acquire socially—that is, through interactions with people who are different. If all the students are the same, then such diverse perspectives aren't available. What's more, learning through these perspectives is a Deweyian exercise, taking place not through books alone but rather through social exchange.

The Insight Resume

Within this general context, Oregon State—a school with a highly homogeneous population—brought two specific motivations to their consideration of their admissions process. One motivation was related to their institutional mission. As admissions director Sandlin explained, Oregon State wanted to be able to assure access that was in line with its land grant mission. A second motivation related to evidence that SAT predictions about how Hispanic students would perform at OSU were, in a word, wrong: "Adding to the concern was a university study finding that for Hispanic students, SAT scores were significantly under-predicting academic performance once students enrolled" (Jaschik, 2007, para. 3). In sum, the impact of the SAT seemed at odds with both OSU's mission and its own data.

Like many institutions, Oregon State's previous admissions process included both SAT scores and grades, and ironically, the standardized test scores carried more weight for students with lower grades. To frame their thinking about how they might redesign their admissions process, Oregon State conducted a comprehensive review of their admissions process. Their findings were as follows:

1. Traditional measures of academic potential such as high school GPA and SAT scores do not give a complete picture of a student's potential for success in college, especially for students with GPAs below 3.25. Research indicates that these measures explain, at best, only 30% of the variation in first-year college GPA, which is a strong indicator of persistence in college.
2. Grade inflation raises additional concerns about the predictive value of high school GPAs below 3.25.
3. Traditional measures vary in reliability for different ethnic groups and genders.
4. Behavioral or non-cognitive factors such as positive self-concept and the ability to overcome obstacles in one's life have been shown to be positively associated with academic success in college, and in conjunction with quantitative measures such as high school GPA, they provide a more holistic assessment of individuals. This is especially true for particular groups of students, including students of color. Research conducted by Dr. William Sedlacek at the University of Maryland has confirmed the ability to measure these non-cognitive factors by asking students to complete a written behavioral assessment based on precisely worded questions. The use of the research-based written behavioral assessment is intended to provide more reliable predictive information than traditional essays or personal statements. (Oregon State University, "Research Analysis," 2003)

Based on these findings, Oregon State created what they call the Insight Resume (IR). This "written behavioral assessment" asks students to write to six questions intended to tap the kind of non-cognitive factors identified by Sedlacek, questions that also permit applicants to speak to their "special experiences." The six questions and their directions include these:

1. **Leadership/group contributions:** Describe examples of your leadership experience in which you have significantly influenced others, helped resolve disputes, or contributed to group efforts over time. Consider responsibilities to initiatives taken in or out of school.
2. **Knowledge in a field/creativity:** Describe any of your special interests and how you have developed knowledge in these areas. Give examples of your creativity; the ability to see alternatives; take diverse perspectives; come up with many, varied, or original ideas; or willingness to try new things.
3. **Dealing with adversity:** Describe the most significant challenge you have faced and the steps you have taken to address this challenge. Include whether you turned to anyone in facing that challenge, the role that person played, and what you learned about yourself.
4. **Community service:** Explain what you have done to make your community a better place to live. Give examples of specific projects in which you have been involved over time.

5. **Handling systemic challenges:** Describe your experiences facing or witnessing discrimination. Tell us how you responded and what you learned from those experiences and how they have prepared you to contribute to the OSU community.
6. **Goals/task commitment:** Articulate the goals you have established for yourself and your efforts to accomplish these. Give at least one specific example that demonstrates your work ethic/diligence. (Oregon State University, "Written Experiential Assessment," 2007).

Students are also advised, as the questions demonstrate, to give "at least one specific example" and to think of their experiences "over time." The advice about time, according to Sandlin, is a key component because the intent is to include in the admissions process "depth of activity" rather than a list of activities. Interestingly, although the responses to the Insight Resume are unique to each individual and thus highly personal, the IR is read "blindly" as an independent document by a committee of faculty and staff. It is not used as a complement or supplement to confirm other evidence but rather as a piece of evidence in its own right. In outlining the IR to applicants, the Admissions Office at OSU is clear about the contribution it makes to the admissions package:

- Understanding of you as a unique, contributing individual.
- Your accomplishments, perspectives, experiences, and talents.
- Your achievements within the context of your social and personal circumstances.
- Participation in activities that develop academic, intellectual, and leadership abilities. (Oregon State University, "Insight Resume," n.d.)

Moreover, the assessment of the IR is consistent with the values ascribed within it: conducted by faculty with a rubric keyed to "critical thinking and reflection on the evidence," which evidence, of course, is selected by the student based on his or her experience. As Vicki Tolar Burton (personal communication, December 6, 2011) explains,

> The IR is scored by professional faculty in the admissions office using a rubric [...] Scorers receive a day of training in which they are introduced to the IR and rubric and practice norming and holistic scoring. The response to each question is rated 1 (low) to 3 (high) and then a total score is given. The criteria do not include grammar or punctuation but do include development of an answer that uses evidence and demonstrates critical thinking and reflection on the evidence. For example, the student who, for the community service question, writes, "I worked in a food bank last Christmas" would get a 1, while the student who gave a fully developed response about working in the food bank and reflected on what they learned would likely get a 3.

In other words, students' experience, observation, and reflection provide the material for the IR, and those are precisely what the assessment values.[2]

And the results? The IR, now counting for about a third of the admission package (with GPA and the SAT counting for the rest), has functioned as designed. One effect of the change shows up in the number of Latina/o students who are now enrolled: in fewer than 10 years, the enrollment of these students at Oregon State has nearly doubled, up to 775 from 432. Using another metric, we could look more broadly at students of color: in two years, the percentage of students of color who were admitted increased from less than a quarter of the entering class to a third. As important, the IR scores are directly related to higher rates of retention:

> The real evidence for the program's success, Sandlin said, is in academic performance. Skeptics of holistic admissions tend to assume that it benefits students who are somehow weaker because their traditional measures (SAT scores and grades) may be lower. But Sandlin said that Oregon State has found a direct correlation between higher scores on the Insight Resume and retention rates. Average GPAs are also going up slightly. She said that the qualities being asked about reward determination, hard work, and other qualities [...] do in fact relate to college success as much as test scores. (Jaschik, 2007, para. 11)

In these terms, the IR works. It works by asking students to write reflectively about experiences that Oregon State recognizes as valuable. It assumes, for example, that we've all witnessed discrimination and that some of us have experienced it. The IR values efforts to overcome adversity, and it recognizes that adversity is no stranger to many students. In other words, the values authorized in this assessment work against racism. This assessment also authorizes students to write about these experiences, and in this way signals that writing is a centerpiece intellectual activity; the activity is thus congruent with the mission and values of the school. Because the IR limits each answer to 100 words, it reminds us all that important insights can be distilled. Likewise, because the IR counts as much as grades and test scores—which is a fairly remarkable proportion for a first introduction—it reduces the influence of standardized test scores as it values student experience. Thus, in welcoming new students, especially students of color—whom the data show *do* succeed— the university has created for all its students an environment offering engagement and reflection.

And not least, these data demonstrate that success in college emerges from something more and other than what we see in conventional measures of success, be they SAT scores or GPAs; in the IR we see another kind of learning, expressed in the student's own voice, that also speaks to what the student brings to higher education. Put in the framework of curricula, we might think of the IR as tapping a different curriculum than that tested by the SAT and GPA. Together, they test some combination of the *delivered* curriculum—ordinarily represented in syllabi, readings, and assignments, for example—and the *experienced* curriculum, which is what students make of that delivered curriculum. But equally important is the third curriculum, the *lived* curriculum. No student walks in the door as a blank slate. Each one brings with him or her a set of prior courses and experiences and connections that contextualize whatever is learned, and this—the lived curriculum, a real if informal curriculum—provides the intellectual material for the IR. What's more, in including this curriculum in its admission and in tracking the success of the admitted students, Oregon State has demonstrated that this lived curriculum is, at the least, the equal of the other two.

We might also pause to note the similarity between the IR and directed self-placement (DSP). DSP, which asks students to reflect on their writing experiences in order to help place them into an appropriate writing class, is a form of reflection focused on self-assessment. As Rachel Lewis Ketai notes in this collection, DSP assumes that students have developed a kind of expertise about their own writing proficiency and about the curricular situation that will best foster their progress (see also Yancey, 2009). The IR, which calls on another kind of expertise, places students more definitively, of course—either into or out of Oregon State—but it likewise does so based students' accounts of their experiences.

Not least, it's worth noting how student expertise is constructed in three very different models of writing assessment: conventional essay tetsing, IR, and DSP. The first model, essay testing, provides the material Bartholomae (1988) refers to in discussing how students need to "invent" the university. New to the discourses of higher education (and of course new to the topic of writing in the essay exam), students, he observes, struggle to find a place to stand, a place from which to speak:

> It is very hard for them to take on the role—the voice, the person—of an authority whose authority is rooted in scholarship, analysis, or research. They slip, then, into the more immediately available and realizable voice of authority, the voice of a teacher giving a lesson or the voice of a parent lecturing at the dinner table. (p. 136)

Students are novices in the university, of course, and they do search for new rhetorical stances, not only when they enter, but as they progress—into majors, internships, and finally, into life beyond the undergraduate experience. At the same time, even upon entering college, they are not completely novices—in writing, in schooling, or in life—which collectively is the point of departure for both DSP and IR. Put differently, the IR and many DSP programs make very different assumptions about students' experiences, about the value of those experiences, and about the values that students bring to the university. DSP operates at the interface of students' past and present experiences as it invites students to tap the past in order to create—to invent—their writing futures. And the IR, through acknowledging and valuing students' experiences, asks students to participate most fully; in this exercise students have both the most agency and the most risk. As I have argued elsewhere, students in this kind of activity are not inventing the university so much as co-inventing it—in the case of IR—even before they matriculate (Yancey, 2009).

One might argue, however, that conventional essay assessments, DSP, and the IR are measuring very different constructs: the claim, as we've seen, is that the IR taps non-cognitive factors; the key word here might be *seems* since it seems to tap the cognitive as well. Writing, of course, is a function of cognition: and the IR calls upon writing. It also requires students to identify a relevant experience and reflect upon it, an activity that also falls into a cognitive domain. The experience being articulated is itself a curriculum, an informal curriculum that complements and informs the formal curricula. In addition, in that the IR asks students to make a judgment—about what counts as adversity, for example—it is also not exclusively a non-cognitive measure. Rather, in asking students to make such judgments, the IR asks them to engage in the highest level of thinking as represented in both Bloom's taxonomy and Perry's developmental schema. The IR asks them to be reflective about that thinking as well. In fact, it is through this capacity—to make a judgment and reflect upon it—that students do well on the IR.[3]

A secondary purpose—connected to consequential validity—of the assessment has developed more recently: to help connect entering students with services at Oregon State that might help them succeed, as explained on the OSU website.

> The purpose of Insight Resume (IR) is to promote student success through more ac-
> curate assessment of student preparedness and academic potential. In addition to its
> potential for making more accurate admissions decisions, this non-cognitive, holistic
> assessment provides OSU with more information on applicants, earlier than we've
> ever had before. With this instrument developed by OSU, and the information it
> provides, we are able to proactively connect students to services that will help them be
> successful when they matriculate to OSU. ("Description," 2009)

Thus far, there is no published information about how this assistance is provided or how well it works. But it's worth noting that this use of the IR—in terms of consequential validity—developed *after* it had been used for admission for several years. In other words, the consequential validity is here a benefit, not a purpose. The purpose is very different: to include the lived curriculum of students, expressed reflectively, to change the kind of student who is admitted and who, the data show, will thrive.

Writing Student Experience

If Oregon State were the only school in the country using the IR, we might applaud it as an iconic practice, interesting but not widely applicable. Since OSU's first use of the IR merely five years ago, however, other schools in Oregon—including Eastern Oregon, Central Oregon, and Western Oregon Universities—as well as schools outside Oregon—including DePaul and Washington State University—have adopted it. Other schools are making similar kinds of changes. Boston College and Tufts University, for example, ask students to submit evidence of creativity as part of their admissions process. Two elite schools, MIT and the University of Pennsylvania, are moving in the same direction: they have redesigned the "admissions essay" into much shorter pieces of writing in hopes of gaining more authentic responses from students.

But closest to the OSU IR, perhaps, is a program at Northeastern University, the Torch Scholars Program, "designed to identify applicants who show leadership potential or have overcome adversity but probably wouldn't qualify for the university based solely on their high-school grades and test scores" (Tomsho, "Boston's Torch Scholars," 2009, para. 1). As part of the admissions process, applicants do the following:

> [Take a personality test] to measure traits such as resolve, resourcefulness, and leadership ability and then are interviewed about their background and goals. They participate in role-playing exercises, meet with current students, even choose a friend, teacher, or relative to speak to administrators on their behalf. (Schworm, 2007, para. 17)

Although these students' SAT scores fall between 200 and 300 points below the median (970 compared to 1250) and their GPAs are likewise lower, the admitted group is doing well.

> School officials are tracking how the students fare academically to test how well the screening process predicts college success, and what personal attributes have the strongest correlation [...] So far, the results are promising. Despite lower high school grades and SAT scores than their Northeastern peers, all 11 students in the second-year program completed their first year this spring, more than half with at least a B average. (Schworm, 2007, para. 18)

In addition, according to university officials, about 90% of these scholars continue into the sophomore year, which is roughly akin to the university-wide average of 92%. And who are these students? The program has enrolled 25 students: 16 who are African American or Hispanic; others who are ELL; and others who are immigrants.

Viewing these changes collectively, we see schools redesigning their traditional essays to tap students' authentic experiences. We see special programs like the Torch Scholars Program rewarding a different kind of knowledge. And we see the Insight Resume that builds in a requirement for that special kind of knowledge for *all* applicants. Of all these programs, of course, the IR is the most robust. It delivers on the campus epistemological need outlined by Soares (2008); it includes all students in its application process; it functions to diversify a student body as intended; and in its selections, it enhances the student body as a whole, as indicated by GPAs. In sum, schools are creating new practices that all point the way to a more accurate and equitable assessment; and in the IR, we have a model for how to widen and sustain this practice so that all students are included.

In Conclusion: The Return To/Of Testing Technology

In the Introduction to *Portfolios in the Writing Classroom*, Lucas (1992) cautions progressive educators about three ways portfolios could go awry, one of which is the impulse to standardize, what Lucas calls "co-option by large-scale testing programs" (p. 7). Valerie Balester in this collection also illustrates how this impulse has shaped the development of writing assessment rubrics. What's true of portfolios, of course, is true of any new assessment exercise, and in this case, of the measurement of (so-called) non-cognitive traits as in the Insight Resume. This caution is already relevant in this case, even though the IR is only five years old. Put differently, such factors will provide a new focus for national assessments, and the historical impulse to standardize is also already in play. In July of 2009, for example, the GRE began including an optional component called the Personal Professional Index (PPI) that is a measure that looks surprisingly like the IR:

> In the index, three or four professors or supervisors—generally those who will also be writing letters of recommendation—will answer a series of questions about candidates' non-cognitive skills in various areas, as well as a more general set of questions. Applicants will be rated on a scale of 1–5 on questions about their abilities in these six areas: knowledge and creativity, communication skills, team work, resilience, planning and organization, and ethics and integrity. Those filling out the forms would also be able to provide narrative answers on each of those areas. (Jaschik, 2008a, para. 3)

Upon examination, of course, we see that this measure is actually very *unlike* the IR. Although it also taps so-called non-cognitive traits, the PPI is scored nationally in ways that aren't explained, and more important, it's an indirect measure in that it taps professors' opinions *of* students, not the students' experience as articulated by the students themselves. But it is a measure of non-cognitive traits; and it is standardized; and the standardization of it is assumed to improve it.

Another non-cognitive measure in development, called by some the SAT III, asks high school students to participate in two endeavors: (1) a listing of activities like leadership and (2) "a situational judgment" exercise in which students are given a scenario—such as being a member of a new group—and asked to make a decision about how they'd behave based on five options, which since there is a right answer (and thus four wrong answers) is actually another form of multiple choice testing. Moreover, since groups behave very differently based on cultural norms, such an exercise with its right and wrong answers is likely to reward white answers in new and disturbing ways. Given this analysis, why would someone want to use this kind of measure rather than the nicely local, student-centered IR? Because, as in the past master narrative, it's more scientific:

> Camara [the Vice President for Research at the College Board] acknowledged that many colleges believe that they already consider factors such as leadership by judging in-person interviews or examining lists of extracurricular activities. But he said that these approaches are not scientific and that many people are less able to judge character in interviews than they believe. A standardized system, he said, is needed. (Jaschik, 2008b, para. 13)

Thus, according to the College Board, what is needed is an approach that is "scientific" and "standardized." Put another way, the caution that Lucas articulated about the co-option of external testing is prescient here: the wheels of standardization are already turning.

And In The Meantime, What Have We Learned?
Basically, Three Lessons.

One: college admissions tests continue to tap multiple constructs, including writing. In the case of the IR, students' lived curriculum is tapped; students are asked to write reflectively and succinctly to articulate what they have learned in life. Moreover, this assessment was designed to meet a specific goal: to admit a more racially diverse student body, one that would succeed in college. As evidenced at Oregon State, such an assessment can be the better measure, the more racially diverse, the more intellectually diverse, *and* the more fair—for individuals and for the university community.

Two: efforts like the Insight Resume will be at odds with a continuing impulse to turn to the traditional technologies of testing—with their affection for science and for standardization—for answers to social problems. It may be that, as one reviewer of this chapter suggested, the IR does itself employ a technology of testing, but even if that's so, the technology is located in very different assumptions, differences that are more of kind than degree. Moreover, where local efforts like the IR are linked—such as at the various Oregon schools and at schools outside the state—we might begin to create a model that crosses individual campuses and that, as it achieves critical mass, begins to counter the rhetoric of scientific testing that is race-blind.

Three: assessment has never produced outcomes innocently; it is itself a construct; it produces outcomes that are ideological even when it pretends otherwise; and it too can be assessed. The ideology of tests past is one located both in class and race; when most of the students who perform well on the tests are white and many students who succeed are students of color, there is something wrong with the test. In this sense, there is a difference between performing on a test and succeeding in life and school, and it was within that gap that the Insight Resume was born. Informed by that gap—that is, by data mapping it—OSU designed another assessment that tapped another source of success, one located in a different kind of curriculum. In doing so, it pluralized both race and class; it admitted a different student body; and it enhanced the intellectual life of the campus.

Writing has always been at the heart of U.S. college admission assessment, and there is increasing agreement that admissions should link more closely to the curriculum; in fact, that argument was one of many put forward by the College Board in announcing the new SAT "writing" test. But as the Insight Resume demonstrates, the school curriculum isn't the only important one; indeed as our students are showing us, the one that might really matter is the one they live.

Notes

---

[1] Affirmative action did affect the enrollment of students of color, of course, and all students of color haven't fared similarly. For instance, Asian American students have excelled, while African American students have not.

[2] During the review process, a question was raised as to how I knew about the Insight Resume and whether I have or had any relationship to Oregon State University. I have no relationship with OSU, nor with the IR. I learned about the IR first, through reading about the practice in *Inside Higher Ed*, and second, by continuing to research its source, its efficacy, and its adoption elsewhere. Given my longstanding interest in reflection and students' lived curricu-

lum, I found the Insight Resume to be a remarkable admissions mechanism—and a better measure of writing than more conventional tests like the SAT. Moreover, the requirement that students write succinctly about an experience of value, from which they make meaning, strikes me as a very sophisticated intellectual task.

[3] There is a line of research in electronic portfolios showing that including students' accounts of their lived curricula is directly related to increased retention. See Cambridge, Cambridge, & Yancey (2009).

CHAPTER TWELVE

Assessment in the French Context: Language Socialization, Socioeconomic Status, and the Implications of the Programme for International Student Assessment

Élisabeth Bautier and Christiane Donahue

French education has traditionally been built on the concepts of equality ("*équité*") and pedagogical effectiveness ("*efficacité*"). Employed throughout French constructivist approaches to learning, such concepts are applied, regardless of students' economic status. We contend, however, that international high-stakes writing assessments such as the Programme for International Student Assessment (PISA) conflict with these traditional concepts; in conflicting with French educational principles, tests such as PISA are most likely to affect French students from lower socioeconomic backgrounds—students who are most often immigrants of certain racial or ethnic backgrounds.

How does PISA disadvantage students *"en difficulté,"* what U.S. readers might call "at-risk" students? We argue that in inviting students to write about personal experiences and opinions grounded in daily life, PISA gives the impression that the exam evaluates mastery of interpreting "ordinary" texts. In answering test questions, students do not need to go beyond individual experience. However, PISA evaluates "full literacy." Full literacy, as first described by Goody and Watt (1963) and further developed most notably by Labov (1987), involves cultural, social, and subjective dimensions that require development and transformation over time, through specific situations rather than formal "exercises." In fact, high-scoring PISA test responses are those that draw on a variety of experiences and can deploy those responses in specific genres and in specific registers. This contradiction creates two problems in the French context. First, while traditional French assessments call on *secondarized*[1] literacy competencies—a concept that we illustrate later in this chapter—use *explicitly* of the personal is rare in French schooling and, in fact, is often penalized by French teachers (Bautier, 1995; Donahue, 2008). While personal experiences shape learning, they are not supposed to serve as the basis for school learning.

Second, assessments like PISA presuppose certain linguistic habits that students *en difficulté* do not develop outside of school but are not typically taught *explicitly* in French school—e.g., the ability to read and use texts as objects of school-based knowledge rather than everyday knowledge. Such habits are the ones that U.S. researchers like Bartholomae (1985) invoke when they talk of students as newcomers to unfamiliar discourse communities and argue for the school's institutional responsibility to facilitate students' access to knowledge. Labov's powerful statement, "the primary cause of school failure is not language difficulty but institutional racism" (Fasold et al., 1987, p. 10), builds out of this concern for the ways in which differences between community and school languages are treated in students' writing.

In this chapter we show that writing activities that are based on one's knowledge, one's everyday experiences, or one's values and opinions can draw on quite different "ways of being" in students' responses to the same prompt. We are not purporting to value or legitimize some ways of reading, writing, or reasoning, such as ways that are found among students from upper socioeconomic classes, over others. Nor are we suggesting a deficit model. Instead, we wish to describe how students' interpretation of PISA prompts is based not only on their non-scholastic linguistic socialization and their relationship to language and to writing, but also the way in which they interpret the academic expectations concerning their work, including language, genre, and content. These different dimensions undergird student writing and connect to sociocultural context. Students thus call on not only their values, sociolinguistic and sociocognitive habits, and resources, but also the way they "make do with" language.

We focus on the *differentiation* resulting from the ways different groups of students work through writing assignments, namely how they respond to the PISA test prompts. *Differentiation* is a term used in France for a long-term and persistent inequality that prevents students from benefiting from what schooling offers. In our research, what differentiates students is what they *mobilize*—i.e., what knowledge they revisit or adapt and the cognitive and linguistic work they do with what they mobilize. To mobilize in secondarized forms of literacy means for students to reflect on what they know, to call on the knowledge needed for a particular task, and to show that knowledge through what they produce (Bautier, 2005). For students at all levels of schooling, each different form of writing (or speaking)—drawing on oneself and one's knowledge, one's everyday experiences, or one's values and opinions—is a quite different "way of being." The differentiating factors in the development of subjects can thus be studied in terms of the activities that require students to mobilize intellectual tools in various ways.

A hypothesis we present here is that *socially differentiating relationships* between the affective and cognitive components mobilized during students' activities, on the one hand, and the constraints that the situations and the assignments construct, along with the students' interpretations of these, on the other hand, clearly exist. Two examples will be explored: one example in a classroom setting as students and a teacher attempt to construct knowledge together and the other example from an analysis of the international comparative PISA assessment. The first example sets the conceptual frame for our argument about assessment, language, and identity, and the second example offers specific arguments about PISA.

The Programme For International Student Assessment

The PISA exam, developed by the Organisation for Economic Co-operation and Development (OECD), is designed to measure lifelong skills in science, mathematics, reading, and critical thinking. The exam is given to between 4,500 and 10,000 students in 50 participating countries, including most European, Asian, and North American counties as well as many developing nations of Africa and South America, for a total of 250,000 students every three years. While the exam scores have resulted in changes in national educational policies and funding patterns in several countries, the OECD itself says the test does not imply better or worse education in different countries.

PISA Test Design

The PISA literature defines literacy as follows: "Understanding, using, and reflecting on written texts, in order to achieve one's goals, to develop one's knowledge and potential and to participate in society" (OECD, 2002, p. 22). In terms of reading and writing prompts, the PISA exam offers students a range of tasks, such as reading documents, giving an opinion, or discussing a chart of survey results. Students are given multiple choice and open-ended questions, which are designed to test their literacy in terms of using information from within or outside of a text, retrieving it, understanding it, and reflecting on content and form. (For a detailed description of the components, see OECD, 2002, p. 23.)

Multiple choice questions account for 45% of the reading test, and open-ended questions account for another 45% of the test. The remaining 10% of reading test questions ask students to construct a written response from a limited range of possible questions (OECD, 2002, p. 25). PISA assesses students' literacy abilities by simulating "the kinds of task encountered in 'authentic' reading situations—i.e., in real life" (OECD, 2002, p. 22). Students are assessed on five dimensions in different types of reading situations, including reading for private use, reading for public use, reading for work, and reading for education. The dimensions are as follows:

1. Forming a broad general understanding (20%)
2. Retrieving information (20%)
3. Developing an interpretation (30%)
4. Reflecting on the content of a text (15%)
5. Reflecting on the form of a text (15%). (OECD, 2002, pp. 22–24)

While PISA is promoted as a reading test, reading ability is tested entirely through writing; the test is in fact a writing assessment. PISA exam responses are evaluated using benchmarked criteria for "good answers."

The reading literacy test is scored on 5 levels with an average score of 500. About two-thirds of students in OECD countries receive scores between 400 and 600 (OECD, 2002, p. 27; see also OECD, 2009).

Critiques of PISA

PISA test designers write that "close attention" is paid to the origin and content of the texts used in the exam:

> The goal is to reach a balance between reflecting the broad definition of reading literacy used in PISA and representing the linguistic and cultural diversity of participating countries. This diversity will help to ensure that no one group is either advantaged or disadvantaged by the assessment context. (OECD, 2002, p. 25)

Yet, the racialized dimensions of PISA test scores have been noted by its critics, such as Lowell and Salzman in their report *Into the Eye of the Storm: Assessing the Evidence on Science and Engineering Education, Quality, and Workforce Demand* (2007).[2] Citing Boe and Shin's analysis of U.S. students' test scores on PISA exams, they note that while overall U.S. test scores are not as high as other countries, U.S. white students "handily outscore students in the Western G5 nations in math and science, albeit they do not do as well as Japanese students" (p. 23). Lowell and Salzman conclude:

> The use of average rates across a diverse group of nations and diverse populations is of limited use in drawing conclusions about global standing economically or educationally [...] The test results indicate that, rather than a policy focus on average science and math scores, there is an urgent need for targeted educational improvement to serve low-performing populations, such as recent immigrants and some minorities [...] Understanding the demographic variation in education performance is important when drawing conclusions and policy recommendations. (pp. 24–25)

Such critiques are instructive for examining diversity and PISA test outcomes in national contexts outside the U.S.

Of course, as numerous scholars have pointed out, there is often an intersection between socioeconomic status and race (APA, 2012a; OECD 2004;

Gillborn & Mirza, 2000; Jencks & Phillips, 1998). While we agree with these critiques, we note that many such critiques do not sufficiently account for how socioeconomic status, race, and national educational context intersect. This intersection becomes more apparent in looking at results from tests such as PISA.

France And The Question Of Race

This chapter presents a discussion about race and assessment in the sense that we target the experiences of students who are most often from particular racial backgrounds—i.e., certain immigrant groups in France. France presents several difficulties in terms of how race and ethnicity can be treated in research studies.[3] For historical reasons linked to the very foundation of the Republic, it is illegal in France to identify an individual, *a fortiori* a French citizen (a child born in France) by his or her racial origins.[4] The term "race" cannot be used as a variable in empirical research; however, the expression "ethnic origin" has sometimes been used to categorize people from a family whose ancestors were not French. A person's racial or ethnic origin appears on no official document, in no social or school statistics. Sociologists often complain about this situation, as it clearly hinders their research and sociological analyses of situations of school failure or difficulty, in particular. Children's first names are the only indication—albeit a very poor one—of a child's race or ethnic background. Some inquiries into the languages spoken in France have looked at languages spoken at home; in this way, we have learned that many students "originating from immigration," even though their parents themselves were born in France, hear languages at home other than French, most often Arabic, Berber, or a sub-Saharan African language. Children from recently immigrated families (in France less than a year), are put into specific classes for *primo-arrivants*[5] where they learn French; children who have been in France for several years or who are born in France of immigrant parents are considered French and receive no particular special educational treatment.

As in most countries with high immigration rates, sociospatial segregation is very strong in major French cities. Entire neighborhoods of cities or their suburbs (e.g., Paris, Lyon, Lille, Marseille) have pauperized populations, with parents who have received little schooling. This population is, in France, a population of immigrant origins, from the Maghreb or Africa in particular, regrouped into almost completely ethnically and socially homogeneous "*cités*" (large housing projects). Given the French school rules about "sectorization"— children are automatically enrolled in the school closest to home—up to 90% of students are "of immigrant origin" in schools in these areas. This is especially the case for schools situated in *zones d'éducation prioritaires*, "zones of educational priority" (ZEP). Such zones were created based on, among other social criteria, parental migratory origins and are targeted for additional attention and funding because they often include many students *en difficulté*.

It is impossible to distinguish for these students the difficulties that come from their social origins (low socioeconomic status, large families with little schooling in their original country, minimal French language proficiency, and high unemployment levels) and the difficulties that come from belonging to a particular racial group in France (and thus potentially subject to certain kinds of social and cultural racism). To study racism in France, one must consider the intersection of these factors.

A Classroom Example Of *Secondarization*

As we have explained, students *en difficulté* are often penalized in French schools because they have not yet learned to transform everyday objects into secondarized objects of study or meta-analysis in ways that are rewarded in French academic contexts. Instead, such students may interpret prompts as a call to spontaneous speaking and writing. In the following example, we use an interaction between a teacher and a group of students to demonstrate the kind of literacy practices expected for success in French schools. This example is based on our previous research (Bautier, 2004; Bautier & Branca-Rosoff, 2002; Bautier & Rochex, 2001, 2004).

An elementary school teacher announces, "Today we are going to talk about water and about how we find water." Some students reply with personal and subjective responses about experiences with water (it can be "chlorinated" or "cold," for example); others interpret the framework of the class discussion in a scholastic register ("water has three forms"); and others collectively explore their academic and non-academic knowledge in order to try to construct a cognitive and collective dialogue of academic responses to the teacher's "question." The assignment is open-ended and does not offer any precise parameters in terms of expected discursive productions, expected forms of response, or expected references to a particular disciplinary discourse. The expression "to find water" is itself ambiguous, yet there is a constructivist expectation to this exercise. Students are to draw on their own knowledge and relate that to academic knowledge. This type of situation occurs often in French classrooms as teachers have been trained in the constructivist tradition regarding knowledge production.

The first student to respond to the teacher's question replies in "good student" mode, with a scholastic answer: *"Water has three forms, boiling water, plain water, and frozen water."* But, in light of the ensuing dialogue with other students, this student realizes that the situation is open to exchange of ideas, debate, and reflections in order to co-construct knowledge that goes beyond what participants knew at the start. She joins the discussion again and calls on her experiences, particularly one discussion with her father, to develop a reflection that puts into play spaces and moments that she constructs as possible sites of knowledge: *"At the expos, there was water [...] My father told me."* Students who succeed in school contexts have learned how to capitalize on this capacity to connect links, to mobilize different knowledge sites and experiences, to work with the inherent heterogeneity of the construction of knowledge. To develop her own thinking, she uses the statements of other students, drawing inspiration from their ideas and formulating her own questions: *"Water can pass through [a towel] because, uh, it is wet, uh [...]"* which then allows her to question, *"So, I think that it is normal for water to pass through things, right?"* These changes in her interpretation of the situation, the use of others' ideas, her experiences, and her own reflections are characteristic of the linguistic abilities a student acquires in order to benefit from the proposed learning situation (and be rewarded academically).

Another, "weak student" interprets the situation quite differently, as requiring him to "respond to the teacher" and to share his personal experiences. He interprets the verb "to find" in terms of felt experience rather than cognitive work: *"Me, sometimes I drink water at my house."* Referring to the chlorinated taste, he says, *"I can tell that the taste comes from the swimming pool."* He refers to his experiences, as does the first student, but his mobilization of the register of personal experience appears linked to a different interpretation of the situation and narrower than that of the "good student." He volunteers participation only once, as if, having once replied to the teacher, he had the sense that he had satisfied school expectations.

These different ways of "being students" in the same situation can be correlated with equally different linguistic socializations—i.e., is language a place to construct meaning or is its function to report experience? The example of the classroom discussion of water illustrates how difficult it can be for students to see what subjectivity to adopt, for "one of the paradoxes of school work is that the [directions often] give few indications about how to articulate what comes from the materiality of the tasks assigned and what constitutes its cognitive benefits" (Rayou, 2004). Students are rarely clued in explicitly to the expectations or benefits attached to a particular activity.

There is a "displacement" in the subjectivity of the first student that allows her to take on different points of view, to be able to choose rhetorical modes that allow this kind of flexibility, to reconfigure the information already present, and to use the mediating and secondarizing dimensions of language to think beyond the description-sharing of immediate, primary experiences. Students who have learned how to displace their point of view can use and change registers between recounting a lived experience and cognitively reconfiguring that experience. This dimension of a student's mastery of writing is one of the dimensions of subjective mobilization—control over organizing ideas about a text, reflecting critically on a text, working with heterogeneous knowledge sources, connecting those sources through language, reconfiguring that knowledge, and ultimately producing a text that inscribes itself in the plurality of voices yet also has authorial control. The second student has not learned to do so with language and, thus, although he is not cognitively inferior to the first student, his response marks him as a "weak student." This echoes findings in U.S. composition studies of student agency and authority (Penrose & Geisler, 1994) and the crucial role they play in enabling student writers to see themselves as endowed with the authorial control necessary to behave as the first student here did.

Language Socialization, Written Culture, And The Study Of PISA

The part of the PISA exam that we analyze in this chapter focuses on the assessment of 15-year-old students' literacy competencies.[6] The following examples, which are typical of PISA reading literacy exam questions, are from the PISA reading exam given in France. A "good" answer to the following prompts assumes that students know how to bring together heterogeneous perspectives, and how to reason with these various perspectives:

- Do you agree with the final judgment of the people surveyed? Explain your response, comparing your attitude to theirs about the films.
- Do you find the results of this survey surprising?
- Think about the key ideas put forth by the five students. With which of these students are you the most in agreement? Using your own words, explain your choice in one or two sentences, based on your personal opinion and the key ideas.
- Put yourself in the place of S. Basing your essay on the data gathered by S., give a reason for your thinking.

The questions we ask in our following analysis of exam responses are: what are the differentiating resources for writing different kinds of text? While some students mobilize only themselves (their immediate lived experiences), other students engage themselves on an axiological level, and still others move from one type of mobilization to another, producing heterogeneous texts. There is a strong relationship between the familiar uses of language and the self-mobilizing register: students who, as described earlier, mobilize only themselves appear to have learned only the use of the language that arises from the immediacy of speaking. These different ways of being in language are not equally distributed; much research in sociolinguistic and sociocognitive practices shows the strong presence of language use that is penalized in the PISA exam responses of students we consider *en difficulté*.

The representative examples here are drawn from a larger study that was designed to show the cultural differences in literacy competencies brought out by the PISA exam (Bautier, Crinon, Rayou, & Rochex, 2005, 2006). That study analyzed 750 PISA exams of students in schools in which the population was from zones of educational priority. We looked at writing from students with PISA scores in the bottom 25%. In that study, we analyzed students' writing in a way that enabled us to cross-reference different indices, including cognitive competencies (inferences, hypotheses about the world) and literacy (understanding and processing of texts as texts), as well as the positions students adopt in the construction of their utterances and in the ways they mobilize commonly accepted knowledge, intrinsic moral values, and affect as they work with different kinds of knowledge and the sources of that knowledge. We also looked at students' school records and their school success overall. The criteria that the research team used in analyzing student responses included a judgment of quality in terms of the degree to which the answer was a simple recopying of the text from which the student drew his or her reply, and in terms of the cognitive and subjective engagement that the student's reply showed.

By analyzing PISA test responses, we identified the characteristics of different student writers and the way different themes create different subject positions invited by everyday or secondarized framing. We found that PISA prompts that encourage personal expression or opinion can act as traps for students *en difficulté*; when self-expression was invited, the school constraints of the prompt became invisible. We concluded that students from marginalized socioeconomic groups were least likely to show secondarization, given their lack of familiarity with expectations for interpreting personal experience in academic writing. Specifically, the weaker responses: (1) did not take information from or refer to the text they were asked to read as part of the PISA question; (2) replied in an essentially affective and moral register, appearing to demonstrate conformity (even collusion?) with opinions that favor the poor, other youth with whom they identify, or moral judgments in general; and (3) repeated utterances from the document they read, often those making a moral judgment (Bautier, Crinon, Rayou, & Rochex, 2005, 2006).[7] In the following discussion, we provide examples of these results.

Referencing The Exam Prompt Text

PISA exam questions may specify that the student should refer to an appended document to look for answers. For example, a document might describe how to put together a bicycle; students were then asked about the criteria that could be used to judge whether the bicycle had been well put together. Students *en difficulté* generally made no reference to the text or the attached documents. They used, instead, their everyday knowledge about bicycles (we hypothesize that they valued this knowledge as more accurate).[8] They might reply, for example, that all you need to do to test whether the bicycle is well put together is to try to ride it—if you fall over, it is not well put together. The following are examples of responses from low-scoring students on another prompt about movies:

> I agree with this kind of movie, but there are others that on the contrary they make us laugh rather than cry.

> The final judgment of people about the movies is ridiculous, because the point of going to the movies is to have fun.

> No because the movies are made to help us change our ideas so it's good to go to the movies every once in a while.

> I think she's right because so many people are dying of hunger, thirst, or sickness, and meanwhile others are shooting off rockets that cost millions of francs.

Our research confirms that students *en difficulté* rely almost entirely on themselves and do not cite the appended documents. They use "auto-reference" (referencing only their own experience and opinions as resources for writing) and everyday pragmatism (reasoning tied to the everyday). These behaviors towards texts have quite powerful consequences in terms of schooling, as academic contexts assume that written text is the basis for work, reasoning, and learning. We are, of course, not suggesting in our study that everyday knowledge and experience are in themselves inadequate; we are simply highlighting the cultural gap between the expectations of the PISA exam and the expectations of students *en difficulté*.

Using Opinion And Common Sense

In another PISA example—a task involving reading charts about children's participation in household chores in different countries—we analyzed students' responses by the difficulties they had in identifying percentages of respondents' opinions. Students *en difficulté* interpreted the responses as accounting for actual practices, and they made judgments about these practices based on their own experiences, as if texts directly describe reality, rather than representing reality.

When the prompt called on forms of reasoning based directly on the elements of a text provided, the students *en difficulté* appeared to not understand the call or to see it as a constraint. Their answers were based on common sense, and the students appeared unfamiliar with language-as-construction. For example, in an assessment that was supposed to show students' competence in scientific reasoning, based on observations noted by a researcher about the difference in death rates between two different birthing centers after an earthquake, students *en difficulté* replied that "earthquakes cannot be the source of death because a woman gives birth in the same way whether there is an earthquake right then or not."

From our analysis, it seemed that students *en difficulté* processed texts differently; they did not appear to understand the objective of the text's author, in the case of the documents being read, nor the cognitive objectives of the task, in the case of the assignment itself. This is consistent with other research that students *en difficulté* respond to assignments differently, whether they address the actual request of the assignment or perhaps translate the assignment into a different task. Most often these students are from ZEPs (Manesse, 2003; Goigoux, 2000).

Repeating Utterances From The Document To Draw A Moral Judgment

We can also analyze students *en difficulté* in terms of their tendency not to see the text as a unit whose meaning must be constructed based on its "*objectifs énonciatifs*" (its objectives as an utterance) and its discursive genre. Students *en difficulté* can typically successfully complete isolated school activities involving recognizing textual aspects, but they have difficulty identifying the genre of discourse in which the text is constructed and its purpose. In other words, they have learned how to carry out certain tasks by recopying elements of the text, as long as they don't need to worry about syntactic relevance. These students can thus be good "picker-outers" without being good "understanders." This tendency is likely related to the fact that many school tasks, especially those used in evaluating students, allow students to "reply" whether they have understood the texts and the cognitive objectives of school tasks or not. Danièle Manesse (2003) notes a high rate of success at simple tasks of recognition that is not carried over when reading activities become more complex. Students recopy an element or use the element they have picked out without necessarily understanding that element in other contexts. Thus to the question, "In the film series, what is the factor that made the people of M. angry?" students give replies such as:

> "A character dead and buried who reappeared transformed into an Arab in the next film" (this is word-for-word what appeared in the text read for the assignment; the student picked out this phrase).

> "The public, who paid two centavos to share in the misadventures of characters, cannot stand this unqualified mockery and broke up all the seats" (the student recopied the exact passage).

Simply recopying the text is clearly a different approach from that of the students who successfully address school expectations. "Good" students paraphrase and argue the ways in which the paraphrased text responds to the question. The students who refer only to themselves, their feelings, and their experiences in writing have not yet learned how to create a new text by weaving their voices with the text's voices.

Conclusion

In our analysis of PISA, we aimed to highlight different modes of mobilization of the self. The students who scored highly on PISA exams were not those who eliminated all personal experience or who eliminated all non-school knowledge from their school discourses (a result we can consider in light of Donahue's 2008 analysis of entering college students' writing in France and the U.S.). Instead, students who scored highly were those who could call on different universes of knowledge and re-construct them to work together in an analytic register, not just an affective one. These are the students who, doubtless because they position themselves as authors of their texts, are able to mobilize their knowledge and to put it in dialogue with other kinds of knowledge from diverse sources—scholastic, experiential, mediated—to craft consistent arguments. More specifically, we can imagine that their subjectivity is not situated solely in affective references or personal feelings. It is these characteristics that, as much cognitively as in terms of school literacy, are positively evaluated. This is a telling difference, since students en difficulté did not re-construct their experiences within a register that would reward them by PISA exam scorers.

Additionally, because PISA's modes of evaluation bear essentially on documents from everyday, non-school life—"how-to" manuals, news stories, students' letters—that can resonate with many students' experiences, we believe they present a kind of trap for students en difficulté, precisely those who are not familiar with ways to secondarize objects that come from everyday contexts, nor with secondarizing uses of language. In this way, PISA effectively presupposes an ease with transforming everyday experience into an object of critical reflection when, in fact, many students respond spontaneously, without secondarizing. The situations that are supposed to engage students' opinions and experiences can, thus, actually be problematic for students *en difficulté*.

In addition to misinterpreting the scope required of exam prompts, students *en difficulté* often do not realize they should draw on the source material provided. In PISA questions, nothing in the prompt orients students' interpretation of the task. They do not require students to cite. Students *en difficulté* are the ones mostly likely to be negatively affected by this lack of explicit guidance.

In regards to race and test outcomes: the difficulty of using "race" as a category in French scholarship is likely to continue to be the case, in spite of some recent movement towards more open discussions of race in French society. What is clear is that racial identity as connected to socioeconomic status is an important embedded factor in French students' academic success and matters in our understanding of writing assessment in the French context.

In the end, scholars have hypothesized that the psychometric approach used in PISA has been afforded more importance than the conceptual approach to literacy used in other forms of contemporary writing instruction and assessment (Bain, 2003; Bautier, Crinon, Rayou, & Rochex, 2006). In other words, the test becomes more important than the literacy it purports to measure. Unless we believe that the ability to exercise subjectivities that permit exploration, construction of knowledge, and understanding and writing of disciplinary genres is not something we want for all students, we must work much more carefully with assessments that penalize students *en difficulté* in every country. The taboo on considering race must make way for an approach to research that allows us to understand the effects of assessments, such as the PISA, for all students.

Notes

---

[1] We use "secondarized" here as it has evolved in French scholarship, building from Bakhtin's treatment of primary and secondary genres (1984), to mean "meta-positioned and critically reflective." U.S. readers might think of this concept as reflection, selection, and integration of sources, including primary and secondary sources, in shaping an argument.

[2] It is important to note that PISA tests students who are 15 years old, not students in a particular grade. While smaller countries test most of their students, larger countries such as the U.S. test a representative sample.

[3] While French scholarship has included many theories of race—Fanon, Balibar, etc.—these theories do not intersect with French scholarship on schooling and literacy.

[4] See, for example, *The Economist* (2009) on ethnic labeling in France.

[5] While the PISA exam is not directly a part of the French curriculum, its international standing is quite influential. Children who have recently arrived in France and do not speak French are integrated into the school system during a 3- to 8-month bilingual education period.

[6] The reading test has been contrasted to a predecessor, the PIRLS test, the explicit purpose of which was to test "the ability to understand and use those written language forms required by society and/or valued by the individual" but which did not include the ability to construct and write responses (Progress in International Reading Literacy Study, 2011, p. 11).

[7] In U.S. composition studies, Flower, an early researcher into the cognitive processes of writing, identified this phenomenon as one aspect of what she called "writer-based prose" (1979).

[8] Identifying and emphasizing the *intelligence* underlying the students' "mistakes" is very much in the tradition of the U.S. composition scholars Shaughnessy (1977) and Rose (1985).

References

AERA, APA, & NCME. (1999). *Standards for educational and psychological testing.* Washington DC: American Educational Research Association.

Allen, B.P., & Niss, J. F. (1990). A chill in the college classroom? *Phil Delta Kappan,* April, 607–609.

National Council on Measurement in Education and American Council on Education. (2006). *Educational Measurement* (4th ed.). Wesport, CT: American Council on Education/Praeger.

American Psychological Association. (2012a). Education and socioeconomic status. Retrieved from http://www.apa.org/pi/ses/resources/publications/factsheet-education.aspx

American Psychological Association. (2012b). Testing information clearinghouse. Retrieved from http://www.apa.org/science/programs/testing/test-clearinghouse.aspx

American Sociological Association. (2002). Statement of the American Sociological Association on the importance of collecting data and doing social scientific research on race. Retrieved from http://www2.asanet.org/governance/racestmt.html

Ampadu, L. (2004). Modeling orality: African American rhetorical practices and the teaching of writing. In E. B. Richardson & R. L. Jackson II (Eds.), *African American rhetoric(s): Interdisciplinary perspectives* (pp. 136–154). Carbondale: SIUP.

Anson, C. M. (1993). The future of writing across the curriculum: Consensus and research. In C. M. Anson, J. E. Schwiebert, & M. M. Williamson (Eds.), *Writing across the curriculum: An annotated bibliography* (pp. xiii–xxiv). Westport: Greenwood.

————— (2002). *The WAC casebook: Scenes for faculty reflection and program development.* New York: Oxford University Press.

————— (2006a). Assessing writing in cross-curricular programs: Determining the locus of activity. *Assessing Writing, 11,* 100–112.

————— (2006b, June). *Writing at the center: WAC, WID & WCs.* Plenary paper presented at the meeting of the European Writing Centers Association, Istanbul, Turkey.

Anson, C. M., Carter, M., Dannels, D., & Rust, J. (2003). Mutual support: CAC programs and institutional improvement in undergraduate education. *Journal of Language and Learning Across the Disciplines, 6*(3), 26–38. Retrieved from http://wac.colostate.edu/llad/v6n3/anson.pdf

Anson, C. M., & Dannels, D. (2009). Profiling programs: Formatives uses of assisted descriptions in the assessment of communication across the curriculum. *Across the Disciplines, 6.* Retrieved from http://wac.colostate.edu/atd/assessment/anson_dannels.cfm

Anson, C. M., Schwiebert, J. E., & Williamson, M. M. (1993). *Writing across the curriculum: An annotated bibliography.* Westport, CT: Greenwood.

Anzaldúa, G. (1987). *Borderlands/La frontera: The new mestiza.* San Francisco: Aunt Lute Books.

Associated Press. (2011, Jan. 11) Universities forced to adapt as demographics shift. *Issues in Higher Education.* Retrieved from http://diverseeducation.com/article/14571/

Attali, Y. (2004). Exploring the feedback and revision features of *Criterion.* Retrieved from http://www.ets.org/Media/Research/pdf/erater_NCME_2004_Attali_B.pdf

Bain, D. (2003) PISA et la lecture: Un point de vue de didacticien. *Revue suisse des sciences de l'éducation, 25,* 59–78.

Bakhtin, M. (1984). *Speech genres and other late essays.* Austin, TX: University of Texas Press. (V.W. McKee, Trans.).

Balester, V. (1993). *Cultural divide: A study of African American college level writers*. Portsmouth, NH: Heinemann-Boynton/Cook.

Ball, A. F. (1992a). *Assessment of student writing in ethnographic contexts: Assessing the written exposition of culturally diverse students*. Retrieved from http://www.stanford.edu/~arnetha/pdf/additionalPDF/Calfee%20Eval%20ArticleA.pdf

——— (1992b). Cultural preference and the expository writing of African American adolescents. *Written Communication, 9,* 501–532.

——— (1995). Text design patterns in the writing of urban African-American students: Teaching to the strengths of students in multicultural settings. *Urban Education, 30*(3), 253–289.

——— (1997). Expanding the dialogue on culture as a critical component when assessing writing. *Assessing Writing, 4*(2), 169–202.

——— (1999). Evaluating the writing of culturally and linguistically diverse students: The case of the African American vernacular English speaker. In C. Cooper & L. Odell (Eds.), *Evaluating writing: The role of teachers' knowledge about text, learning, and culture* (pp. 225–248). Urbana, IL: NCTE.

——— (2005). Teaching writing in culturally diverse classrooms. In C. A. MacArthur, S. Graham, & J. Fitzgerald (Eds.), *Handbook of writing research* (pp. 293–310). New York: Guilford.

——— (2009) Expanding the dialogue on culture as a critical component when assessing writing. In B. Huot & P. O'Neill (Eds.), *Assessing writing: A critical sourcebook.* (pp. 357–386). Boston: Bedford/St. Martin's.

Ball, A. F., Christensen, L., Fleischer, C., Haswell, R., Ketter, J., Yagelski, R., & Yancey, K. (2005). The impact of the SAT and ACT timed writing tests. Retrieved from http://www.ncte.org/library/files/About_NCTE/Press_Center/SAT/SAT-ACT-tf-report.pdf

Ball, A. F. & Lardner, T. (1997). Teacher constructs of knowledge and the Ann Arbor Black English case. *College Composition and Communication, 48*(4), 469–485.

——— (2005). *African American literacies unleashed: Vernacular English and the composition classroom*. Carbondale, IL: Southern Illinois University Press.

Baron, Dennis. (1992, July 1). Why do academics continue to insist on "proper English"? *Chronicle of Higher Education*. Retrieved from http://chronicle.com/article/Why-DoAcademics-Continue-to/79938/

Barnett, T. (2000). Reading whiteness in English Studies. *College English, 63*(1), 9–37.

Bartholomae, D. (1985). Inventing the University. In M. Rose (Ed.). *When a writer can't write: Studies in writer's block and other composing-process problems* (pp. 134–166). New York and London: The Guilford Press.

——— (1993). The tidy house: Basic writing in the American curriculum. *Journal of Basic Writing, 12*(1), 4–21.

Bauman, M. (1997). What grades do for us, and how to do without them. In S. Tchudi (Ed.), *Alternatives to grading student writing* (pp. 162–78). Urbana: NCTE.

Bautier, E. (1995). *Pratiques langagières, pratiques sociales*. Paris: L'Harmattan.

——— (2004). Formes et activités scolaires: Secondarisation, reconfiguration, et différenciation sociale, In N. Ramognino & P. Verges (Eds.), *La langue française hier et aujourd'hui* (pp. 49–68). Aix-en-Provence: Presses Universitaires de Provence.

——— (2005). Mobilisation de soi, exigences langagières scolaires et processus de différenciation. *Langage et société, 111,* 51–72.

Bautier, E., & Branca-Rosoff, S. (2002). Pratiques linguistiques des élèves en échec scolaire et enseignement. *VEI Enjeux, 130,* 196–213.

References203

Bautier, E., Crinon, J., Rayou, P., & Rochex, J-Y. (2005). Les performances en littéracie et l'hétérogénéité des univers mentaux mobilisés par les élèves. *Giornale Italiano di Pedagogia Sperimentale, 13*(2), 43–64.

—— (2006). Performances en littéraci, modes de faire et univers mobilisés par les élèves: Analyses secondaires de l'enquête PISA. *Revue Française de Pédagogie, 157*, 72–85.

Bautier, E. & Rochex, J-Y. (2001). Rapport aux savoirs et travail d'écriture en philosophie et sciences économiques et socials. In B. Charlot (Ed.), *Les jeunes et le savoir* (pp. 133–154). Paris: Anthropos.

—— (2004). Activité conjointe ne signifie pas significations partagées. *Raisons éducatives, 8,* 199–220.

Baxter, M. (1976). Educating teachers about educating the oppressed. *College English, 37*(7), 677–681.

Bazerman, C. (1991). The second stage in writing across the curriculum. *College English, 53*(2), 209–212.

Bazerman, C., Little, J., Bethel, L., Chavkin, T., Fouquette, D., & Garufis, J. (2005). *Reference guide to writing across the curriculum.* West Lafayette, IN: Parlor Press.

Bazerman, C., & Russell, D. R. (Eds.). (1994). *Landmark essays on writing across the curriculum.* Davis, CA: Hermagoras.

Bedore, P., & Rossen-Knill, D. F. (2004). Informed self-placement: Is a choice offered a choice received? *WPA: Writing Program Administration, 28*(2), 55–78.

Beech, J. (2004). Redneck and hillbilly discourse in the writing classroom: Classifying critical pedagogies of whiteness. *College English, 67*(2), 172–186.

Behm, N. (2008). *Whiteness, white privilege, and three first-year guides to writing.* (Doctoral dissertation, Arizona State University). Retrieved from http://books.google.com/books/about/Whiteness_white_privilege_and_three_firs.html?id=uk5R29SjSUwC

Belanoff, P., & Dickson, M. (Eds.). (1991). *Portfolios: Process and product.* Portsmouth: Boynton/Cook.

Belanoff, P., & Elbow, P. (1986). Using portfolios to increase collaboration and community in a writing program. *Journal of Writing Program Administrators, 9,* 27–39.

Berthoff, A. E., & Clark, W. G. (1975). Responses to "The Students' Right to Their Own Language." *College Composition and Communication, 22*(2), 216–217.

Bishop, G. K. (1986). An investigation to determine if significant differences exist in writing skills instruction in demographically similar schools in Pennsylvania. (Doctoral dissertation, Temple University, Philadelphia, PA. *DAI-A, 47*(03), 784.

Bizzell, P. (1982). Cognition, convention, and certainty: What we need to know about writing. *PRE/TEXT, 3,* 213–143.

—— (1994). "Contact zones" and English studies. *College English, 56,* 163–169.

Black, L., Daiker, D., Sommers, J., & Stygall, G. (Eds.). (1994). *New directions in portfolio assessment: Reflective practice, critical theory, and large-scale scoring.* Portsmouth, NH: Boynton/Cook.

Black, L., et al. (1994). Writing like a woman and being rewarded for it: Gender, assessment, and reflective letters from Miami University's student portfolios. In L. Black, D. Daiker, & J. Sommers (Eds.), *New directions in portfolio assessment: Reflective practice, critical theory, and large-scale scoring.* (pp. 235–247). Portsmouth, NH: Boynton/Cook Publishers.

Blakesley, D. (2002). Directed self-placement in the university. *WPA: Writing Program Administration, 25*(3), 9–40.

Bleich, D. (1997). What can be done about grading. In L. Allison, L. Bryant, & M. Hourigan (Eds.), *Grading in the post-process classroom: From theory to practice* (pp. 15–35). Portsmouth: Boynton/Cook.

Bond, L. (1995). Unintended consequences of performance assessment: Issues of bias and fairness. *Educational Measurement: Issues and Practice, 14*(4), 21–24.

Bonilla-Silva, E. (2001). *White supremacy and racism in the post-civil rights era.* Boulder: Lynne Rienner P.

——— (2006). *Racism without racists: Color-Blind racism and the persistence of racial inequality in the United States.* (2nd ed.). Lanham, Maryland: Rowman & Littlefield P.

Bourdieu, P. (1997). *Pascalian meditations.* Trans. Richard Nice. Stanford: Stanford UP.

Bowie, R., & Bond, C. (1994). Influencing future teachers' attitudes toward black English: Are we making a difference? *Journal of Teacher Education, 45,* 112–118.

Bowman, J. P. (1973). Problems of the grading differential. *Journal of Business Communication, 11*(1), 22–30.

Brandt, D. (1995). Accumulating literacy: Writing and learning to write in the twentieth century. *College English, 57*(6), 649–668.

Breland, H., M. Kubota, K. Nickerson, C. Trapani, & M. Walker. (2004). *New SAT writing prompt study: Analyses of group impact and reliability.* New York: College Board Publications.

Broad, B. (1997). Reciprocal authorities in communal writing assessment: Constructing textual value within a "new politics of inquiry." *Assessing Writing, 4*(2), 133–167.

——— (2000). Pulling your hair out: Crises of standardization in communal writing assessment. *Research in the Teaching of English, 35,* 213–260.

——— (2003). *What we really value: Beyond rubrics in teaching and assessing writing.* Logan, UT: Utah State UP.

——— (2006). More work for teacher? Possible futures of teaching writing in the age of computerized writing assessment. In P. Ericsson & R. Haswell (Eds.), *Machine scoring of student essays: Truth and consequences* (pp. 221–233). Logan: Utah State UP.

Broad, B., Adler-Kassner, L., Alford, B., Detweiler, J., Estrem, H., Harrington, S., McBride, M., Stalions, E., & Weeden, S. (Eds.). (2009). *Organic writing assessment: Dynamic criteria mapping in action.* Logan, UT: Utah State UP.

Brodkey, L. (1987). *Academic writing as social practice.* Philadelphia, PA: Temple University Press.

Brooks, M.P., & D. Houck. (2010). Introduction. In M. P. Brooks & D. Houck (Eds.), *The speeches of Fannie Lou Hamer: To tell it like it is.* (pp. xi–xxxi). Jackson, MS: UP of Mississippi.

Bulinski, M., Dominguez, A., Inoue, A. B., Jamali, M., McKnight, M., Seidel, S., & Stott, J. (2009, March). "Shit-plus," "AWK," "frag," and "huh?": An empirical look at a writing program's commenting practices. Paper presented at the Conference on College Composition and Communication, San Francisco, CA.

Burstein, J., Chodorow, M., & Leacock, C. (2004). Automated essay evaluation: The *Criterion* Online Writing Service. *AI Magazine, 25*(3), 27–36.

Butler, S. (1998). Race and gender in an internet-based history course. *Works and Days, 16*(1/2), 193–216.

California State Fresno. (2009). English 5A: Experiencing academic literacy by entering conversations about being and becoming American. Department of English. Syllabus.

——— (2009). Final regularly admitted first-time freshmen proficiency, Fresno. Retrieved from http://www.asd.calstate.edu/proficiency/2009/Prof_Fre_fall2009.htm

Callahan, S. (1995). Portfolio expectations: Possibilities and limits. *Assessing Writing, 2*(2), 117–151.

——— (1999). All done with the best of intentions: One Kentucky high school after six years of state portfolio tests. *Assessing Writing, 6*(1), 5-40.

Cambridge, B., Kahn, S., Tompkins, D. P., & Yancey, K. B. (Eds.). (2001). *Electronic portfolios: Emerging practices in student, faculty, and institutional learning.* Washington, DC: American Association for Higher Education.

Cambridge, D., Cambridge, B., & Yancey, K. B. (2009). *Electronic portfolios 2.0.* Washington, DC: Stylus.

Campbell, K. E. (2004). We is who we was: The African/American rhetoric of *Amistad.* In E. B. Richardson & R. L. Jackson II (Eds.), *African American rhetoric(s): Interdisciplinary perspectives* (pp. 204-220). Carbondale: SIUP.

——— (2005). *Getting' our groove on: Rhetoric, language, and literacy for the hip hop generation.* African American life series. Detroit, MI: Wayne State University Press.

Canagarajah, A. S. (2006a). The place of world Englishes in composition: Pluralization continued. *College Composition and Communication, 57*(4), 586-619.

——— (2006b). Toward a writing pedagogy of shuttling between languages: Learning from multilingual writers. *College English, 68*(6), 589-604.

Carroll, P., & D. Noble. (1992). *The free and the unfree: A new history of the United States.* New York: Penguin.

Carter, M. (2003). A process for establishing outcomes-based assessment plans for writing and speaking in the disciplines. *Language and Learning Across the Disciplines, 6*(1), 4-29.

Center, C. (2007). Representing race in basic writing scholarship. *Journal of Basic Writing, 26*(1), 20-42.

Chen, C.-F.E., & Cheng, W.-Y. E. (2008). Beyond the design of automated writing evaluation: Pedagogical practices and perceived learning effectiveness in EFL writing classes. *Language, Learning & Technology, 12*(2), 94-112.

Chesnutt, C. (2011). *The conjure woman and other tales.* New York: CreateSpace. (Original work published in 1899).

Chodorow, M., Gamon, M., & Tetrault, J. (2010). The utility of grammatical error detection systems for English language learners: Feedback and assessment. *Language Testing, 27,* 419-436.

Cohodas, N. (1997). *The band played Dixie: Race and the liberal conscience at Ole Miss.* New York: Free Press.

College Board. (2010). *Spelman College. At a glance.* Retrieved from http://collegesearch.collegeboard.com/search/CollegeDetail.jsp?collegeId=662&profileId=

Conference on College Composition and Communication. (1974). Background statement. *College Composition and Communication, 25*(3), 1-18.

Conference on College Composition and Communication. (1988). CCCC Guideline on the national language policy. Retrieved from http://www.ncte.org/cccc/resources/positions/nationallangpolicy

Conference on College Composition and Communication. (2003). Students' rights to their own language Retrieved from http://www.ncte.org/cccc/resources/positions/srtolsummary.

Conference on College Composition and Communication. (2009). Writing assessment: A position statement. Retrieved from http://www.ncte.org/cccc/resources/positions/writingassessment

Condon, F. (2007). Beyond the known: Writing centers and the work of anti-racism. *The Writing Center Journal, 27*(2), 19-38.

Condon, W. (2011). Reinventing writing assessment: How the conversation is shifting. *Writing Program Administration, 34*(2), 162–182.

Connors, R. J. (2000). The erasure of the sentence. *College Composition and Communication, 52*(1), 96–128.

Cooper, M. M. (2004). Nonessentialist identity and the national discourse. In K. Gilyard and V. Nunley (Eds.), *Rhetoric and Ethnicity.* (pp. 87-102). Portsmouth, NH: Boynton/Cook.

Crenshaw, K. W. (1995). Race, reform, and retrenchment: Transformation and legitimation in antidiscrimination law. In K. W. Crenshaw, N. Gotanda, G. Peller, & K. Thomas (Eds.), *Critical race theory: The key writings that formed the movement.* (pp. 103-122). New York: The New Press.

Cronbach, L. J. (1988). Five perspectives on validity argument. In Wainer, H. (Ed.), *Test validity.* (pp. 3-17). Hillsdale, NJ: Lawrence Erlbaum.

———— (1989). Construct validation after thirty years. In. R. E. Linn (Ed.), *Intelligence: Measurement, theory and public policy* (pp. 147-171). Urbana: University of Illinois Press.

Crowley, S. (1998). *Composition in the university: Historical and polemical essays.* Pittsburgh, PA: University of Pittsburgh Press.

Danielewicz, J., & Elbow, P. (2009). A unilateral grading contract to improve learning and teaching. *College Composition and Communication, 61*(2), 244-268.

Davidson, M., Howell, K. W., & Hoekema, P. (2000). Effects of ethnicity and violent content on rubric scores in writing samples. *The Journal of Educational Research, 93*(6), 367-373.

Delgado, R. (1989) Legal storytelling: Storytelling for oppositionists and others: A plea for narrative. *Michigan Law Review,* 87, 2411-2441.

Delpit, L. (1988). The silenced dialogue: Power and pedagogy in educating other people's children. *Harvard Educational Review, 58*(3), 280-298.

———— (1995a). Skills and other dilemmas of the progressive educator. *Other people's children: Cultural conflict in the classroom.* New York: New Press.

———— (1995b). The silenced dialogue. *Other people's children: Cultural conflict in the classroom.* New York: New Press.

———— (2004). What should teachers do? Ebonics and culturally responsive instruction. In S. J. Nero (Ed.), *Dialects, Englishes, creoles, and education* (pp. 93-104). New Jersey: Lawrence Erlbaum.

Diederich, P. B. (1974). *Measuring growth in English.* Urbana, IL: NCTE.

Donahue, C. (2008). *Ecrire à l'université: Analyse comparee en France et aux Etats-Unis.* Villeneuve d'Ascq: Presses Universitaires du Septentrion.

———— (2011). *Considering the international in international research.* Paper presented at Writing Education Across Borders Conference, State College, PA.

Donahue, P. (2002). Strange resistances. *WAC Journal, 13,* 31-41. Retrieved from http://wac.colostate.edu/journal/vol13/donahue.pdf

D'Souza, D. (1995). *The end of racism.* New York: Free Press.

Duffy, J. (2007). *Writing from these roots: Literacy in a Hmong-American community.* Honolulu: University of Hawai'i Press.

Duncan, A. (2009). HBCUs and higher education: Beyond the iron triangle Remarks of Arne Duncan to National Historically Black Colleges and Universities Conference. Retrieved from http://www2.ed.gov/news/speeches/2009/09/09022009.html

Dyer, R. (1993). *In the matter of images: Essays on representations.* New York: Routledge.

Economist. (2009). Collecting ethnic information in France. Retrieved from http://www.economist.com/world/europe/displaystory.cfm?story_id=13377324

Elbow, P. (1993). Ranking, evaluating, and liking: Sorting out three forms of judgment. *College English*, 55(2), 187–206.

——— (1996). Writing assessment in the 21st century: A utopian view. In L. Z. Bloom, D. A. Daiker, & E. M. White (Eds.), *Composition in the twenty-first century: Crisis and change* (pp. 83–100). Carbondale: Southern Illinois University Press.

Elliot, N. (2005). *On a scale: A social history of writing assessment in America*. New York: Peter Lang.

Elliot, N., Briller, V., & Joshi, K. (2007). Portfolio assessment: Quantification and community. *Journal of Writing Assessment*, 3(1), 5–30.

Enright, M.K., & Quinlan, T. (2010). Complementing human judgment of essays written by English language learners with *e-rater* scoring. *Language Testing*, 27, 317–334.

Ericsson, P. F., & Haswell, R. (Eds.). (2006). *Machine scoring of student essays: Truth and consequences*. Logan, UT: Utah State UP.

Essed, P. (2002). Everyday racism: A new approach to the study of racism. In P. Essed & D. T. Goldberg (Eds.), *Race critical theories* (pp. 176–194). Malden, MA: Blackwell.

ETS. (2007a). ETS's *Criterion*SM online writing evaluation wins top honor for global learning impact. Retrieved from http://www.ets.org/newsroom/news_releases/criterion_honored_global_impact

——— (2007b). The *Criterion* teaching guide: Using the *Criterion* Online Evaluation Service for differentiated instruction in the college classroom: A guide for faculty and administrators. Retrieved from http://www.ets.org/Media/Resources_For/Higher_Education/pdf/ Criterion_Teacher_Guide_web_6487.pdf

——— (2011a). *Criterion*SM Online Writing Evaluation. Retrieved from http://www.ets.org/ criterion/

——— (2011b). *Criterion*SM Online Writing Evaluation. Higher education. Retrieved from http://www.ets.org/criterion/higher_ed/about

——— (2012). Frequently asked questions about the *Criterion*® Online Writing Evaluation Service. Retrieved from http://www.ets.org/criterion/higher_ed/about/faq/

Evans, D., & He, H. (2007). *The Washington State University Writing Portfolio. Seventh findings: June 2005–May 2007.* Office of Writing Assessment Internal Report #8. Pullman, WA: Washington State University.

Farr, M., & Daniels, H. (1986). *Language diversity and writing instruction*. ERIC Clearinghouse on Urban Education.

Farr, M., & Nardini, G. (1996). Essayist literacy and sociolinguistic difference. In E.M. White, W. D. Lutz & S. Kamusikiri (Eds.), *Assessment of writing: Politics, policies, practices* (pp. 108–119). New York: The Modern Language Association of America.

Fasold, W., Labov, W., Vaughn-Cooke, F., Bailey, G., Wolfram, W., Spears, A., Rickford, J. (1987). Are black and white vernaculars diverging: Papers from the NWAVE XIV panel discussion. *American Speech*, 61(1), 3-80.

Feagin, J. R. (2010). *Racist America: Roots, current realities, and future reparations*. (2nd ed.). New York: Routledge.

Feagin, J. R., & H. Vera. (1995). *White racism: The basics*. New York: Routledge.

Feagin, J. R., H. Vera, & N. Imani. (1996) *The agony of education: Black students at white colleges and universities*. New York: Routledge.

Florida State University. (2011). Freshman admissions. The process. Retrieved from http:// admissions.fsu.edu/freshman/parents/admissions.cfm.

Flower, L. (1979). Writer-based prose: A cognitive basis for problems in writing. *College English*, 41(1), 19-37.

Frankenberg, R. (1997). Introduction: Local whitenesses, localizing whiteness. In R. Frankenberg (Ed.), *Displacing whiteness: Essays in social and cultural criticism* (pp. 1-33). Durham: Duke UP.

Freedle, R. O. (2003). Correcting the SAT's ethnic and social-class bias: A method for reestimating SAT scores. *Harvard Educational Review, 73*(1), 1-43.

Freedman, S. H. (1996). Moving writing research into the 21st century. In L. Z. Bloom, D. A. Daiker, & E. M. White (Eds.), *Composition in the twenty-first century: Crisis and change* (pp. 183-193). Carbondale, IL: Southern Illinois University Press.

Fulwiler, T. (1984). How well does writing across the curriculum work? *College English, 46,* 113-125.

Fulwiler, T., & Young, A. (Eds.). (1982). *Language connections: Writing and reading across the curriculum.* Urbana, IL: National Council of Teachers of English.

————— (1990). *Programs that work: Models and methods for writing across the curriculum.* Portsmouth, NH: Boynton-Cook.

Gallagher, C. (2010). Assess locally, validate globally: Heuristics for validating local writing assessments. *Journal of the Council of Writing Program Administration, 34*(1), 10-32.

Garcia, O., & K. Mencken. (2006). The English of Latinos from a plurilingual transcultural angle: Implications for assessment and schools. In S. J. Nero (Ed.), *Dialects, Englishes, creoles, and education* (pp. 167-83). New Jersey: Lawrence Erlbaum.

Gere, A. R. (Ed.). (1985). *Roots in the sawdust: Writing to learn across the disciplines.* Urbana, IL: National Council of Teachers of English.

Gere, A. R., Aull, L., Green, T., & Porter, A. (2010). Assessing the validity of directed self-placement at a large university. *Assessing Writing, 15*(3), 154-176.

Gillborn, D., & Mirza, H.S. (2000). *Educational inequality: mapping race, class and gender–a synthesis of research evidence.* Report HMI 232. London: Office for Standards in Education.

Gilroy, P. (2000). *Against race: Imagining political culture beyond the color line.* Cambridge, MA: Harvard University Press.

Gilyard, K. (1991). *Voice of the self: A study of language competence.* Detroit: Wayne State University Press.

————— (1999a). African American contributions to composition studies. *College Composition and Communication, 50*(4), 626-644.

————— (1999b). Higher learning: Composition's racialized reflection. In K Gilyard (Ed.), *Race, rhetoric, and composition* (pp. 44-52). Portsmouth, NH: Boynton/Cook.

Goigoux, R. (2000). *Les élèves en difficulté de lecture et les enseignements adaptés.* Suresnes: Editions du CNEFEL.

Goldberg, D. T. (1994). *Racist culture: Philosophy and the politics of meaning.* Malden, MA: Blackwell.

————— (1997). *Racial subjects: Writing on race in America.* New York: Routledge.

————— (2002). *The racial state.* Malden, MA: Blackwell.

Goody, J., & Watt, I. (1963). The consequences of literacy. *Comparative Studies in Society and History, 5*(3), 304-345.

Gottschalk, K. K. (1991). Training TAs across the curriculum to teach writing: Embracing diversity. In J. D. Nyquist (Ed.), *Preparing the professoriate of tomorrow to teach: Selected readings in TA training* (pp. 168-174). Dubuque, Iowa: Kendall/Hunt.

Gould, S. J. (1996). *The mismeasure of man.* New York: W.W. Norton & Co.

Graff, G. (2003). *Clueless in academe: How schooling obscures the life of the mind.* New Haven: Yale University Press.

Hairston, M. (1981). Not all errors are created equal: Nonacademic readers in the professions respond to lapses in usage. *College English, 43,* 794-806.

Halasz, J., Brinckner, M., Gambs, D., Geraci, D., Queeley, A., & Solovyova, S. (2006). Making it your own: Writing fellows re-evaluate faculty "resistance". *Across the Disciplines, 3.* Retrieved from http://wac.colostate.edu/atd/articles/halasz2006.cfm

Hall Kells, M. (2006). Tex Mex, metalinguistic discourse, and teaching college writing. In S. J. Nero (Ed.): *Dialects, Englishes, creoles, and education* (pp. 185-201). New Jersey: Lawrence Erlbaum.

Hamer, F.L. (2010). We are on our way. In M.P. Brooks & D. Houck, (Eds.), *The speeches of Fannie Lou Hamer: To tell it like it is* (pp. 46-56). Jackson, MS: UP of Mississippi.

Hamp-Lyons, L. (2009). The challenges of second-language writing assessment. In B. Huot & P. O'Neill (Eds.), *Assessing writing: A critical sourcebook* (pp. 343-356). Boston: Bedford/St. Martin's.

Hamp-Lyons, L., & Condon, W. (2000). *Assessing the portfolio: Principles for practice, theory and research.* Cresskill, NJ: Hampton Press.

Hannaford, I. (1996). *Race: The history of an idea in the west.* Washington, DC: Woodrow Wilson Center Press.

Hanson, F. A. (1993). *Testing testing: Social consequences of the examined life.* Berkeley: University of California Press.

Harber, K.D. (1998). Feedback to minorities: Evidence of a positive bias. *Journal of Personality and Social Psychology, 74*(3), 622-628.

Harrington, S., Rhodes, K., Fischer, R. O., & Malenczyk, R. (Eds.). (2005). *The outcomes book: Debate and consensus after the WPA outcomes statement.* Logan, UT: Utah State UP.

Hartwell, P. (1985). Grammar, grammars, and the teaching of grammar. *College English, 47*(2), 105-127.

Haswell, R. H. (1995). *The WSU Writing Portfolio. First findings (Feb. 1993–May 1995).* Office of Writing Assessment Internal Report #2. Pullman, WA: Washington State University.

———— (1998a). Multiple inquiry in the validation of writing tests. *Assessing Writing, 5*(1), 89-109.

———— (1998b). Rubrics, prototypes and exemplars: Categorization and systems of writing placement. *Assessing Writing, 5*(2), 231-268.

———— (2000). Documenting improvement in college writing: A longitudinal approach. *Written Communication, 45,* 220-236.

———— (Ed.) (2001). *Beyond outcomes: Assessment and instruction within a university writing program.* Westport, CT. Ablex.

Haswell, R., Johnson-Shull, L., and Wyche-Smith, S. (1994). Shooting Niagara: Making portfolio assessment serve instruction at a state university. *Writing Program Administration, 18*(1/2), 44-53.

Haswell, R. & Wyche, S. (1996). A two-tiered rating procedure for placement essays. In T. W. Banta (Ed.), *Assessment in Practice: Putting Principles to Work on College Campuses* (pp. 204-207). San Francisco: Jossey-Bass.

Haymes, S. N. (1995). White culture and the politics of racial difference: Implications for multiculturalism. In C. E. Sleeter & P. L. McLaren (Eds.), *Multicultural education, critical pedagogy, and the politics of difference* (pp. 105-127). Albany: SUNY Press.

Heath, S. B. (1983). *Ways with words: Language, life, and work in communities and classrooms.* New York: Cambridge UP.

Henry, J. (1994). A narratological analysis of WAC authorship. *College English, 56,* 810-824.

Herrington, A., & Curtis, M. (2000). *Persons in progress: Four stories of writing and personal development in college.* Urbana, IL: National Council of Teachers of English.

Herrington, A., & Moran. C. (Eds.). (1992). *Writing, teaching, and learning in the disciplines.* New York: Modern Language Association.

———— (2001). What happens when machines read our students' writing? *College English, 63,* 480–499.

———— (Eds.). (2005). *Genre across the curriculum.* Logan, UT: Utah State University Press.

———— (2006). WritePlacer *Plus* in place: An exploratory case study. In P. Ericsson & R. Haswell (Eds.), *Machine scoring of student essays: Truth and consequences* (pp. 114–129). Logan, UT: Utah State UP.

———— (2009). Writing, assessment, and new technologies. In M. Paretti & K. Powell (Eds), *Assessment of writing.* Tallahassee FL: Association of Institutional Researchers.

Hesse, D. (2005). Who owns writing? *College Composition and Communication, 57,* 335–357.

Hillocks, G. (1999). *Ways of thinking, ways of teaching.* New York: Teachers College Press.

———— (2002). *The testing trap: How state writing assessments control learning.* New York: Teachers College Press.

Hirsch, L., Nadal, J., & Shohet, L. (1991). Adapting language across the curriculum to diverse linguistic populations. In L. C. Stanley & J. Ambron (Eds.), *Writing across the curriculum in community colleges* (pp. 71–78). San Francisco: Jossey-Bass.

Holmes, D. G. (1999). Fighting back by writing Black: Beyond racially reductive composition theory. In. K. Gilyard (Ed.), *Race, Rhetoric, and Composition.* (pp. 53-66). New Hampshire: Boynton/Cook.

Hong, W.P., & Youngs, P. (2008). Does high-stakes testing increase cultural capital among low-income and racial minority students? *Education Policy Analysis Archives, 16*(6). Retrieved from http://epaa.asu.edu/epaa/v16n6/

Hoover, M., & Politzer, R. (1981). Bias in composition tests with suggestions for a culturally appropriate assessment technique. In M. F. Whiteman (Ed.), *Writing: The nature, development, and teaching of written communication, Vol. 1: Variation in writing: Functional and linguistic-cultural differences* (pp. 197–204). Hillsdale, NJ: Erlbaum.

Horner, B., & Lu, M-Z. (2007). Resisting monolingualism in "English": Reading and writing the politics of language." In V. Ellis, C. Fox, & B. V. Street (Eds.), *Rethinking English in schools: Towards a new and constructive stage* (pp. 141–157). New York: Continuum International Pub. Group.

Horner, B., & Trimbur, J. (2002). English Only and U.S. college composition. *College Composition and Communication, 53,* 594–630.

Howard, R. M. (2000). Applications and assumptions of student self-assessment. In J. B. Smith & K. B. Yancey (Eds.), *Self-Assessment and development in writing: A collaborative inquiry* (pp. 35–59). Cresskill, NJ: Hampton Press.

Huot, B. (1990). Reliability, validity, and holistic scoring: What we know and what we need to know. *College Composition and Communication, 41*(2), 201–213.

———— (2002a). *(Re)Articulating writing assessment for teaching and learning.* Logan, UT: Utah State University Press.

———— (2002b). Toward a new discourse of assessment for the college writing classroom. *College English, 65*(2), 163–180.

Huot, B., & Neal, M. (2006). Writing assessment: A techno-history. In C. MacArthur, S. Graham, & J. Fitzgerald (Eds.), *Handbook of writing research.* (pp. 417–432). New York: Guilford Press.

Huot, B., & P. O'Neill (Eds.). (2009). *Assessing writing: A critical sourcebook*. Boston: Bedford/St. Martin's.

Huot, B., O'Neill, P., & Moore, C. (2010). A useable past for writing assessment. *College English, 72*(5), 495–517.

Hurston, Z. N. (2006). *Their eyes were watching God*. New York: Harper. (Originally published in 1937).

Hutchison, D. (2007). An evaluation of computerized essay marking for national curriculum assessment in the UK for 11-year-olds. *British Journal of Educational Technology, 38*(6), 977–989.

Inoue, A. B. (2004). Community-based assessment pedagogy. *Assessing Writing, 9*(3), 208–238.

——— (2008). Program assessment and DSP validation study: First-Year writing program and its pilot DSP. Report. Retrieved from http://www.csufresno.edu/english/undergraduate/firstyear/documents/FYW%20Program%20Assessment-AY07-08v4.pdf

——— (2009a). Self-assessment as programmatic center: The first year writing program and its assessment at California State University, Fresno. *Composition Forum, 20*. Retrieved from http://compositionforum.com/issue/20/calstate-fresno.php

——— (2009b). The technology of writing assessment and racial validity. In Christopher S. Schreiner (Ed.), *Handbook of research on assessment technologies, methods, and applications in higher education* (pp. 97–120). Hershey, PA: IGI Global.

Jackson, J. S. (2007, April). *Disaggregating race and ethnicity in behavioral and social science research*. Decade of Behavior Distinguished Lecture presented at the meeting of the American Educational Research Association, Chicago, IL.

Jaschik, S. (2007). Making holistic admissions work. *Inside Higher Education*, March 2. Retrieved from http://www.insidehighered.com/news/2007/03/02/holistic

——— (2008a). Non-cognitive qualities join the GRE. *Inside Higher Education*, May 22. Retrieved from http://www.insidehighered.com/news/2008/05/22/ets

——— (2008b). If you can't beat 'em, join 'em. *Inside Higher Education*. May 22. Retrieved from http://www.insidehighered.com/news/2008/09/29/predict

Jencks, C., & M. Phillips. (1998). *The black-white test score gap*. Washington, DC: Brookings Institute.

Johnson, T. S. (1986). A comment on "Collaborative Learning and the Conversation of Mankind." *College English, 48*, 76.

Jolliffe, D. A. (Ed.). (1988). *Writing in academic disciplines*. Norwood, NJ: Ablex.

Jones, R., & Comprone, J. J. (1993). Where do we go next in writing across the curriculum? *College Composition and Communication, 44*, 59–68.

Kamusikiri, S. (1996). African American English and writing assessment: An Afrocentric approach. In E. M. White, W. D. Lutz, and S. Kamusikiri (Eds.), *Assessment of writing: Politics, policies, practices.* (pp. 187–203). New York: The Modern Language Association of America.

Keating, A. L. (1995). Interrogating "whiteness," (de)constructing "race." *College English, 57*(8), 901–918.

Kelly, L. (1974). Is competent copyreading a violation of students' right to their own language? *College Composition and Communication, 25*(4), 254–258.

Kelly-Riley, D. (2006). A validity inquiry into minority students' performances in a large-scale writing portfolio assessment. (Doctoral dissertation, Washington State University). *DAI*, A-67/08.

——— (2011). Validity inquiry of race and shared evaluation practices in a large-scale, university-wide writing portfolio assessment. *Journal of Writing Assessment, 4*(1), Retrieved from http://www.journalofwriting assessment.org/article.php?article=53

Kemp, F. (1992). Who programmed this? Examining the instructional attitudes of writing support software. *Computers and Composition*, *10*, 9–24.

Kent, T. (1991). On the very idea of a discourse community. *College Composition and Communication*, *42*(4), 425–445.

Ki-moon, Ban. (Sept. 2 2011). Literacy has capacity to "unlock capacity of individuals'" says secretary-general, calling it fundamental aspect of human dignity in message for International Day. Retrieved from http://www.un.org/News/Press/docs/2011/sgsm13769 .doc.htm

King, J. (1991). Dysconscious racism: Ideology, identity, and the miseducation of teachers. *Journal of Negro Education*, *60*, 133–146.

Kinloch, V. (2005). Revisiting the promise of *Students' Right to Their Own Language*: Pedagogical strategies. *College Composition and Communication*, *57*(1), 83–113.

———— (2010). "To not be a traitor of Black English": Youth perceptions of language rights in an urban context. *Teachers College Record*, *112*(1), 103–141.

Klein, S. (2003). Language and diversity. In I. Clark (Ed.), *Concepts in composition* (pp. 413–425). Mahwah, NJ: Erlbaum.

Knapp, J. V. (1976). Contract/Conference evaluations of freshman composition. *College English*, *37*(7), 647–653.

Kohn, A. (1993). *Punished by rewards: The trouble with gold stars, incentive plans, A's, praise, and other bribes*. Boston: Houghton Mifflin.

Kolln, M. (2007). *Rhetorical grammar: Grammatical choices, rhetorical effects*. New York, NY: Longman.

Kucer, S. B. (2009). *Dimensions of literacy*. New York, NY: Routledge.

Labov, W. (1970). *The study of nonstandard English*. Champaign, IL: NCTE.

———— (1972). *Language in the inner city: Studies in the Black English vernacular*. Philadelphia, PA: University of Pennsylvania Press.

———— (2010). Unendangered languages, endangered people: The case of African American vernacular English. *Transforming Anthropology*, *18*, 15–27.

Latta, S., & Lauer, J. (2000). Student self-assessment: Some issues and concerns from postmodern and feminist perspectives. In J. B. Smith & K. B. Yancey (Eds.), *Self-Assessment and Development in Writing: A Collaborative Inquiry* (pp. 25–35). Cresskill, NJ: Hampton Press.

Lave, J., & Wenger, E. (1991). *Situated learning: Legitimate peripheral participation*. Cambridge England: Cambridge University Press.

LeCourt, D. (1996). WAC as critical pedagogy: The third stage? JAC, *16*(3). Retrieved from http://www.jacweb.org/Archived_volumes/Text_articles/ V16_I3_LeCourt.htm

Lemann, N. (1999). *The Big Test*. New York: Farrar, Straus and Giroux.

Lewicki-Wilson, C., Sommers, J., & Tassoni, J.P. (2000). Rhetoric and the writer's profile: Problematizing directed self-placement. *Assessing Writing*, *7*, 165–183.

Lippi-Green, R. (1997). *English with an accent: Language, ideology, and discrimination in the United States*. London: Routledge.

Lovejoy, K. B. (2003). Practical pedagogy for composition. In G. Smitherman & V. Villanueva (Eds.), *Language diversity in the classroom: From intention to practice: Studies in writing & rhetoric* (pp. 89–108). Carbondale: Southern Illinois University Press.

Lowell, L., & Salzman, H. (2007). *Into the eye of the storm: Assessing the evidence on science and engineering education, quality, and workforce demand*. Washington, DC: The Urban Institute.

Lu, M. Z. (1994). Professing multiculturalism: The politics of style in the contact zone. *College Composition and Communication*, *45*, 442–458.

———— (2006). Living-English work. *College English*, *68*(6), 605–618.

Lu, M. Z., Matsuda, P.K., & Horner, B. (Eds.). (2006) Special issue: Cross-language relations in composition. *College English, 68*(6).

Lucas, C. (1992). Introduction: Writing portfolios-changes and challenges. In Yancey, K. B. (Ed.), *Portfolios in the writing classroom: An introduction* (pp. 1–12). Urbana: NCTE.

Lundstrum, K., & Baker, W. (2009). To give is better than to receive: the benefits of peer review to the reviewer's own writing. *Journal of Second Language Writing, 18*, 30–43.

Lynne, P. (2004). *Coming to terms: A theory of writing assessment.* Logan, UT: Utah State University Press.

Mabry, L. (1999). Writing to the rubric: Lingering effects of traditional standardized testing on direct writing assessment. *Phi Delta Kappan, 80* (9), 673–679.

MacArthur, C. A., Graham, S., & Fitzgerald, J. (Eds.). (2006). *Handbook of writing research.* New York: Guilford.

MacCannell, D. (1989). *The tourist: A theory of the leisure class.* New York: Schocken.

Madaus, G. (1990). *Testing as a social technology: The inaugural Boisi lecture in education and public policy.* Boston: Center for the Study of Testing Evaluation and Educational Policy, Boston College.

——— (1993). A national testing system: Manna from above? An historical/technological perspective. *Educational Assessment, 1*(1), 9–26.

——— (1994). A technological and historical consideration of equity issues associated with proposals to change the nation's testing policy. *Harvard Educational Review, 64*(1), 76–95.

Madaus, G., & Clarke, M. (2001). The adverse impact of high-stakes testing on minority students: Evidence from one hundred years of test data. In G. Orfield & M. L. Kornhaber (Eds.), *Raising standards or raising barriers? Inequality and high-stakes testing in public education* (pp. 85–106). New York: Century Foundation.

Madaus, G., & Horn, C. (2000). Testing technology: The need for oversight. In A. Filer (Ed.), *Assessment: Social practice and social product* (pp. 47–66). London: Routledge/Falmer.

Mahala, D. (1991). Writing utopias: Writing across the curriculum and the promise of reform. *College English, 53*(7), 773–789.

Maimon, E. P. (1982). Writing across the curriculum: Past, present, and future. In Griffin, C. W. (Ed.), *Teaching writing in all disciplines* (pp. 67–73). San Francisco: Jossey-Bass.

Mandel, B. J. (1973). Teaching without judging. *College English, 34*(5), 623–633.

Manesse, D. (2003). *Le français en classes difficiles. Le college entre langue et discours.* Lyon: INRP.

Martin, D., & Penrod, D. (2006). Coming to know criteria: The value of an evaluating writing course for undergraduates. *Assessing Writing, 11*(1), 66–73.

Mason, W. (2010). College essay advice. Responses to this entry. Retrieved from http://blogs.oberlin.edu/applying/applying/college_essay_a.shtml

Matarese, M., & Anson, C. M. (2010). Teacher response to AAE features in the writing of college students: A case study in the social construction of error. In J. B. Smith (Ed.), *The elephant in the classroom: Race and writing* (pp. 111–136). Cresskill, NJ: Hampton Press.

Matsuda, P. K. (2006). The myth of linguistic homogeneity in U.S. college composition. *College English, 68*, 637–651.

McCabe, C. (1994, March 14). Making a difference: Expo inspires school for the "useful arts." *Providence Journal-Bulletin.* Retrieved from http://www.projo.com/cgi-in/include.pl/specials/women/94root10.htm

McLeod, S. H. (Ed.). (1988). *Strengthening programs for writing across the curriculum.* San Francisco: Jossey-Bass.

——— (1989). Writing across the curriculum: The second stage, and beyond. *College Composition and Communication, 40*, 337–343.

McLeod, S. H., Miraglia, E., Soven, M., & Thaiss, C. (Eds.). (2001). *WAC for the new millennium: Strategies for continuing writing-across-the-curriculum programs.* Urbana, IL: National Council of Teachers of English.

McLeod, S. H., & Soven, M. I. (Eds.). (2006). *Composing a community: A history of writing across the curriculum.* West Lafayette, IN: Parlor Press.

Mead, L. (1986). *Beyond entitlement: The social obligations of citizenship.* New York: Free Press.

Meloni, J. (2009). *Beyond the writing placement exam: Writing experiences of students placed into English 100 (1998–2008).* Internal report. Office of Writing Assessment. Pullman, WA.

Mercer, K. (1990). Welcome to the jungle: Identity and diversity in postmodern politics. In J. Rutherford (Ed.), *Community, culture, difference* (pp. 43–71). London: Lawrence and Wishart.

Messick, S. (1989a). Meaning and values in test validation: The science and ethics of assessment. *Educational researcher, 18*(2), 5–11.

———— (1989b). Validity. In Linn, R. L. (Ed.), *Educational measurement.* 3rd ed. (pp. 13–103). New York: American Council on Education and Macmillan.

Miller, S. (1991). *Textual carnivals: The politics of composition.* Carbondale, IL: Southern Illinois University Press.

Miraglia, E., & McLeod, S. (1997). Whither WAC? Interpreting the stories/histories of enduring WAC programs. *Writing Program Administration, 20,* 46–65.

Moller-Wong, C., & Eide, A. (1997). An engineering student retention study. *Journal of Engineering Education, 86*(1), 7–15.

Moore, C., O'Neill, P. & Huot, B. Creating a culture of assessment in writing programs and beyond. *College Composition and Communication, 61*(1), 107–132.

Morrison, T. (1992). *Playing in the dark: Whiteness and the literary imagination.* New York: Vintage Books.

Moss, P. A. (1992). Shifting conceptions of validity in educational measurement: Implications for performative assessment. *Review of Educational Research, 62*(3), 229–258.

———— (1994). Can there be validity without reliability? *Educational Researcher, 23*(4), 5–12.

———— (1998). Testing the test of the test: A response to "multiple inquiry in the validation of writing tests." *Assessing Writing, 5*(1), 111–122.

Mountford, R. (1999). Let them experiment: Accommodating diverse discourse practices in large-scale writing assessment. In C. R. Cooper and L. Odell (Eds.), *Evaluating writing: The role of teachers' knowledge about text, learning, and culture* (pp. 366–396). Urbana, IL: National Council of Teachers of English.

Murphy, S. (2007). Culture and consequences: The canaries in the coal mine. *Research in the Teaching of English, 42*(2), 228–244.

———— (In press). Some consequences of writing assessment. In A. Havnes & L. McDowell (Eds.), *Balancing dilemmas in assessment and learning in contemporary education.* Routledge.

Myers, G. (1986). Reality, consensus, and reform in the rhetoric of composition teaching. *College English, 48,* 154–174.

National Center for Education Statistics. (2009). Projection of education statistics to 2018. 37th edition. U.S. Department of Education. Washington DC. Retrieved from http://nces.ed.gov/pubs2009/2009062.pdf

NCTE-WPA Task Force on Writing Assessment. NCTE-WPA white paper on writing assessment in colleges and universities. Retrieved from http://wpacouncil.org/whitepaper

Nelson, G. L. (1997). How cultural differences affect written and oral communication: The case of peer response groups. In D. L. Sigsbee & B. W. Speck (Eds.), *Approaches to teaching nonnative English speakers across the curriculum* (pp. 77–84). San Francisco, CA: Jossey-Bass.

Nelson, J. & Kelly-Riley, D. (2001). Students as stakeholders: Maintaining a responsive assessment. In R. H. Haswell (Ed.), *Beyond outcomes: Assessment and instruction within a university writing program* (pp. 143–160). Westport, CT: Ablex.

Nettles, A., & Nettles, M. (1999). *Measuring up: Challenges minorities face in educational assessment.* Boston: Kluwer.

Noguchi, R. (1991). *Grammar and the teaching of writing: Limits and possibilities.* Urbana, IL: NCTE.

Nunley, V. L. (2004). From the harbor to da academic hood: Hush harbors and an African American rhetorical tradition. In E. B. Richardson & R. L. Jackson II (Eds.), *African American rhetoric(s): Interdisciplinary perspectives* (pp. 221–241). Carbondale: SIUP.

O'Conner, P. T. (2003). *Woe is I: The grammarphobe's guide to better English in plain English.* New York: Riverhead Books.

OECD. (2002). *Programme for international student assessment: Sample tasks from the PISA 2000 assessment of reading, mathematical, and scientific literacy.* Paris: OECD.

——— (2004). *Learning for tomorrow's world – First results from PISA 2003.* OECD Publications, 2 rue André-Pascal, Paris Cedex 16.

——— (2005). Counting Immigrants and Expatriates in OECD Countries: A New Perspective. *Trends in International Migration.* Retrieved from http://www.oecd.org/dataoecd/46/33/37965376.pdf

——— (2009). *PISA 2006 technical report.* Paris: OECD.

O'Hagan, L. K. (1997). It's broken—Fix it! In S. Tchudi (Ed.), *Alternatives to grading student writing* (pp. 3–13). Urbana, IL: NCTE.

Olmstead, A. (1999). *Juilliard: A history.* Urbana: University of Illinois Press.

Omi, M., & Winant, H. (1994). *Racial formations in the United States: From the 1960s to the 1990s.* Second Edition. New York: Routledge.

O'Neill, P. (1998). *Writing assessment and the disciplinarity of composition.* (Doctoral dissertation, University of Louisville). (UMI No. 9907059).

——— (2003). Moving beyond holistic scoring through validity inquiry. *Journal of Writing Assessment, 1*(1), 47–65.

O'Neill, P., Moore, C., & Huot, B. (2009). *A guide to college writing assessment.* Logan, UT: Utah State UP.

Oregon State University. (2003). Undergraduate admissions policy proposal. Retrieved from http://oregonstate.edu/senate/ committees/aac/agen/reports/20030115.html

——— (2007). Insight Résumé. Written experiential assessment. Retrieved from http://oregon state.edu/admissions/sites/.../insight_resume_worksheet.pdf

——— (2009). Insight Résumé. Retrieved from http://icoregon.technologypublisher.com/technology/2759

——— (n.d.). Admission requirements. Retrieved from http://oregonstate.edu/admissions/admission-requirements-0

Orfield, G., & Kornhaber, M. (Eds.). (2001). *Raising standards or raising barriers? Inequality and high-stakes testing in public education.* New York: Century Foundation.

Paris, D. (2009). "They're in my culture, They speak the same way": African American language in multiethnic high schools. *Harvard Educational Review, 79*(3), 428–447.

Penrose, A. M., & Geisler, C. (1994). Reading and writing without authority. *College Composition and Communication, 45*(4), 505–520.

Piche, G. L., Rubin, D. L., Turner, L. J., & Michlin, M. L. (1978). Teachers' subjective evaluations of standard and black nonstandard English compositions: A study of written language and attitudes. *Research in the Teaching of English, 12,* 107–118.

Pinter, R., & Sims, E. (2003). Directed self-placement at Belmont University: Sharing power, forming relationships, fostering reflection. In D. J. Royer & R. Gilles (Eds.), *Directed self-placement: Principles and practices* (pp. 107–125). Cresskill: Hampton Press.

Pixton, W. H. (1975). An open letter of congratulation to the NCTE for the 1974 resolutions. *College English, 37*(1), 92–94.

Plata, M. (1995). Success of Hispanic college students on a writing examination. *The Journal of Educational Issue of Language Minority Students.* Available at http://www.ncela.gwu.edu/files/rcd/BE021059/Success_of_Hispanic.pdf

Poe, M. (2006a). Race, representation, and writing assessment: Racial stereotypes and the construction of identity in writing assessments. (Doctoral dissertation—University of Massachusetts Amherst). Retrieved from http://scholarworks.umass.edu/dissertations/AAI3206201/

————— (2006b, September). *Not just a test: Race and power in the essay test.* Paper presented at the 10th International Conference of the EARLI Special Interest Group on Writing, Antwerp, Belgium.

Porter, J. E. (1986). Intertextuality and the discourse community. *Rhetoric Review, 5*(1), 34–47.

Pratt, M. L. (1991). Arts of the contact zone. *Profession, 91,* 33–40.

Prendergast, C. (1998). Race: The absent presence in composition studies. *College Composition and Communication, 50*(1), 36–53.

————— (2003). *Literacy and racial justice: The politics of learning after Brown v. Board of Education.* Carbondale: Southern Illinois UP.

Prior, P. (2006). A sociocultural theory of writing. In C. A. MacArthur, S. Graham, & J. Fitzgerald (Eds.), *Handbook of writing research* (pp. 54–66). New York: Guilford, 2006.

Progress in International Reading Literacy Study (PIRLS). (2011). Overview of IEA's PIRLS assessment. Retrieved from timss.bc.edu/pirls2011/downloads/PIRLS2011_Frame-work.pdf

Quinlan, T., Higgins, D., & Wolff, S. (2009). Evaluating the construct-coverage of e-rater scoring engine. Retrieved from http://www.ets.org/Media/Research/pdf/RR-09-01.pdf

Ratcliffe, K. (2000). Eavesdropping as rhetorical tactic: History, whiteness, and rhetoric. *JAC, 20*(1), 87–119.

————— (2005). *Rhetorical listening: Identification, gender, whiteness.* Carbondale: Southern Illinois University Press.

Rayou, P. (2004). Note critique d'A. Barrère. *Revue Française de Pédagogie, 147,* 129–131.

Redd, T. M. (2001). *"How I got ovah": Success stories of African American composition students, part II.* Paper presented at the annual meeting of the Conference on College Composition and Communication, Denver, CO.

Redd, T. M., & Webb, K. S. (2005). *A teacher's introduction to African American English.* Illinois: NCTE.

Retzer, M. W. (1998). *The Effects on attitude and achievement of a cognitive apprenticeship approach to college-level algebra.* (Doctoral dissertation, Northern Illinois University). *DAI-A* 59/05, 1501.

Reynolds, E. J. (2003). The role of self-efficacy in writing and directed self-placement. In D. J. Royer & R. Gilles (Eds.), *Directed self-placement: Principles and practices* (pp. 73–103). Cresskill: Hampton Press.

Rhode Island School of Design Catalog, 2008–09. (2008). Providence, RI: Rhode Island School of Design.

Rhymes, B., & Anderson, K. (2004). Second language acquisition for all: Understanding the interactional dynamics of classrooms in which Spanish and AAE are spoken. *Research in the Teaching of English, 39*, 107–135.

Richardson, E. (2002). "To protect and serve": African American female literacies. *College Composition and Communication, 53*(4), 675–704.

——— (2003a). *African American literacies.* New York: Routledge.

——— (2003b). Race, class(es), gender, and age: The making of knowledge about language diversity. In G. Smitherman & V. Villanueva (Eds.), *Language diversity in the classroom: From intention to practice: Studies in writing & rhetoric* (pp. 40–66). Carbondale: Southern Illinois University Press.

——— (2004). Coming from the heart: African American students, literacy stories, and rhetorical education. In E. B. Richardson & R. L. Jackson II (Eds.), *African American rhetoric(s): Interdisciplinary perspectives* (pp. 155–169). Carbondale: SIUP.

Rickford, J. R. (1999). *African American Vernacular English: Features, evolutions, educational implications.* Oxford: Blackwell.

RISD. (2012a). About RISD. RISD's ongoing mission. (n.d.). Retrieved from http://www.risd.edu/About/History_Mission_Governance/Mission/

——— (2012b). Admissions. Apply. Freshman applicants. Retrieved from http://www.risd.edu/Admissions/Apply/Freshmen/.

Ritter, K. (2009). *Before Shaughnessy: Basic writing at Yale and Harvard, 1920–1960.* Carbondale: Southern Illinois University Press.

Rochex, J-Y. (1996). Lecture, écriture et travail du sujet: Des papiers pour quelle identité? *Le français aujourd'hui, 113*, 33–41.

Ronda, J. P. (1984). *Lewis and Clark among the Indians.* Lincoln: University of Nebraska Press.

——— (2006, April 5) "And in conclusion": James Ronda sums up Lewis and Clark. lecture. Washington State University, Pullman, WA.

Roozen, K. (2008). Journalism, poetry, stand-up comedy, and academic literacy: Mapping the interplay of curricular and extracurricular literate activity. *Journal of Basic Writing, 27*(1), 5–34.

——— (2009a). "Fan fic-ing" English studies: A case study exploring the interplay of vernacular literacies and disciplinary engagement. *Research in the Teaching of English, 44*(2), 136–169.

——— (2009b). From journals to journalism: Tracing trajectories of literate development. *College Composition and Communication, 60*(3), 541–572.

Roozen, K., & Herrera, A. (2010). "Indigenous interests": Reconciling literate identities across extracurricular and curricular contexts. In C. Ortmeier-Hooper, J. Jordan, M. Cox, & G. Schwartz (Eds.), *Inventing identities in second-language writing* (pp. 139–162). Urbana, IL: NCTE.

Rose, M. (1985). *When a writer can't write: Studies in writer's block and other composing problems.* New York: Guilford Press.

Royer, J. D., & Gilles, R. (1998). Directed self-placement: An attitude of orientation. *College Composition and Communication, 50*(1), 54–70.

——— (2000). Basic writing and directed self-placement. *Basic Writing e-Journal, 2*(2). Retrieved from http://orgs.tamu-commerce.edu/cbw/ASU/summer_2000_V2N2.htm#dan

——— (2003). *Directed self-placement: Principles and Practices.* Cresskill, NJ: Hampton Press.

Royster, J. J. (1996). When the first voice you hear is not your own. *College Composition and Communication, 47*(1), 29–40.

Rubin, D. L., & M. Williams-James. (1997). The impact of writer nationality on mainstream teachers' judgments of composition quality. *Journal of Second Language Writing,* 6(2), 139–154.

Ruble, S. M. (1975). On students' right to their own language. *College Composition and Communication,* 37(1), 94–95.

Russell, D. R. (1990). Writing across the curriculum in a historical perspective: Toward a social interpretation. *College English,* 52(1), 52–73.

———— (1991). *Writing in the academic disciplines, 1870–1990: A curricular history.* Carbondale, IL: Southern Illinois University Press.

Ruth, L., & Murphy, S. (1988). *Designing writing tasks for the assessment of writing.* Norwood: Ablex.

Sacks, P. (1999). *Standardized minds: The high price of America's testing culture and what we can do to change it.* Cambridge, MA: Perseus.

Santelices, M., & Wilson, M. (2010). Unfair treatment? The case of Freedle, the SAT, and the standardization approach to differential item functioning. *Harvard Educational Review,* 80(1), 106–142.

Schworm, P. (2007). Torch program lights their way to college. *Boston Globe.* August 2. Retrieved from http://www.boston.com/news/local/articles/2007/08/03/torch_program_lights_their_way_to_college/?page=full

Segall, M. T., & Smart, R. A. (2005). *Direct from the disciplines: Writing across the curriculum.* Portsmouth, NH: Boynton/Cook.

Seymour, E., & Hewitt, N. M. (1994). *Talking about leaving: Factors contributing to high attrition rates among science, mathematics and engineering undergraduate majors.* Final Report to the Alfred P. Sloan Foundation on an Ethnographic Inquiry at Seven Institutions. Boulder: University of Colorado Bureau of Sociological Research.

Shapiro, N., Wright, S., Joseph, C, Walsh, S., & Huot, B. (2006). *Community: The result of cross-institutional collaboration.* Paper presented at the Conference on College Composition and Communication, Chicago, IL.

Shaughnessy, M. P. (1976). Diving in: An introduction to basic writing. *College Composition and Communication,* 27, 234–239.

———— (1977). *Errors and expectations: A guide for the teacher of basic writing.* New York: Oxford UP.

Shor, I. (1996). *When students have power: Negotiating authority in a critical pedagogy.* Chicago: U of Chicago Press.

Shor, I. (1997). Our Apartheid: Writing instruction and inequality. *Journal of Basic Writing, (16),* 91–104.

Simons, H. W. (1989). *Rhetoric in the human sciences.* London: Sage.

Smit, D. W. (1989). Some difficulties with collaborative learning. *JAC, 9,* 45–58.

Smith, W. L. (1993). Assessing the reliability and adequacy of using holistic scoring of essays as a college composition placement technique. In M. M. Williamson & B. A. Huot (Eds.), *Validating Holistic scoring for writing assessment: Theoretical and empirical foundations* (pp.142–205). Cresskill, NJ: Hampton Press.

Smitherman, G. (1977). *Talking and testifying: The language of Black America.* Boston: Houghton Mifflin.

———— (1979). Toward educational linguistics for the first world. *College English,* 41(2), 202–211.

———— (1987). Toward a national public policy on language. *College English,* 49(1), 29–36.

———— (1992). Black English, diverging or converging? The view from the National Assessment of Educational Progress. *Language and Education, 6*(1), 47–61.

———— (1993). "The blacker the berry, the sweeter the juice": African American student writers and the National Assessment of Educational Progress. National Council of Teachers of English Conference, Pittsburgh, PA, November 17–22, 1993. ERIC Document Reproduction Service, ED 366 944.

———— (2000). *Talking that talk: Language, culture, and education in African America.* New York: Routledge.

———— (2003). The historical struggle for language rights in CCCC. In G. Smitherman & V. Villanueva (Eds.), *Language diversity in the classroom: From intention to practice: Studies in writing & rhetoric* (pp. 7–39). Carbondale: Southern Illinois University Press.

———— (2004). Meditations on language, pedagogy, and a life of struggle. In K. Gilyard & V. Nunley (Eds.), *Rhetoric and ethnicity* (pp. 3–14). Portsmouth, NH: Boynton Cook/Heinemann.

Soares, J. A. (2008). An open letter to faculty on Wake Forest's new admissions policy. May 27. Retrieved from http://www.wfu.edu/wowf/2008/sat-act/soares/

Soliday, M. (2002). *The politics of remediation: Institutional and student needs in higher education.* Pittsburgh: University of Pittsburgh Press.

Solorzano, D. G., & T. J. Yosso. (2002) Critical race methodology: Counter-storytelling as an analytical framework for education research. *Qualitative Inquiry, 8*(1), 23–44.

Sorcinelli, M. D., & Elbow, P. (Eds.). (1997). *Writing to learn: Strategies for assigning and responding to writing across the disciplines.* San Francisco: Jossey-Bass.

Spidell, C., & Thelin, W. H. (2006). Not ready to let go: A study of resistance to grading contracts. *Composition Studies, 34*(1), 35–57.

Stanley, J. (2010). *The rhetoric of remediation: Negotiating entitlement and access to higher education.* Pittsburgh: University of Pittsburgh Press.

Stanley, S. (2009). *Writing a path toward social change: A critical pedagogy of grammatical choice.* Paper presented at the Conference on College Composition and Communication. San Francisco, CA.

Steele, C. M. (1997). A threat in the air: How stereotypes shape intellectual identity and performance. *American Psychologist, 52*(6), 613–629.

Steele, S. (1991). *Content of our character: A new vision of race in America.* New York: HarperPerennial.

Sternberg, R. J. (2010). *College admissions for the 21st century.* Cambridge, MA: Harvard UP.

Sternglass, M. S. (1997). *Time to know them: A longitudinal study of writing and learning at the college level.* Mahwah, NJ: Erlbaum.

Stockwell, R.J., Bowen, D., & Martin, J.W. (1965). *The grammatical structures of English and Spanish.* Chicago: University of Chicago Press.

Strauss, M. J., & Fulwiler, T. (1987). Interactive writing and learning chemistry. *Journal of College Science Teaching, 16,* 256–262.

Supovitz, J. A., & Brennan, R. T. (1997). Mirror, mirror on the wall, which is the fairest test of all? An examination of the equitability of portfolio assessment relative to standardized tests. *Harvard Educational Review, 67*(3), 472–506.

Takaki, R. (1979). *Iron cages: Race and culture in 19th-century America.* New York: Knopf.

Taylor, D. (1997). *Many families, many literacies: An international declaration of principles.* Portsmouth, NH: Heinemman.

Thaiss, C. (1988). The future of writing across the curriculum. In S. H. McLeod (Ed.), *Strengthening programs for writing across the curriculum* (pp. 91–102). San Francisco: Jossey-Bass.

———— (2001). Theory in WAC: Where have we been, where are we going? In S. H. McLeod, E. Miraglia, M. Soven, & C. Thaiss (Eds.), *WAC for the new millennium: Strategies for continuing writing-across-the-curriculum programs* (pp. 299-325). Urbana, IL: National Council of Teachers of English.

———— (2009, March). *Challenging standard views of teaching, curriculum, and learning in higher education: Results and implications of the International WAC/WID Mapping Project.* Paper delivered at the Conference on College Composition and Communication, San Francisco, CA.

Thaiss, C., & Zawacki, T. (2006). *Engaged writers, dynamic disciplines: Research on the academic writing life.* Portsmouth, NH: Boynton/Cook Heinemann.

Todd, J. G. (1989). The liberal education of studio artists in the post-modern age. *Art & Academe: A Journal for the Humanities and Sciences in the Education of Artists, 1*(2), 1-16.

Tolar Burton. V. (2010). Activity systems, genre, and research on writing across the curriculum. *College Composition and Communication, 61*(3), 583-596.

Tomsho, R. A. (2009). Adding personality to the college admissions mix. *Wall Street Journal,* Aug. 20. Retrieved at http://online.wsj.com/article/SB10001424052970203612504574342732853413584.html

Trimbur, J. (1996). Response: Why do we test writing?. In E. M. White, W. D. Lutz, & S. Kamusikiri (Eds.), *Assessment of writing: Politics, policies, practices.* (pp. 45-48). New York: MLA.

———— (2006). Linguistic memory and the politics of U.S. English. *College English, 68*(6), 575-588.

University of California. (2010). StatFinder. Retrieved from http://statfinder.ucop.edu/library/tables/table_126.aspx

U.S. Census Bureau. (2009). Census bureau estimates nearly half of children under age 5 are minorities. Retrieved from http://www.census.gov/newsroom/releases/archives/population/cb09-75.html

van Dijk, T. A. (2002). Discourse and racism. In D. Goldberg & J. Solomos (Eds.), *The Blackwell companion to racial and ethnic atudies* (pp. 145-159). Oxford: Blackwell.

Villanueva, V. (1993). *Bootstraps: From an American academic of color.* Urbana, IL: NCTE.

———— (1997). Maybe a colony: And still another critique of the comp community. *JAC, 17,* 183-190.

———— (2001). The politics of literacy across the curriculum. In S. H. McLeod, E. Miraglia, M. Soven, & C. Thaiss (Eds.), *WAC for the new millennium: Strategies for continuing writing-across-the-curriculum programs* (pp. 165-178). Urbana, IL: National Council of Teachers of English.

———— (2003). On rhetoric and the precedents of racism. In V. Villanueva (Ed.), *Cross-talk in comp theory: A reader.* (2nd ed.). (pp. 829-845). Urbana, IL: NCTE.

Walvoord, B. E. (1992). Getting started. In S. H. McLeod & M. Soven (Eds.), *Writing across the curriculum: A guide to developing programs* (pp. 9-22). Newbury Park, CA: Sage.

———— (1996). The future of writing across the curriculum. *College English, 58*(1), 58-79.

Walvoord, B. E., & McCarthy, L. P. (1990). *Thinking and writing in college: A naturalistic study of students in four disciplines.* Urbana, IL: National Council of Teachers of English.

Waters, M. C. (1990). *Ethnic options: Choosing identities in America.* Berkeley: University of California Press.

Weigle, S.C. (2010). Validation of automated scoring of TOEFL iBT tasks against non-test indicators of writing. *Language Testing, 27,* 335-353.

West, C. (1993). *Race matters.* Boston: Beacon P.

West, T. (1997). The racist other. *JAC, 17,* 215-226.

White, E. M. (1985). *Teaching and assessing writing.* San Francisco: Jossey-Bass.

———— (1996). Response: Assessment as a site of contention. In E. M. White, W. Lutz, & S. Kamusikiri (Eds.), *Assessment of writing: Politics, policies, practices* (pp. 301–304). New York: Modern Language Association of America.

———— (2001). The opening of the modern era of writing assessment: A narrative. *College English, 63*(3), 306–320.

White, E. M., & Thomas, L. (1981). Racial minorities and writing skills assessment in the California State University and colleges. *College English, 43*(3), 276–83.

Widdowson, H. G. (1994). The ownership of English. *TESOL Quarterly, 28*(2), 377–392.

Williams, J. (1981). The phenomenology of error. *College Composition and Communication, 32*(2), 152–168.

Williamson, M. M. (2003). Validity of automated scoring: Prologue for a continuing discussion of machine scoring student writing. *Journal of Writing Assessment, 1*(2), n.p. Retrieved from http://journalofwritingassessment.org/archives.php?issue=X12

Williamson, M. M., & Huot, B. A. (1993) *Validating holistic scoring for writing assessment: Theoretical and empirical foundations.* Cresskill, NJ: Hampton Press.

Wilson, M. (2006). *Rethinking rubrics in writing assessment.* Portsmouth, NH: Heinemann.

Wolcott, W., & Legg, S. M. (1998). *An overview of writing assessment: Theory, research and practice.* Urbana: NCTE.

Wolfram, W., & Thomas, E. R. (2002). *The development of African American English.* Oxford, UK: Blackwell Publishers.

Writing Center. Spelman College. (2009). First-year writing portfolio guidelines 2009–2010: A part of the SpEl.Folio project at Spelman College. "What does 'resubmit' mean." Retrieved from http://www.spelman.edu/wcenter/cwp/FIRST_YR_PORTFOLIO.html

Yancey, K. B. (1997). *Reflection in the writing classroom.* Logan, UT: Utah State University Press.

———— (1999). Looking back as we look forward: Historicizing writing assessment *College Composition and Communication, 50*(3), 483–503.

———— (2009). Reflection and electronic portfolios: Inventing the self and reinventing the university. In Cambridge, D., Cambridge, B., & Yancey, K. B. (Eds.), *Electronic portfolios 2.0.* (pp. 5–7). Washington, DC: Stylus.

Yancey, K. B., & Huot, B. (Eds.). (1997). *Assessing writing across the curriculum: Diverse approaches and practices.* Greenwich, CT: Ablex.

Yancey, K. B., & Weiser, I. (Eds.) (1997). *Situating portfolios: Four perspectives.* Logan, UT: Utah State University Press.

Yosso, T. J. (2002). Toward a critical race curriculum. *Equity & Excellence in Education, 35,* 93–107.

Yosso, T. J., L. Parker, D. G. Solorzano, & M. Lynn. (2004). From Jim Crow to affirmative action and back again: A critical race discussion of racialized rationales and access to higher education. *Review of Research in Education, 28,* 1–25.

Young, A., & Fulwiler, T. (Eds.). (1986). *Writing across the disciplines: Research into practice.* Upper Montclair, NJ: Boynton/Cook.

Young, V. A. (2007). *Your average nigga: Performing race, literacy, and masculinity.* Detroit: Wayne State UP.

———— (2009). "Nah, we straight": An argument against code switching. *JAC, 29*(1), 49–76.

———— (2011). *Code meshing as world English: Policy, pedagogy, performance.* Champaign: NCTE.

Yood, J. (2004). The next stage is a system: Writing across the curriculum and the new knowledge society. *Across the Disciplines, 2.* Retrieved from http://wac.colostate.edu/ atd/articles/ yood2004.cfm

Zamel, V. (1995). Strangers in academia: The experiences of faculty and ESL students across the curriculum. *College Composition and Communication, 46*(4), 506–521.

Zawacki, T. M., & Williams, A. T. (2001). Is it still WAC? Writing within interdisciplinary learning communities. In S. H. McLeod, E. Miraglia, M. Soven, & C. Thaiss (Eds.), *WAC for the new millennium* (pp. 109–140). Urbana, IL: NCTE.

Contributors

Chris M. Anson is University Distinguished Professor and Director of the Campus Writing and Speaking Program at North Carolina State University. He has published and spoken widely on the learning and teaching of writing. He is currently Associate Chair of the Conference on College Composition and Communication.

Valerie Balester is the Executive Director of the University Writing Center, which hosts the writing-and-speaking-in-the-disciplines program at Texas A&M University. She is the author of *Cultural Divide* (1993) and the editor, with Michelle Hall Kells, of *Attending to the Margins* (1999) and, with Victor Villanueva and Michelle Hall Kells, of *Latino/a Discourses* (2004).

Élisabeth Bautier is professor at l'Université de Paris 8 in sociology of language and education. She focuses on language issues as relevant to social differences, difference in learning, in teaching, and in construction of knowledge. She works to understand the evolution of school, curricula, and teaching, and its impact on educational and social inequality.

Nicholas Behm, an assistant professor of English at Elmhurst College, studies composition pedagogy and theory, ancient rhetoric, postmodern rhetorical theory, and critical race theory. He teaches undergraduate and graduate courses in composition theory and rhetoric, and he frequently leads workshops about composition theory, writing assessment, writing-in-the-disciplines, and graduate education.

Christiane Donahue is Director of the Institute for Writing and Rhetoric at Dartmouth and associate professor of linguistics. She publishes in Europe and the United States on cross-cultural analysis of student writing and writing instruction, writing program administration, and research methods. She is a member of the Théodile-CIREL research group at l'Université de Lille III.

Judy Fowler has taught English and occasionally history since Fall 1962, first in middle school and later in senior high. Since 1987, she has taught courses in rhetoric and writing at the post-secondary and graduate levels. She has taught at four state universities, two in Maryland and two in North Carolina, one of which was an HBCU. Fowler has supervised student teachers of

English and is professionally interested in cooperative instructional ventures between secondary and post-secondary schools.

Anne Herrington is Distinguished Professor of English and Site Director of the Western Massachusetts Writing Project at the University of Massachusetts Amherst. With Charles Moran and Kevin Hodgson, she co-edited *Teaching the New Writing: Technology, Change, and Assessment* (2009), and with Marcia Curtis, she co-authored *Persons in Process: Four Stories of Writing and Personal Development in College* (NCTE, 2000), recipient of the David H. Russell Award for Distinguished Research in the Teaching of English, NCTE, 2002.

Asao B. Inoue is an associate professor of Rhetoric and Composition at California State University, Fresno, where he also is the Special Assistant to the Provost for Writing Across the Curriculum. His areas of research are writing assessment, validity studies, and racism. He's published articles in various edited collections as well as in *Assessing Writing*, the *Journal of Writing Assessment*, and *Composition Forum*. Currently, he is the Book Review Editor for *Composition Studies* and is working on a monograph that theorizes writing assessment as a technology.

Zandra L. Jordan is an assistant professor of English at Spelman College, where she coordinates first-year composition; co-directs SpEl.Folio, Spelman's electronic portfolio program; and teaches primarily in the writing minor. Her writing courses include composition, argumentation, and ethnographic writing. Her research focuses on African American language, literacies, and rhetoric in college writing and the Black Church.

Diane Kelly-Riley directs the Writing Assessment Program and Writing Program at Washington State University, which received the 2008–09 CCCC Writing Program Certificate of Excellence. Her research interests include race and writing assessment, validity theory, critical thinking, writing-across-the-curriculum, and writing program administration. She is the co-editor of the *Journal of Writing Assessment*.

Rachel Lewis Ketai teaches composition at El Camino College. She earned her PhD in Rhetoric, Composition, and the Teaching of English from the University of Arizona in 2010, where she specialized in composition theory, composition pedagogy, issues of access to higher education for Latino/a students, developmental composition, writing assessment, and genre theory. Currently, her work focuses on applications of this research in the community college context.

Anthony Lioi is an associate professor of Liberal Arts and English at the Juilliard School in New York City. He is the founding director of Juilliard's Writing and Communication Center. His research interests include ecocomposition, American literature, popular culture, and the essay as a genre. His work has been published in *Interdisciplinary Studies in Literature and Environment*, *MELUS*, *ImageTexT*, *Feminist Studies*, *CrossCurrents*, and *TransFormations*, and in a number of edited volumes.

Nicole M. Merola is associate professor of Ecocriticism and American Literature at the Rhode Island School of Design. Her research and teaching interests include twentieth-century U.S. environmental literature, visual art, and film; critical animal studies; science studies; and environmental theory. Her work has been published in *JAC*, *TransFormations*, *Journal of Postcolonial and Commonwealth Studies*, *Reader*, and *Green Letters* and is forthcoming in *American Literature*.

Keith D. Miller is a professor of English at Arizona State University. His newest book is *Martin Luther King's Biblical Epic: His Great, Final Speech*; he previously wrote *Voice of Deliverance: The Language of Martin Luther King, Jr., and Its Sources*. His essays have appeared in such journals as *College Composition and Communication*, *College English*, *Rhetoric Society Quarterly*, *PMLA*, and *Journal of American History*. In 2007 he won the Theresa Enos Award for best essay of the year published in *Rhetoric Review*.

Robert Ochsner directs the Center for Research on Teaching Excellence at the University of California, Merced. Informed by applied linguistics scholarship and second-language studies, Ochsner's research attends to issues of language use that encompass literacy politics, rhetorical theory, and design and administration of academic programs. As a teacher, he is committed to serving linguistically and culturally diverse college students.

Mya Poe is assistant professor of English at Penn State University. Her research focuses on writing in the disciplines, writing assessment, and racial identity. Her publications include *Learning to Communicate in Science and Engineering: Case Studies from MIT* (MIT Press, 2010), which won the CCCC 2012 Advancement of Knowledge Award, as well as articles in *College Composition and Communication* and the *Journal of Business and Technical Communication*. She is currently working on a book entitled *The Consequences of Assessment*.

Sarah Stanley is an assistant professor of English and Director of Composition at the University of Alaska Fairbanks. Her research interests entail how the disparate fields of linguistics and social theory inform writing instruction, classroom practices, and curriculum. As a teacher and writing administrator, she is committed to learning more about the linguistic and cultural resources of diverse student populations.

Kathleen Blake Yancey is Kellogg W. Hunt Professor of English and Distinguished Research Professor at Florida State University, where she directs the Graduate Program in Rhetoric and Composition. She has served as President of NCTE; as Chair of CCCC; and as President of WPA. Yancey's research—focusing on composition studies; on writing assessment, especially print and electronic portfolios; and on the intersections of culture, literacy and technologies—has been published in 11 scholarly books, and more than 70 articles and book chapters. Since 2010, she has edited *College Composition and Communication*.

Index

L

language
    change, 112
    diversity, 48, 71, 97, 98, 100–103,
        106, 108
    proficiency, 46, 192
    socialization, 170, 194
Latino/a, 6, 9, 64, 112, 130, 138, 160
linguistic
    diversity, 65, 190
    socialization, 188, 193
    variation, 9, 14, 45, 46, 68, 95, 98
low-income populations, 111

M

meritocracy, 129, 157, 159
mobilize, 188–189, 193, 194–195, 198
monolingualism, 49, 137
multiculturalism, 17, 65, 75, 134
multilingualism, 46, 65, 69, 137
multiphase essays, 113, 116, 124

N

NAEP, 8, 52, 98
national language policy, 48
Native American, 27, 64, 84, 130
naturalization, 129, 130
No Child Left Behind, 137
non-cognitive (factors or measures), 10,
    176, 180, 182–183

O

objectifs énonciatifs, 197

P

personal experience, 135, 187, 193, 195,
    198
PISA, 10, 170, 187–199
placement testing. *See* assessment
plagiarism, 124, 174
portfolios. *See* assessment
power relations, 13, 127, 135
PRAXIS exam, 123–124

privilege, 127
    See also white privilege

R

racial
    identity, xi, 2, 24, 35, 161, 199
    politics, 96, 127–128
racism, 6, 10, 13, 26, 65, 96, 127–136,
    138, 142, 145, 146, 148, 158, 178,
    188, 192
    new, 129
    See also anti-racism
reader bias, 126
reflection, 29, 83, 85, 149, 171, 177–178,
    179, 193, 199
register, 58–59, 187, 192, 193, 194, 195,
    198
reliability. *See* assessment
remediation, 54, 86, 93, 141
rubric. *See* assessment

S

SAT, 11, 94, 155, 156, 169, 171, 172,
    173–176, 178, 179, 181, 183, 194
scholastic, 192, 198
secondarized, 187, 188, 192, 195, 199
shared evaluation methods. *See* assessment
socioeconomic status, xi, 2, 3, 170, 187,
    190–191, 192, 199
sociolinguistic, 65, 133, 188, 195
Spanish, 52, 86, 112, 114, 119, 125
Spanish-influenced writing, 96, 113, 118
Standard American English, 51
    See also Edited American English
students of color, 1, 7–9, 10, 14, 24, 25,
    26, 29, 30–42, 84, 94, 131, 132–137,
    139, 140, 143–146, 161, 163, 165,
    169, 171, 172, 176, 178, 184
Students' Right to Their Own Language,
    48, 95, 97, 103, 137

T

teacher
    bias, 111–112, 113
    education, 111, 123

STUDIES IN COMPOSITION AND RHETORIC

Edited by LEONARD A. PODIS

This series welcomes both individually-authored and collaboratively-authored books and monographs as well as edited collections of essays. We are especially interested in books that might be used in either advanced undergraduate or graduate courses in one or more of the following subjects: cultural or multicultural studies and the teaching of writing; feminist perspectives on composition and rhetoric; postmodernism and the theory and practice of composition; "post-process" pedagogies; values, ethics, and ideologies in the teaching of writing; information technology and composition pedagogy; the assessment of writing; authorship and intellectual property issues; and studies of oppositional discourse in the academy, particularly challenges to exclusionary or hegemonic conventions. We also seek proposals in the following areas: the role of autobiography and of identity issues in both writing and writing pedagogy; the influence of social context on composing; the relationship of composition and rhetoric to various disciplines and schools of thought; collaborative learning and peer tutoring; facilitating and responding to student writing; approaches to empowering marginalized learners; the role or status of composition studies within English studies and the academy at large; and the role or status of student writers within the fields of composition and English studies.

For additional information about this series or for the submission of manuscripts, please contact:

Peter Lang Publishing, Inc.
Acquisitions Department
29 Broadway
New York, NY 10006

To order other books in this series, please contact our Customer Service Department at:

(800) 770-LANG (within the U.S.)
(212) 647-7706 (outside the U.S.)
(212) 647-7707 FAX

or browse online by series at:

WWW.PETERLANG.COM